AB The Legend

A Photographer's Tribute

Author Pradeep Chandra with Amitabh Bachchan

AB The Legend

A Photographer's Tribute

Pradeep Chandra

Rupa & Co

Copyright © Pradeep Chandra 2006

Published in 2006 by

Rupa & Co

7/16, Ansari Road,
Daryaganj,
New Delhi 110 002

Sales Centres:
Allahabad, Bangalore, Chandigarh, Chennai,
Hyderabad, Jaipur, Kathmandu, Kolkata, Mumbai,
Pune

Project Editor: Pradeep Chandra
Designed by: Arundeep Creations
Cover Photograph: Pradeep Chandra

All rights reserved.
No part of this publication may be reproduced, stored in a retrieval system, or transmitted, in any form or by any means, electronic, mechanical, photocopying, recording or otherwise, without the prior permission of the publisher.

ISBN 81-291-0881-X

Printed in India by:
Ajanta Offset Ltd., New Delhi

Dedicated to

My family

Veena • Vibhor • Priyanka • Vikas • Stuti

फुल्ल कमल,
गोद नवल,
मोद नवल,
गेह में विनोद नवल।

बाल नवल,
लाल नवल,
दीपक में ज्वाल नवल।

दूध नवल
पूत नवल,
वंश से विभूति नवल,

नवल दृश्य,
नवल दृष्टि,
जीवन का नव भविष्य,
जीवन की नवल सृष्टि।

Dr Harivanshrai Bachchan wrote this poem on the birth of his son Amitabh Bachchan

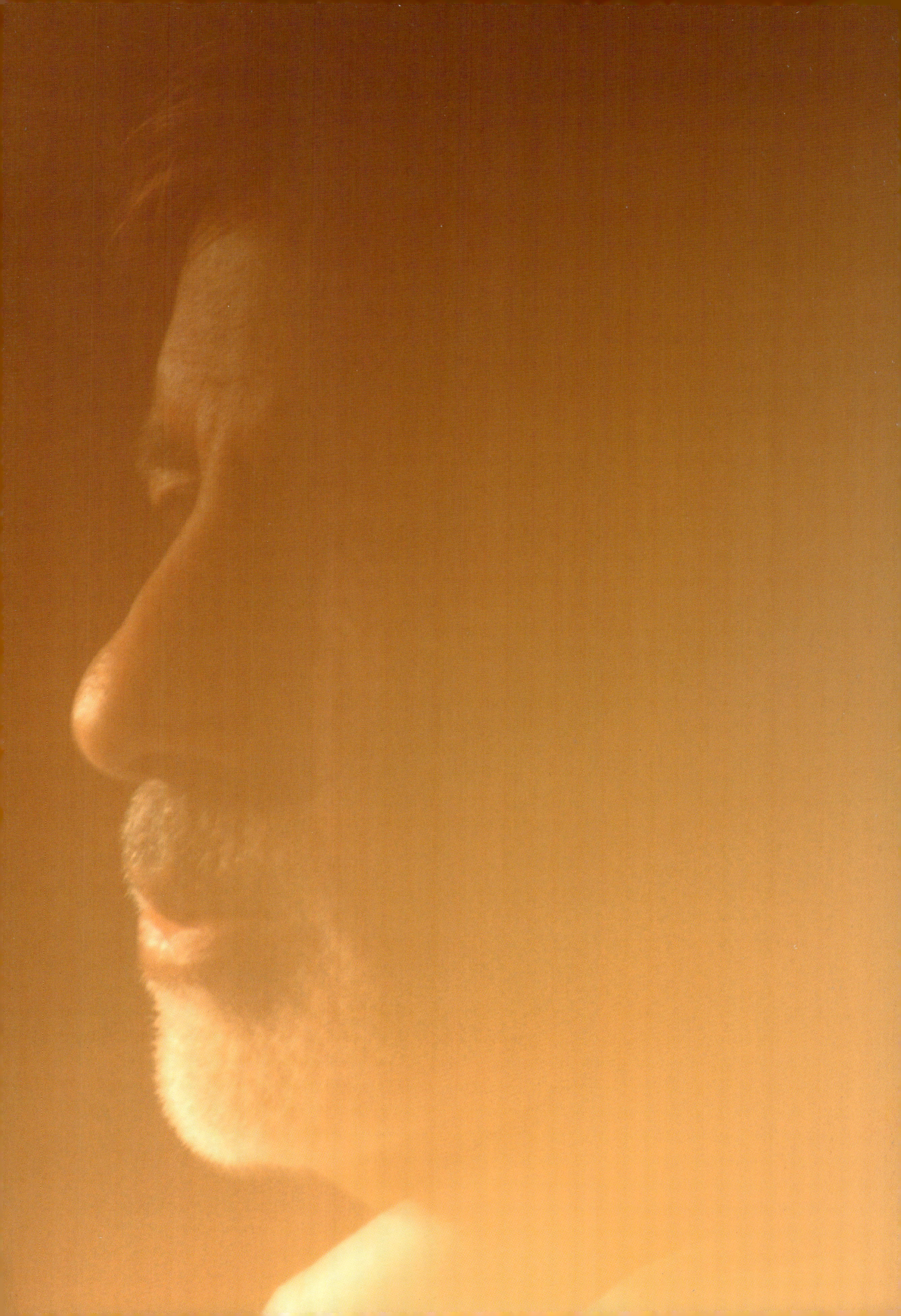

Contents

The Early Days
One thing that ran through Bachchan's long years of anonymity as a fever in his blood was his love of make-believe and play acting. This passion for acting stayed on in his mind.

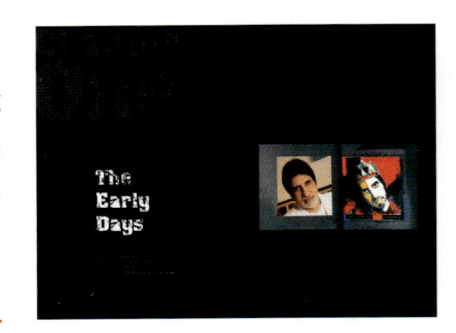

18

The Struggle
They say in the Hindi film industry that a newcomer whose first film is a flop is definitely going to make it big. The bigger the flops, the greater the success. Bachchan must have definitely stretched the rule to the limit.

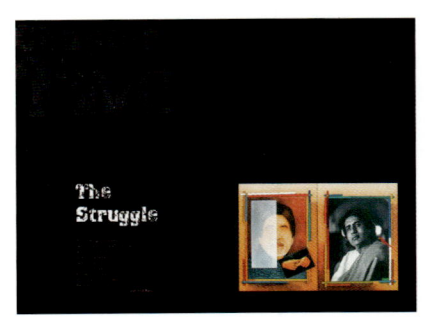

46

The Angry Young Man
Bachchan's role in *Zanjeer* marked the watershed point in his career. The film made Amitabh Bachchan an icon of the masses. The Angry Young Man phase captured and held the imagination of the country.

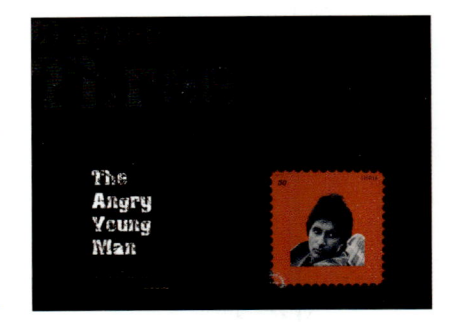

74

A Search For Identity
After a successful reign of nearly twenty years at the Hindi movie box-office, Bachchan was longing for something else. Introspection followed, interspersed with some serious globetrotting.

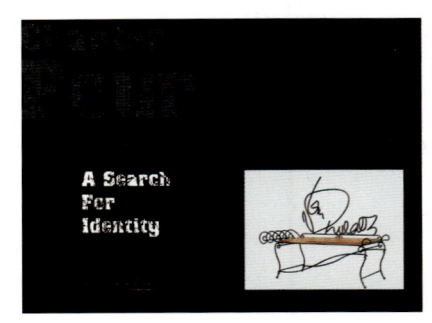

102

The Return Of The King
It was in 1999 that Bachchan met up with a man who had an unusual but exciting offer. He wanted Bachchan to host a game show on his TV channel.

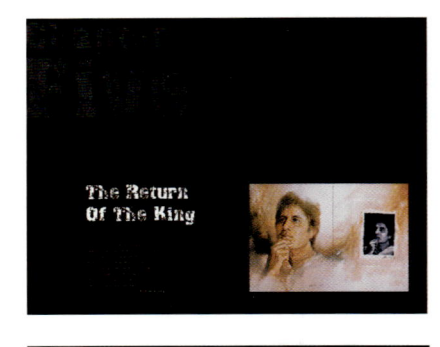

140

Still Here
Facing the darkness, and living through trying times has endowed Bachchan with a newfound confidence. The kind that blossoms from within.

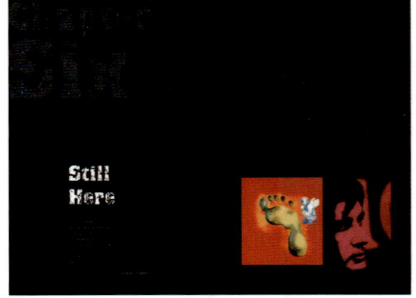

174

Guest Columns

Pritish Nandy

My intent here is modest. All I attempt is a personal glimpse into why AB, as he is better known these days, has emerged as such an iconic figure of our times. But to understand that you have to first understand the man.

10

Rauf Ahmed

Nobody could have imagined that a tall, gawky guy with deep-set brooding eyes would rule the marquee for more than two decades. This phenomenon not just defied convention and logic, but bent the very flow of time.

68

T.R. Gopaalakrishnan

As a very junior hack in Delhi, I still remember getting to see his movie *Naseeb* on the first day. It required a police escort from the local police station to get me that much-prized ticket.

100

Govind Nihalani

Amit *ji* is now a liberated actor: liberated from the pressure of maintaining the number one position, from the pressure of always succeeding in a big way at the box office, from the pressure of maintaining any kind of image.

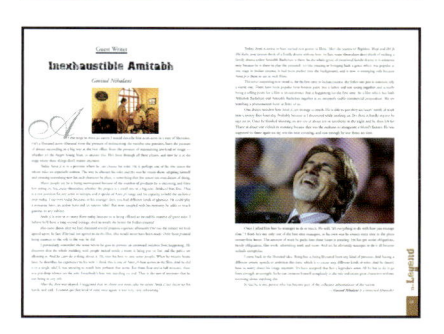

138

Srinivas Hebbar

I wouldn't call him the Teflon man on whom nothing sticks. He is more like an escape artist: handcuff him, tie him up, put him in a box and drop him into the sea and soon you see him emerging, his old hearty self.

170

Shobhaa Dé

To call Amitabh Bachchan an enigma, is to fall back on a cliché. But he, more than any other actor of our times, truly fits that description. I have watched him with interest (most of the time) and some indifference, over a period of thirty years.

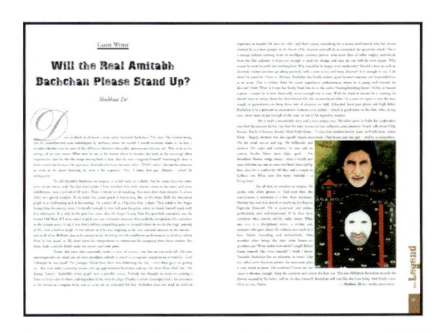

200

Preface -14, Introduction - 16, The Writer Amitabh Bachchan - 46, Notes - 202, Captions - 204, Acknowledgements - 207

Foreword

So Many Lives In One Lifetime

Pritish Nandy

What can one write about Amitabh Bachchan that does not sound like a tired, shop soiled cliché? But I can't say no because I have known Pradeep Chandra for two decades now, as a friend, colleague and exceptional chronicler of the fleeting moment. He has also been a Bachchan aficionado for ages, long before it was fashionable to be so. This book is his tribute to the man. A man I have known and admired as a friend for years now.

My intent here is modest. All I attempt is a personal glimpse into why AB, as he is better known these days, has emerged as such an iconic figure of our times. But to understand that you have to first understand the man.

One of the simplest ways to understand Amit is to realise that he has lived many lives in one lifetime and, like most successful Indians, reached where he has through a strange graph of success and failures. There are many others I know who have done the same. But few have reached the amazing heights that Amit has. Few have plumbed the depths he has, wracked by failure and disappointment. Both success and failure have knocked on his door with equal persistence. His highs and his lows have almost gone hand in hand, in a yin yang of sorts. But like Sisyphus in the Greek myth, he is best remembered for rolling the boulder uphill. While the Gods may have given him everything he ever craved for, they also made sure he suffered enough to remember to thank them.

My own life has intersected with Amit's at several critical junctures and even though I cannot really claim to be a close friend of his, I have known him for a while. No, I did not know him through his struggling years as an actor. Nor did I know him all that well during his years of spectacular stardom. I came to know him when his stardom was on a decline and he had begun to experience his first series of flops. But being the huge star he still was, no one was ready to acknowledge that. The film industry in any case survives on lies and hypocrisy. So when I did my first cover story on him in *The Illustrated Weekly of India*, which I edited in the eighties, it did not make me very popular with either him or his fan clubs.

Then Amit entered politics, as the best friend of Rajiv and Sonia. The media went ballistic as he campaigned and won the Allahabad seat for the Congress. They welcomed him as the new political avatar of India's greatest living star. A messiah almost. Bigger, sexier, more powerful than MGR or NTR. My somewhat sceptical cover story in *Filmfare*, which I also edited in those days, suggested that the poor guy was destined to flop in politics. The reasoning was simple. He was such a big star only because he was the Angry Young Man who could stand up to the might of the brute, ugly political system. Every young person in India identified with him and the roles he played, fighting what you could describe as an almost epic battle against the forces of evil and corruption. He was the hope of the common man, the fire that kept the nation alive during some of its worst years. For him to now switch over and become a part of the very same corrupt political establishment that the Congress and Rajiv represented was such a terrible letdown that I feared he would lose his credibility as well as his ability to deliver sustainable political goals.

It did not require rocket science to predict this but since I was the only journalist saying so, ostensibly in his moment of glory, it did not win me many friends. History, however, endorsed my worst fears. Within months of Amit's joining politics, the knives came out. The party he went to serve became his private battlefield. His image went for a toss. So did his mass following. What's worse, he sank into the cesspool of politics without a bubble.

The rest is history. Bofors happened. Amit got dragged into it. The media which, till then was acclaiming him as the next big thing to happen to Indian politics after Rajiv, were the first to implicate him in the scam. They were encouraged to do so by Rajiv's own coterie, anxious to make a scapegoat out of him. For the Opposition, he was an easy prey. Targeting Amit was like targeting Rajiv. Ultimately, fed up with what he could neither fully comprehend nor cope with, Amit resigned from Parliament and politics and swore to stay away from both for life. He spent his next few years defending himself against the Bofors charges. That's when I came to his support, much to the surprise of everyone, including Amit's closest friends and political colleagues, who promptly called me to flood me with gratuitous bits of evidence to prove his complicity in the notorious howitzer deal.

Meanwhile, in his anxiety to clear his name, Amit went on overdrive against Rajiv's detractors of those days, mainly led by Vishwanath Pratap Singh, another friend of mine, who was once Rajiv's close ally and finance minister. Singh had an open spat with Rajiv, manipulated by two warring business houses of the time and abetted of course by the media. An infuriated Singh went on to spearhead a revolt within the Congress. He saw in Amit, Rajiv's Achilles heel and went for him hammer and tongs. Since all the investigating agencies reported to Singh, he (rather unjustly) unleashed their full power against him. It was his way of showing India that he was not afraid of Rajiv or his friends.

But it was not Singh so much as Rajiv's own friends and sycophants who instigated the entire campaign against Amit and tried their best to lay the blame of Bofors at his doorstep. I must have been given lunch by every powerful friend and advisor of Rajiv in those days. Every lunch ended with the request that Amit should be exposed as the key man behind Bofors. I ignored the requests but warned Amit that his own friends and partymen were more dangerous than those he thought were the enemy. But he was too naïve and idealistic. He trusted Rajiv implicitly. As a result, he got dragged more and more into the quagmire. Worse, he also got dragged into the Ambani-Wadia feud that, in those days, defined the twists and turns Indian politics took.

It would be stupid of me to now retrace the entire campaign against Amit. It's enough to record that every effort was made to drag him into the Bofors muck, hoping he would sink forever, taking away with him all the unanswered questions about the deal. This, Rajiv's political strategists thought, would close the chapter on one of the most tumultuous periods of our political history and make life that much easier for both Rajiv and the Congress. But Amit had wised up by now. He knew he could not give up the battle midway. His enemies would have destroyed him forever. So he fought back all the charges and, after some initial faltering, managed to win a complicated legal battle overseas. That victory was then flaunted here to affirm his innocence. But politics was over, as far as he was concerned. He returned to what he was best at, movies—and tried to refashion his career there.

It did not work. As I said before, his Angry Young Man image had lost its sheen. And politics had made him both weary and cynical. He knew he had to return to familiar turf. He knew he had to reclaim his kingdom. He tried to do this, one step at a time. He founded ABCL, India's first entertainment corporate. It was a great idea but perhaps a bit premature. In barely a year's time it went bankrupt and eventually landed up in BIFR. But instead of letting that demoralise him, Amit persisted. Since his movies were not getting anywhere, he turned to the small screen.

Everyone thought it was a huge mistake. But he knew where he was going. Television had already become very big worldwide and Sameer Nair of Star managed to persuade him to host KBC. The rest is history. KBC upstaged the entire hierarchy of Indian television and made Star Plus the No. 1 channel overnight. Entertainment history was rewritten. All of a sudden, television began to look much bigger than cinema and Amit was back on top.

I remember the last time he came home. Jaya, Rina, Amit and I went to Anil Ambani's wedding in town. Anil, who was one of my closest friends in those days, barely knew Amit. He fought with me because I had turned up late. I explained that Amit's big van took a bit of time negotiating through the late evening traffic. That evening eventually laid the foundation for a famous friendship—Amit and Anil's.

Slowly, over the next few years, the star morphed into the legend. The huge success of KBC brought Amit back onto the big screen, this time as an actor of remarkable range and talent. You could call it his home coming. Some described it as a second coming.

We even made a movie together, *Kaante*. Sanjay Dutt greenlighted the idea. Amit played a kind of role he had never attempted before. It was yet another breakthrough. The audience loved the fact that he was experimenting with his characterisations. Despite the advice of his friends, Amit became braver with each film and cast aside the old stereotypes. He deliberately chose roles that allowed him to break out of his tired star image and attempt new things. At the same time, he also did conventional roles to keep his old fans happy. The experiments paid off. Even clangers like *Boom* contributed to his repertoire. While the hits brought him back, centrestage. This time, as the nation's most versatile actor. Be it *Black* or *Bunty aur Babli*, he's on a roll.

His iconic presence straddles the entire world of entertainment today. He endorses more products than anyone else. Good, bad, indifferent brands, they all sign him on for fees unheard of. Cadbury, when it was reeling under a scandal, signed him on as their image doctor. They were soon back in business. The public had forgiven them the worms in their chocolates. From Parker pens to ayurvedic tonics, AB promotes anything and everything today. He is the ultimate Daddy Cool of showbiz. Give him any role and he makes it work. Give him any product and he brings it instant credibility. He works round the clock, defying myasthenia gravis and indifferent health. He's never late on the sets and rarely goes back on a commitment made. He is generous to a fault. He writes immaculate letters, many of which I have kept away just to show my children how a man's genius manifests itself in so many different ways. He is rich, famous, successful. Everything everyone in India dreams of becoming.

Our lives have touched at times, in different places, on different occasions and I have always felt enriched by the experience. Is he a friend? I would like to believe he is—though it's a long time since we last met or spent some time together.

Among my most prized possessions remains the Bulgari pen he gave me on my 45th birthday and a stunning terracotta sculpture which still adorns my drawing room. But, to be honest, my most cherished memory of Amit is that enchanting wintry day we spent together in Kolkata when he, Anupam and Satish Kaushik turned up to enact a Sanskrit street play to launch an exhibition of my poems in a tiny gallery on Shakespeare Sarani. The same evening he launched an album of my poems.

How long ago was that? I have no idea but it seems like yesterday.

Isn't that what friendship is all about.

Preface

What do I say of a man to whom reams and reams of pages have already been devoted?

My first meeting with Amitabh Bachchan was soon after his marriage: he was visiting Delhi, where I was then based. Accompanied by a journalist friend, I went to meet the newly-wed couple at the Oberoi's and was welcomed by his mother Teji *ji*. We waited awhile to see the bride, Jaya Bachchan, and after some time enquired, 'When will Jaya *ji* come?' Teji *ji* answered, *'Abhi toh main apni bahu se khud nahi mil paayi hoon aur aap log aa gaye. Intezar kijiye.'* (I haven't seen my own daughter-in-law yet, and you have arrived. Please wait.) And then, in walked Amitabh Bachchan. He sat across the table from us wearing a red, round-neck T-shirt with a huge gold chain around his neck.

Some years later, I shifted base to Mumbai in search of a full-time career in photojournalism. I would often visit studios in search of a good photograph. I did see Bachchan a couple of times, and even then I found him to be a very humble man. One day, as I was sitting under a tree at Mohan Studio in Andheri, I saw him cycle from one set to another to meet director Hrishikesh Mukherjee. I can still see that image vividly — Amitabh Bachchan cycling.

My first job in the city was as a photo editor with a magazine called *Super*, published by Namita Gokhale and her late husband Rajiv Gokhale. At that time, Bachchan was not talking to the Press. We decided to do a cover story on him and travelled to several places, including Allahabad, Nainital and Kolkata, to find out about his early days. But our story was incomplete without his interview. My colleague Malvinder Grewal and I met several people — including Dr Harivanshrai Bachchan — to see if they could set up an interview with Amitabh Bachchan for us. Nothing worked. Finally, we tracked him down at a film shoot. We went up to him and requested an interview. He politely declined saying that he was staying away from the Press. He even refused a photo shoot.

Once Bachchan resumed shooting after his accident, the Press was invited to meet him. I subsequently attended many film shootings and photographed him on several occasions. However, all my shots have been candid ones, and taken from a long distance. He rarely looked into my camera, while I enjoyed shooting from a distance.

I have interviewed him myself on a few occasions, like the time when he was voted 'Man of the Year'. Though Bachchan was extremely hard-pressed for time, he accommodated me. I did a telephonic interview while he was on his way to Breach Candy Hospital. I requested him for a photograph which he said was difficult because he was pressed for time. I persisted, as, being a photojournalist, my article was incomplete without a photograph. He obliged, and found time for that as well.

A couple of years ago, I decided to do an exhibition of paintings, photographs, furniture and poems on his sixty-first birthday. I requested him to inaugurate my show — held at JW Marriott — and to my surprise he agreed. It was a pleasant evening, one that I will always remember.

My many images of him in his various moods and during the myriad situations he has faced in life are like little time capsules of how a man faces, with dignity, whatever life throws at him. And this is a man we all look up to. A man who carries a little bit of every Indian's hopes with him at all times.

I have continued to photograph and admire the actor and the man from a distance. And, like his audience, I too know a little about the legend through his films and through the media. But my most intimate connection to him remains my photographs. Hundreds of them shot over the span of my career as a photojournalist.

I can't pinpoint how and when the idea of writing this book struck me. In this youth-centric world, very few of our icons have already finished half the glass of the elixir called life. Bachchan remains one of the few people who inspires me to be the best I can, as he does millions of people across the country. When I am low, I revisit my memories of the times I was privileged enough to spend with him and others I admire like M.F. Husain, Dev Anand and J.P. Singhal.

In my musings about Bachchan, I realise what a continued inspiration he remains not just to me but my family as well. I, of course, have been a fan since *Deewar;* my children used to dance to his songs through school and college; and I was astounded recently when my toddler granddaughter, Stuti, pointed to one of his photographs and started singing *Holi Khele Raghuveera.* She has since moved on to *Kajra re.*

At sixty-four, Bachchan remains the biggest and most successful star of all time, in India at least, if we're not counting his fans among the Indian diaspora. Superstars like Dilip Kumar and Ashok Kumar have seen a resurgence in their popularity in their middle ages, but none have seen the adulation that Bachchan continues to receive.

Fame doesn't sit lightly on him, though. Bachchan puts in forty hours' worth of work in the twenty-four that we all get. If I were to divide a lifetime into Shakespeare's seven stages, he has made every one of them count.

In an era where youth is king, he is a lesson on the value of the vintage. He represents an entire generation of India. One that has refused to fade away. His old world charisma sits easily alongside the youthful charm of son Abhishek. Here's to both of them. Live on Mr Bachchan. And Abhishek, here's to you and the dreams of your generation. Live on and sing on.

Introduction

Bachchan, the movie legend; Bachchan, the TV star; Bachchan, the actor non pareil.

The czar of Hindi cinema continues to rule. God knows, his golden era has lasted long enough, and how! But don't attribute it to luck alone, hand it to him — for his sheer dedication, hard work and the honesty with which he plays his roles.

'Do you realise what it has taken me to make an ass of myself?' Bachchan queried in 1982. (The inevitable response to that being, whatever it is, the audience loves it.) Like the philosopher's stone, every little thing he touches seems to turn into gold. Five hits in 2005 and a hit TV show to boot, Amitabh Bachchan is the new age Midas. And when one begins to consider the sheer variety and virtuosity that went into each of these roles, one begins to appreciate the capacity and talent of the man once dismissed as a flop hero.

On screen, he created magic at the box office for over two decades. But it was a run punctuated by many trials. Then came his self-imposed exile in the late Nineties after *Khuda Gawah*, with Sridevi, another superstar with a troubled aurorae.

And then his return to the film industry in 1995, but with a corporate image. He came back to the business as the brand ambassador of Amitabh Bachchan Corporation Limited (ABCL). As a star, he was contracted to his own company. Everything looked rosy. Bachchan seemed capable of making the enterprise a success solely on the strength of his personality and popularity. Even though the first movie he did for the corporation, *Mrityudaata,* didn't do well, Bachchan's onscreen clout and some savvy casting helped him hold his own in his next two releases, *Major Saab* and *Bade Miyan Chhote Miyan.*

From then on, Bachchan lived through the ideals put forth by Rudyard Kipling in the celebrated poem *If.* He staked all his earnings on a 'single game of pitch-and-toss' that was ABCL. He lost everything.

The period that followed turned out to be the nadir of his life. The corporation faced bankruptcy and Bachchan suddenly found himself out of work. However, he kept his wits about him in a situation where others might have lost it. He started again, from the beginning, without bewailing his loss in public. He began looking for work with the sole aim of paying off all his debts. He met with a great deal of media scrutiny regarding his financial status, but his path back from the brink was a journey he accomplished with the same grace and principled approach that has been the trademark of his career.

Mohabbatein — produced by Yash Raj films in 2000 — saw him return to the silver screen with a bang. Young director Aditya Chopra pitted him against Chopra mascot and current superstar Shah Rukh Khan, who was cast opposite screen queen Aishwarya Rai. The film also had three pairs of teenyboppers, including the director's brother Uday Chopra. Not an easy prospect for any actor seeking a comeback, let alone one in his fifties. Any other middle-aged actor would have been eclipsed. Anyone, that is, other than Bachchan. His performance demonstrated clearly that he was still an actor to reckon with.

But Bachchan didn't rest with this. The volume of debt he was facing meant more challenges had to be taken. Undaunted, he began endorsing products, something he had refrained from doing throughout his career. The offers poured in. In 2000, Bachchan successfully broke ground in another path, another medium: the small screen. The Star network approached Bachchan with an offer to host a game show, *Kaun Banega Crorepati* (KBC). No established film actor had ever ventured into television programming before. It was another tough call, but he decided to take the plunge, much against his wife's wishes (Jaya Bachchan thought his aura would diminish if he appeared on television). And what a plunge it was! Bachchan's charm worked its magic; his years in show business, his experiences, his trials, had all lent him a maturity which, coupled with his magnetic screen presence, surrounded him like a nimbus and bowled the audience over. Clearly Bachchan's star was on the rise once more.

Bachchan is not just the only big movie star to enter television, he is also the only film actor to have succeeded so overwhelmingly. Today, the makers of KBC have such confidence in Bachchan, they have signed him on for a second season comprising eighty-five episodes, which will be telecast through the second half of 2005.

Bachchan's versatility is such that he is able to shoot these shows while simultaneously acting in films. Another first in the history of Indian entertainment: no star who has made the transition to TV has ever returned to the big screen successfully, and in a sustained manner. Even younger actors like Karisma Kapoor and Raveena Tandon have not yet set out to do this. Madhuri Dixit is the only actor to have come back to the big screen successfully with *Devdas* after her short foray into television.

Today, there is a marked difference in the roles that Bachchan does. While he typified the Angry Young Man, and possibly the Angry Middle-Aged Man in the past, it is a more sensitive, brooding man that we see now. Previously stuck with the tag of being a 'popular entertainer', Bachchan now no longer lags behind on the creativity stakes. Not only is he the first fifty-plus star to have such massive, widespread appeal, he is also the only one to comprehensively regain all his erstwhile glory.

Whereas earlier, he was heralded as a superstar, Bachchan's newly regained stardom has made him a figure of awe among the other members of the industry. With over four hits in the first half of 2005 alone, Amitabh Bachchan is no longer on a 'comeback' trail. Also, having paid off all his debts and with his company AB Corp doing well, he is sitting pretty on the financial side of his life too.

And what a delight it is to watch Bachchan act now. There is more variety in his roles. The authoritarian of *Mohabbatein* and *Kabhi Khushi Kabhi Gham* is balanced by the playful principal of *Kyon! Ho Gaya Na* and the new age father in *Waqt*. The only role that can be compared with his role as Dashrath Singh in *Bunty Aur Babli* could be Bachchan's own turn in *Zanjeer* — and, he's arguably bettered himself. And is there any precedent at all for his Devraj Sahai in *Black*? His role as Vidyadhar Patwardhan in *Viruddh* is in a different league altogether. *Viruddh*, as one reviewer puts it, is 'an Amitabh Bachchan movie: Carefully keeping away from the classy mannerisms which have been his mainstay, he brings alive the very identifiable qualities that a majority of the middle class lives by — die-hard honesty, sincerity and grit.'

The icing on Bachchan's cake, however, is his son Abhishek's recent success. Indeed, two of his four major hits in 2005 were films in which he shared screen time with Abhishek.

There has been no one quite like Amitabh Bachchan in the film industry. Of course, there have been many superstars like him, but none that have come back in their sixties to dominate the Indian psyche as Bachchan has. Shahnaz Anand, Bachchan's co-star in his first film *Saat Hindustani,* who also shared the screen with him briefly in *Black,* says: 'He could definitely be called a legend. Perhaps Dilip Kumar too could be classified as a legend, but nobody else. Rajesh Khanna had his time, but I would not call him a legend. He was a superstar. I think Amitabh has surpassed the "superstar" status and has gone on to become a legend.'

Chapter One

The Early Days

Then to the rolling Heav'n itself I cried,
Asking 'What Lamp has Destiny to guide
Her little children stumbling in the dark?'
And — 'A blind Understanding!' Heav'n replied.
　　　　　　　–The Rubaiyat of Omar Khayyam

To dear Amitji with love n Regards

MACBETH

IS THIS A DAGGER THAT I SEE BEFORE ME?

Through Amitabh Bachchan's childhood, a love for make-believe and play-acting ran through his blood like a fever. Nothing in his childhood had influenced this passion for acting, but it stayed on in Bachchan's mind, only to emerge well into his adulthood.

Bachchan was born the year the Quit India movement began: 1942. The movement was a massive social phenomenon that was a precursor of a great change. Like Salman Rushdie's Saleem Sinai, Amitabh's life 'dissolves into episodes and as a character..., who grows up in a society experiencing a process of modernisation, is built up from moment to moment through these episodes. His life is narrated by focusing on particular visual details; the "remake" of his life shows how circumstantial, transitory and fragile individuality is. Only step by step or look by look through the circular hole in the sheet does Dr Aziz succeed in making "a badly fitting collage" of Saleem's grandmother-to-be; in the same way Saleem is a collage rather than a whole person[1]. Similarly, most of Amitabh's life can be described through a series of visual images that are his films.

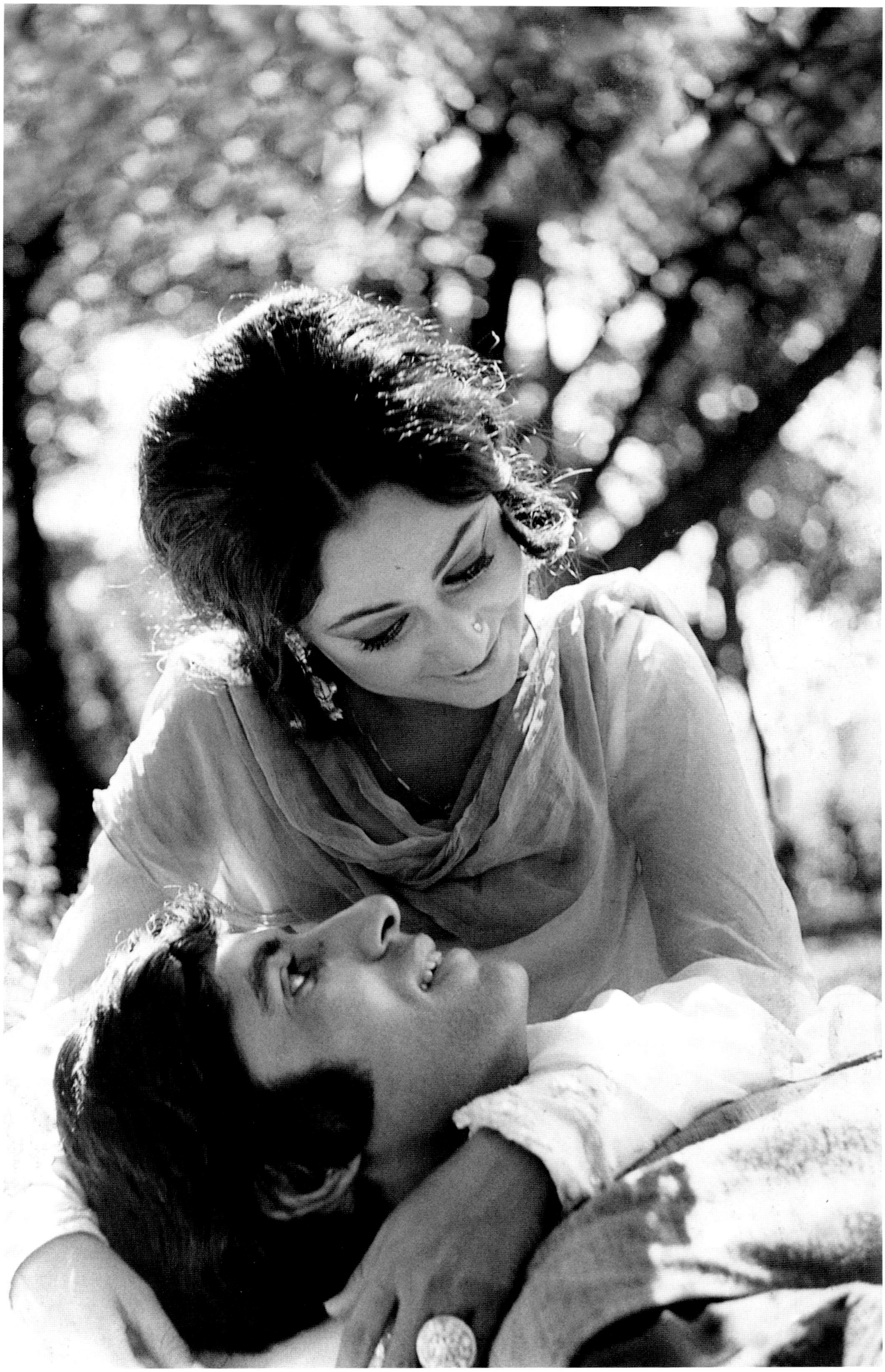

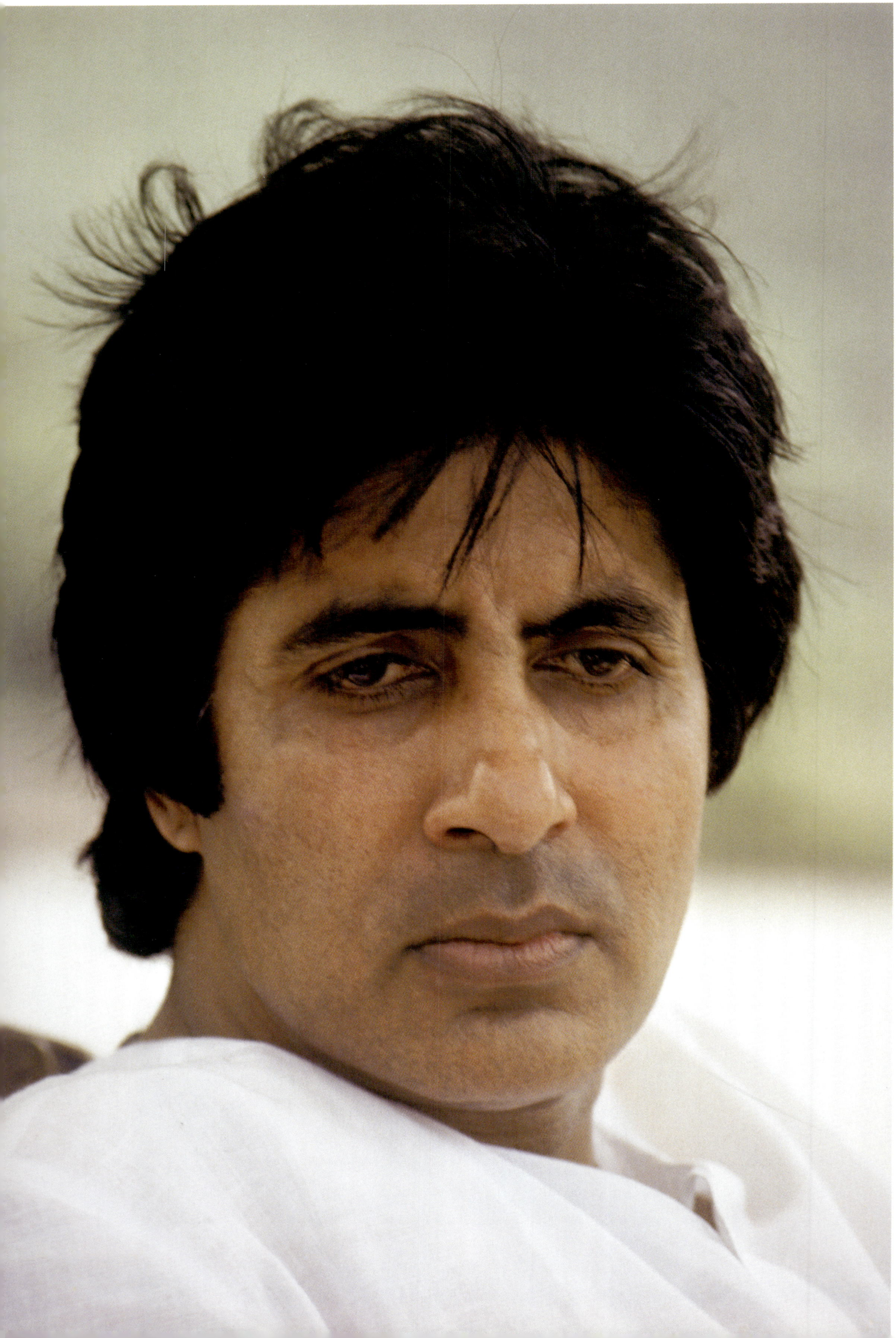

A child of famous parents has to spend a considerable part of his or her life under the charged halo of their personas. The young Amitabh was no exception. Though a keen follower of literature, he didn't want to enter this realm that his father, Harivanshrai Bachchan, dominated. His middling looks did not in any way mark him out as a likely successor to his mother Teji, a famed beauty from an affluent Sikh family of Lahore, the centre of glitz and sophistication at the time.

However, his mother inculcated a sense of order and aesthetics in her young son. Lessons that the grown man would always remember. Herself an aesthete, she inculcated in him a sense of good taste and manners. Teji Bachchan wanted her son to be an all-rounder. She encouraged him to take an equal interest in games as well as studies.

Pushpa Bharati[2], a family friend of the Bachchans, remembers the young Amitabh as a resilient child. She recounts how once, when the four-year-old Amitabh was gored by a bull in the head, the child did not cry even once, as his mother washed the wound with stinging spirit and he eventually had to be taken to a doctor. He was also a dependable child. On being told that they had to return before sunset, Amitabh and his brother Ajitabh would run back home at the stipulated time, sometimes even abandoning a game midway.

Amitabh was a keen pugilist in school. However, he scored more on interest rather than success in boxing bouts. His father encouraged him, once even gifting his son a book on boxing with a quote from Yeats inscribed in it which said: 'Good hard blows are a delight to the mind'. Amitabh's lean physique didn't help him much, though his tenacity earned him several admirers. In his final year at Sherwood College, Nainital, Amitabh pugnaciously held on, eventually losing narrowly on a points decision in the final round. He won appreciation as a determined, but fair, sportsperson though. This quality has remained with him all his life. 'He's like Mohammed Ali. He can come back when he wants. He has tremendous reserves as an actor,' says old acquaintance, Amar Bedi.

Bachchan's time at school was fairly uneventful. Not many of the staff that taught him at Sherwood actually still remain. In any case, the quiet boy is likely to have escaped attention; he had impeccable manners and was inherently disciplined. And teachers as a rule only tend to recall the naughty children in a class, the ones who have to be hauled up frequently.

Bundu, the school barber, still remains though, and has no complaints. 'He would stand quietly while I cut his hair. The other boys were always fidgeting and complaining, "barber, *jaldi kaat do*". If I told him to get me sohan halwa from Delhi, he would bring back a box full when he returned after the holidays.'

A keen theatre person and elocutionist, Bachchan took part in various play. Though he didn't get very far in elocution competitions, he was very good at acting. Ms M. Murch, his teacher and the mother of Delhi theatre personality Marcus Murch, and Santosh, the school's master in-charge of Hindi plays, shaped and moulded the style and mannerisms that would become famous across India. 'Amit, do something with your hands, don't keep them dangling,' they would instruct him. His turn as Mr Pond, the headmaster in John Dighton's *The Happiest Days of Your Life,* during the 1956 term was remarkable as it was a part meant for a much older actor. Yet, Amitabh showed restraint and maturity, remarkable things in a fourteen-year-old.

The next year saw another challenge: he was given the role of the mayor in Nicolai Gogol's

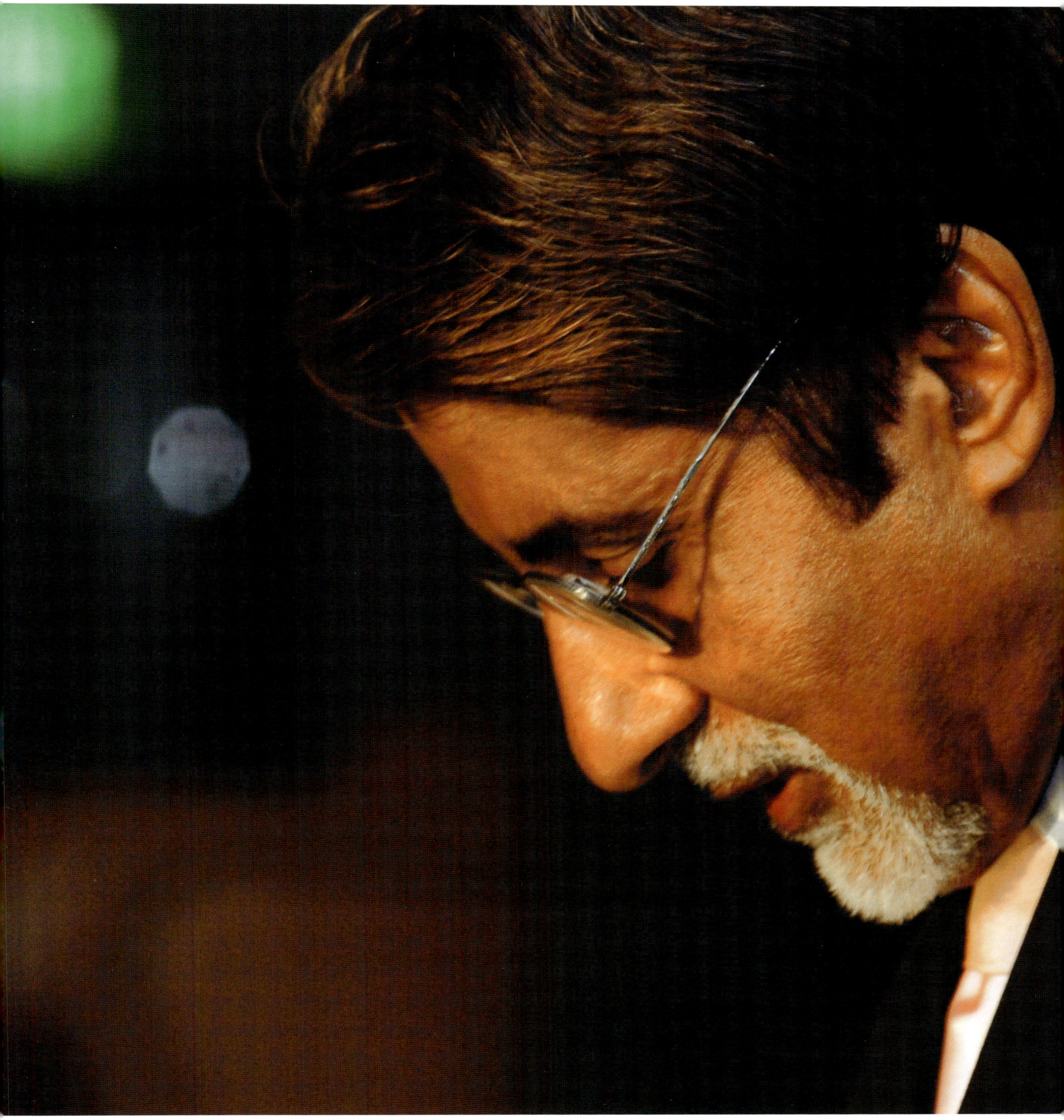

The Legend

26

Inspector General. Again, the part required an older actor. The talented boy carried the audience along with him. He most definitely deserved the Kendall Cup which he won that year for Best Actor: it was presented to him by the legendary Geoffrey Kendall, Shakespearean actor and Shashi Kapoor's father-in-law.

Amitabh finished his education with a degree in science from Delhi's Kirori Mal College. Frank Thakurdas, the head of the college's drama society Players, which has had other illustrious members like Rajendra Nath, Dinesh Thakur and Kulbushan Kharbanda, remembers hearing Amitabh's voice while passing through the corridors one day. He realised how

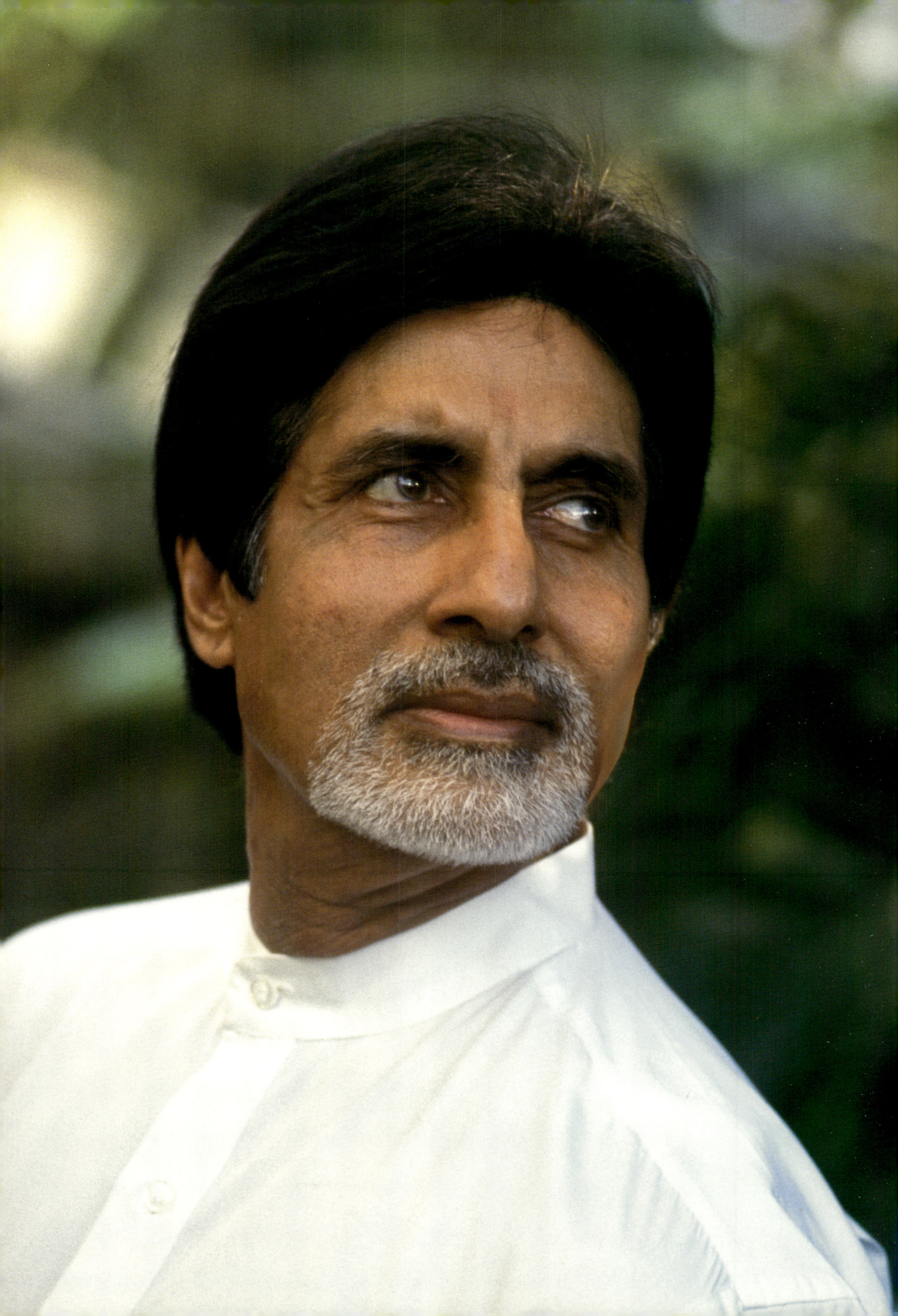

well the voice would suit the stage and took him on in a play he was staging.

That year, theatre personality Pratap Sharma's brother had been cast in the lead role. However, for some reason he was suddenly unable to do it. In the ensuing panic, Amitabh quietly told the master that he could step in. Thakurdas dithered as he thought Amitabh's height might detract attention from the character, but let him play the part as he knew the role by heart. Amitabh went on to do a wonderful job. 'We would love to have him back on the stage, even for a few minutes,' says Thakurdas[3].

During his college days, Amitabh got the chance to act in the annual theatre production organised by Miranda House: a well known event in Delhi. The play was *Rape of the Belt* by Benn Levy, and he played a minor part: that of Zeus. The person who really shone that year was a young actor from Miranda

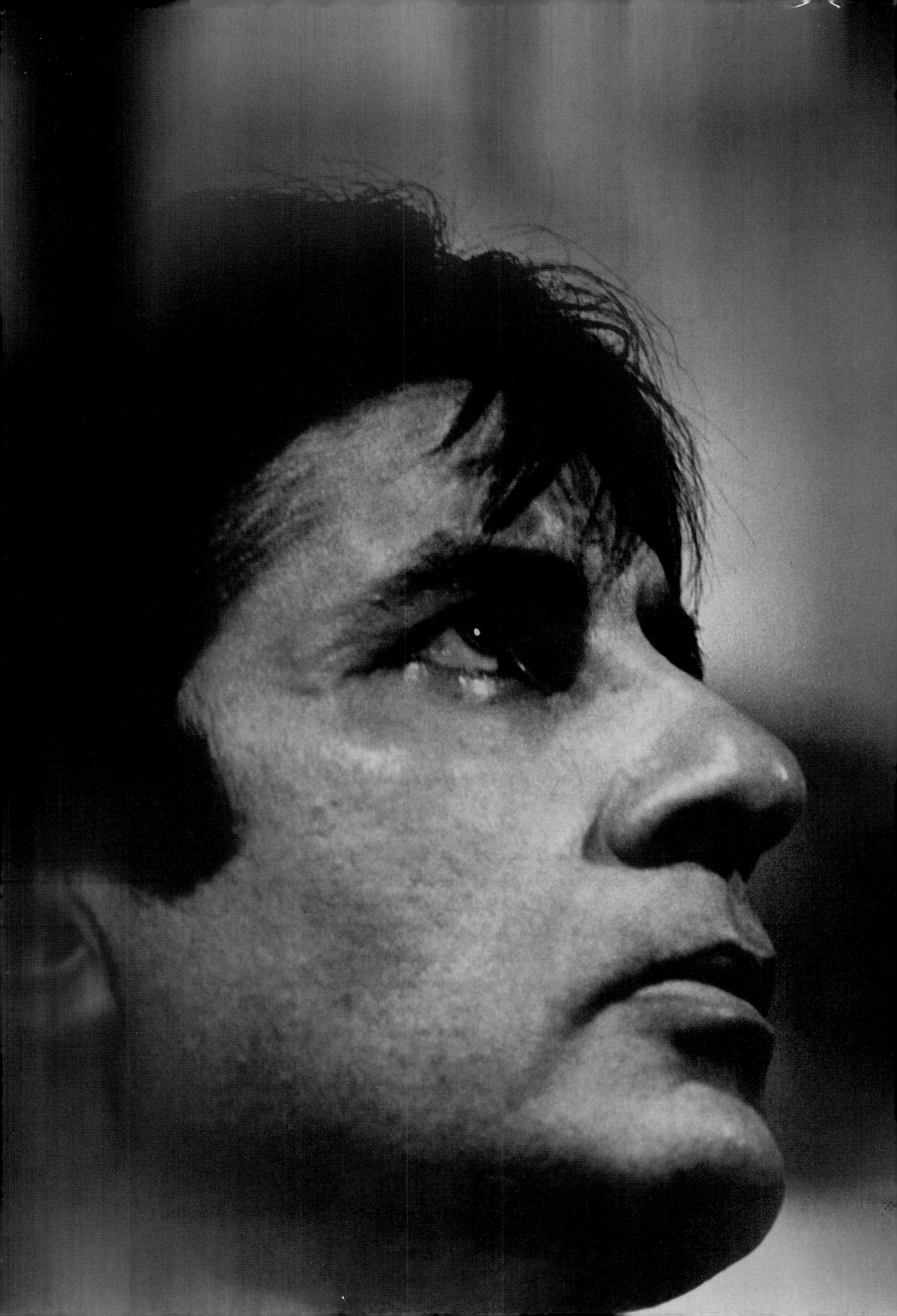

House, who would go on to become a very famous face in Mumbai theatre, Dolly Thakore.

Thakore and Bachchan didn't know each other well then, 'but his brother Bunty and he belonged to the same so-called circle in a sense, that I belonged to while we were in college,' she says. Preminder Premchand, one of the first women to work in media, used to hold get-togethers and soirees for which she used to invite this circle of friends. Ajitabh, who seems to have been the more extroverted brother, Bachchan, Thakore and Vijay Crishna were all part of this group.

'Vijay Crishna's mother was personal secretary to Indira Gandhi at the time. So we used to get invited for Christmas or some big party every year. The whole gang used to go. Bunty used to be a regular, but Amitabh came only once or twice. What I remember was he used to sit in a corner — very quiet, very shy. Bunty was the handsome one, not Amitabh,' remembers Thakore.

After college Amitabh started working with Calcutta's Bird and Co., then a leading business concern with a long lineage. His boss, David Gilani,

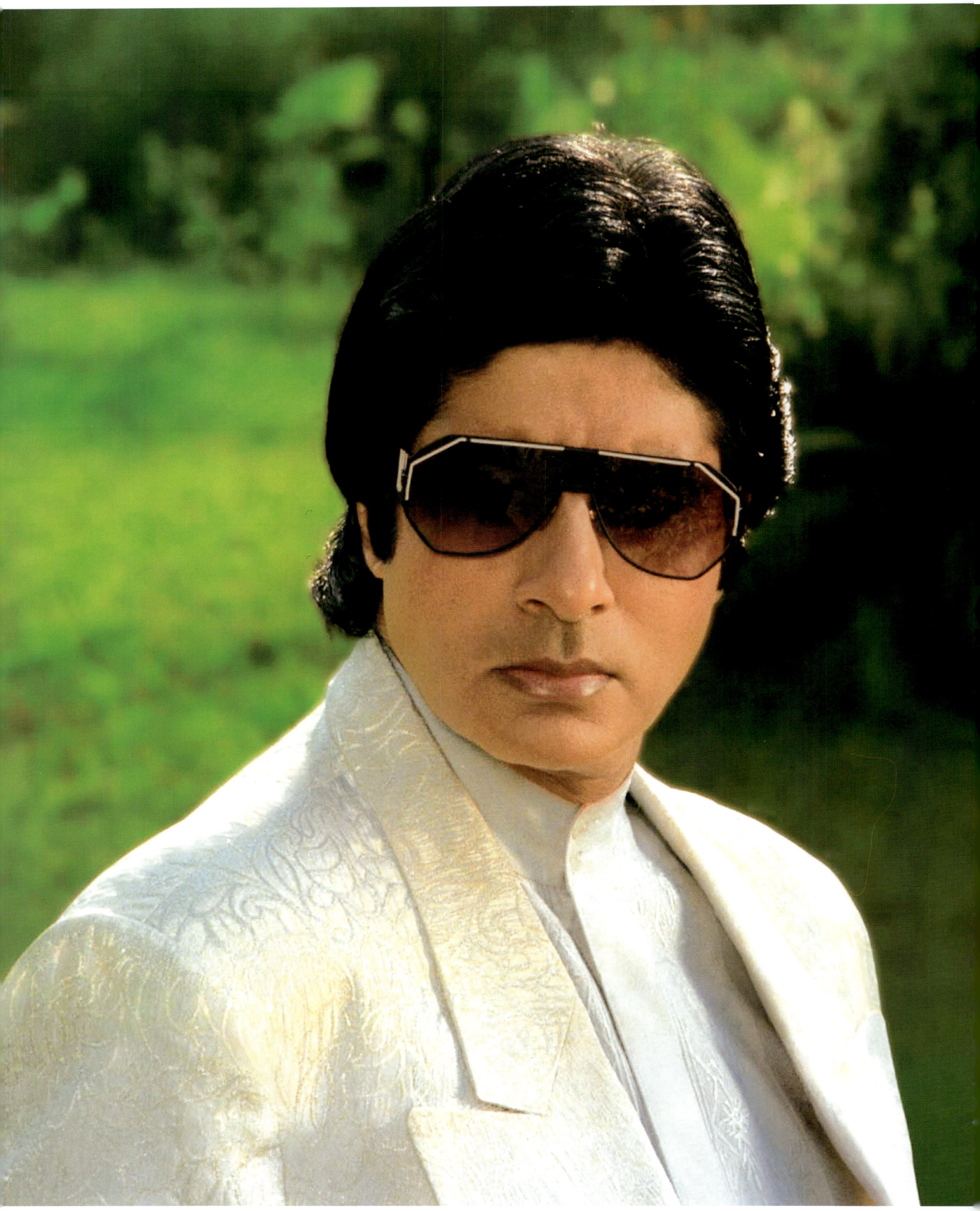

remembers him as serious and conscientious. 'His principal asset, even in business, was his charm and good manners, but while his mind was in business his heart was clearly somewhere else,' he says[4].

While in Calcutta, Amitabh joined the Calcutta Amateur Theatre Society. Through his stellar performances, he established himself in the local theatre circuit and earned a lot of respect both from his peers as well as the audience. Gilani remembers him as doing both serious plays as well as comedies. 'I've seen a lot of plays in London and on Broadway and I can say that Amitabh's performances ranked with the best,' says Gilani.

Gerson D'Cunha, respected theatre personality and director of Bombay First, said recently, 'I had heard of him as an actor of English theatre in Calcutta from my friend Noel Godin. My personal feeling is that he should give theatre a chance. But the problem with theatre is that it demands time. Theatre and cinema are very different — don't think that if you can do one, you can do the other. When Amitabh decides to do theatre, he will be a great actor... But he will do it because he instinctively perceives his audience....'

'Theatre has always interested me. Prior to joining films, there was never a year when I was not on stage. [These days] Time has been a constraint. I don't think I will be able to do it now. I don't think I have the confidence to do a play,' Bachchan confessed ruefully once.

It must have been a very comfortable life for Amitabh. He changed jobs after a couple of years to join the freight brokering firm Blacker and Co. for a post that offered double his previous salary as well as a Morris Minor car. As a single, newly-independent man, life was good. He had a well-paying job and several friends. He could have stayed where he was. But he chose to make a change.

According to American mythologist Joseph Campbell, the standard path of a hero's mythological

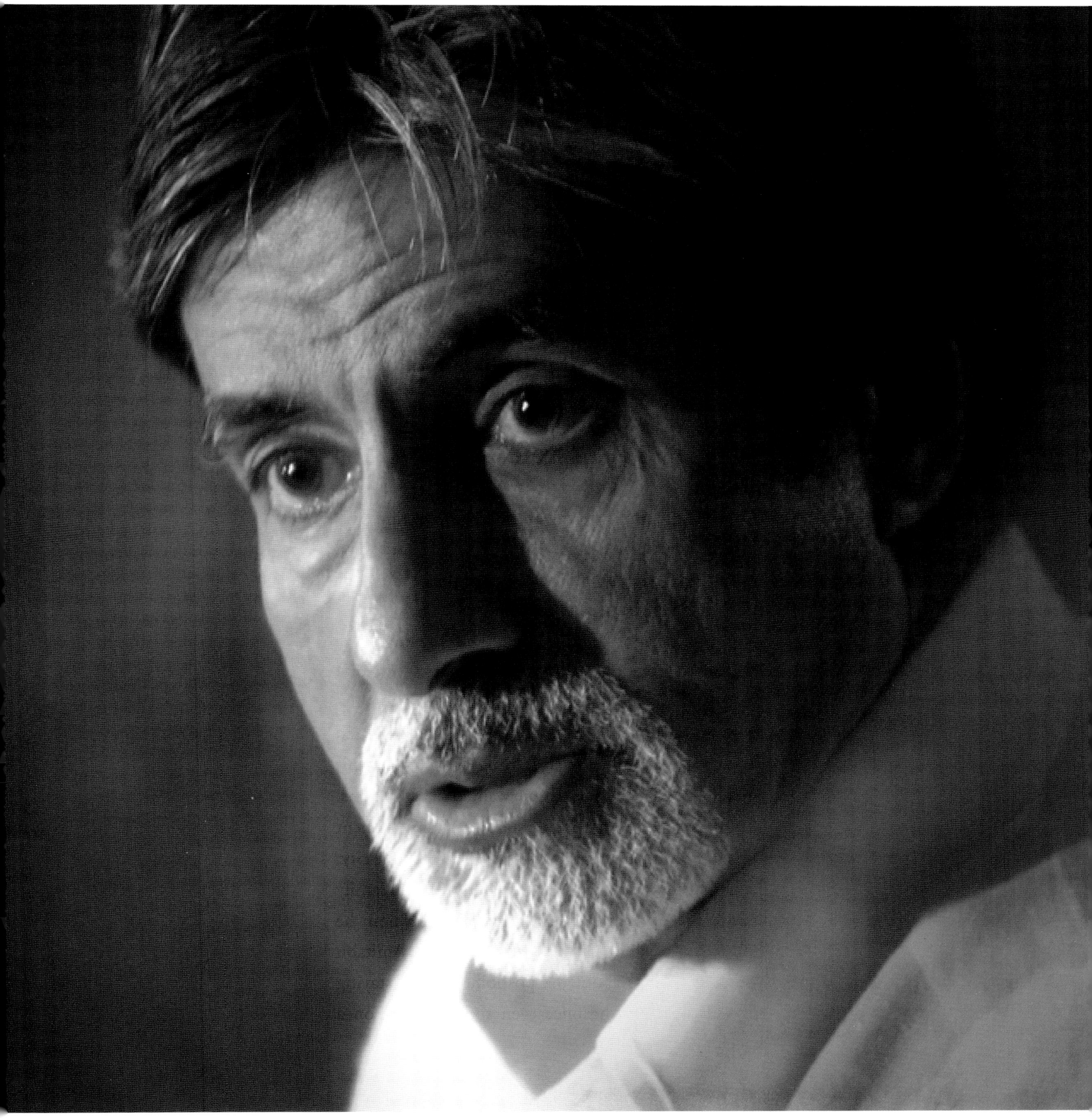

adventure is a magnification of the formula represented in the rites of passage: separation — initiation — return[5]. A hero ventures forth from the common every day world into a region of supernatural wonder: fabulous forces are there encountered and decisive victory is won: the hero comes back from the mysterious venture to bestow boons on his fellow man[6].

The journey into the magical realm of films was primed to start any time. The call to adventure had begun. And Amitabh, the artist, heard the keening cry. All he had to do was take the plunge.

His brother Ajitabh sensed his dilemma. He clicked photographs of Amitabh around Victoria Memorial in Calcutta and sent them to the Filmfare–Madhuri talent contest: a nationwide search for new stars. Amitabh didn't make it. But after this initial brush, he decided that he wanted to act in films. Having made the decision, he started making frequent trips to Bombay. Amitabh wasn't rudderless in the city: he had his brother's house there, besides several family friends including the Khaitan family, with whom he housed for a while. But the well-mannered Amitabh was so conscious about the possibility of overstaying his welcome, that he once even spent a night on a bench at Marine Drive.

Actor Tinnu Anand, who was originally to play a part in *Saat Hindustani,* recalls how Amitabh was

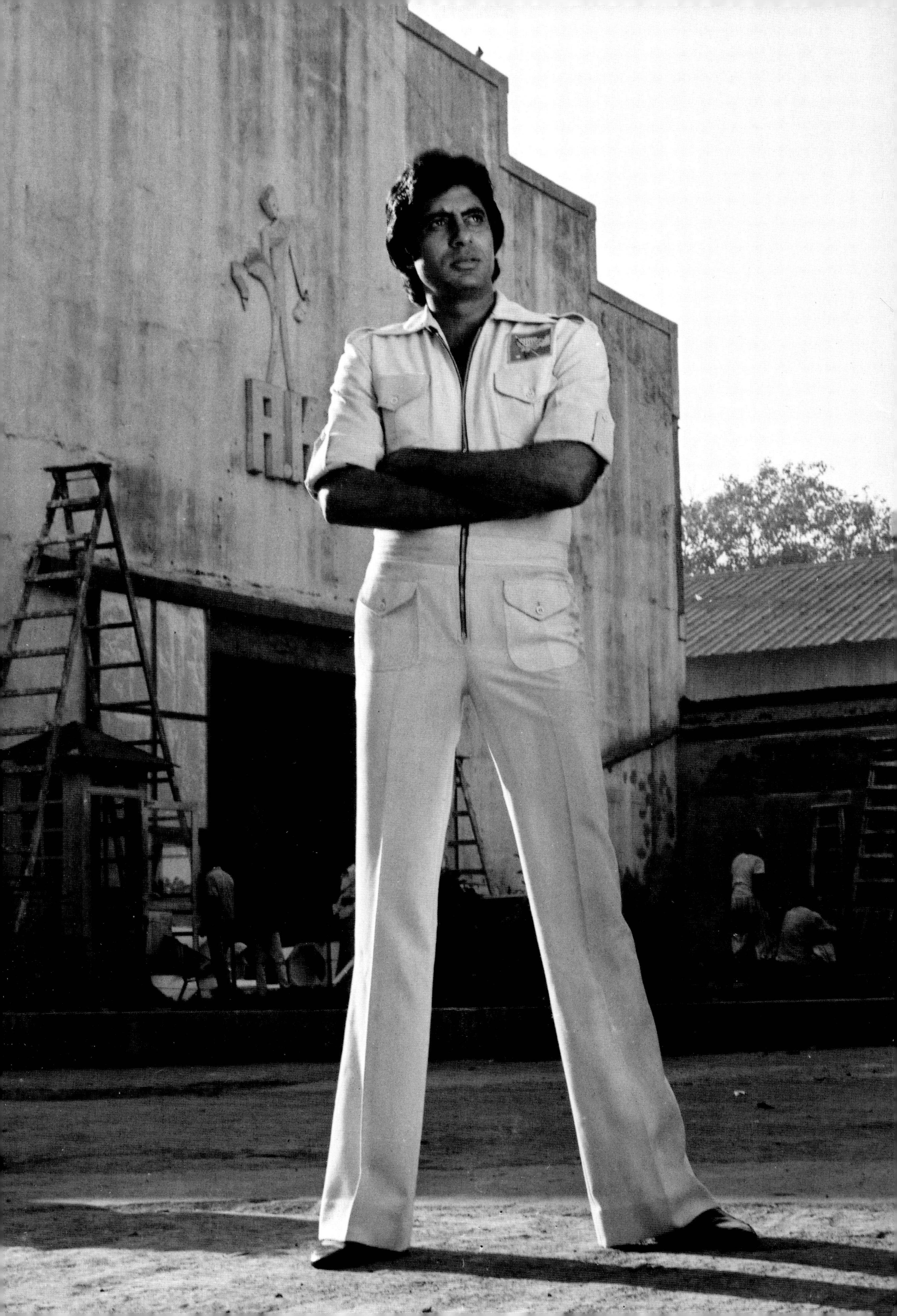

cast in the movie. Anand was asked by a mutual friend and one of the heroines of the movie, Neena Singh, to show a friend's photographs to K.A. Abbas, the director. 'The photos were of Amitabh outside Victoria Memorial and that was handed over to Abbas *sahab* through me. I was just the conduit, the catalyst[7].

'When Abbas *sahab* saw the pictures he said *theek hai*. Tell Neena *ji* to call her friend to see me. Amitabh came to Bombay and went straight to Abbas *sahab's* office. While we were waiting to see him, he wanted to use the washroom. I escorted him to my house, which was in the same building. When we were there, I introduced him to my father, who asked Amitabh whether he was related to Dr Harivanshrai Bachchan. He replied that Dr Bachchan was his father. My father then told him that our family was acquainted with Teji *ji's* family. And we exchanged a few pleasantries.

'Then we went to meet Abbas *sahab* and Amitabh left after the interview. Abbas *sahab* settled with me that Amitabh would act in his film and would receive Rs 5,000 as a fixed salary irrespective of how

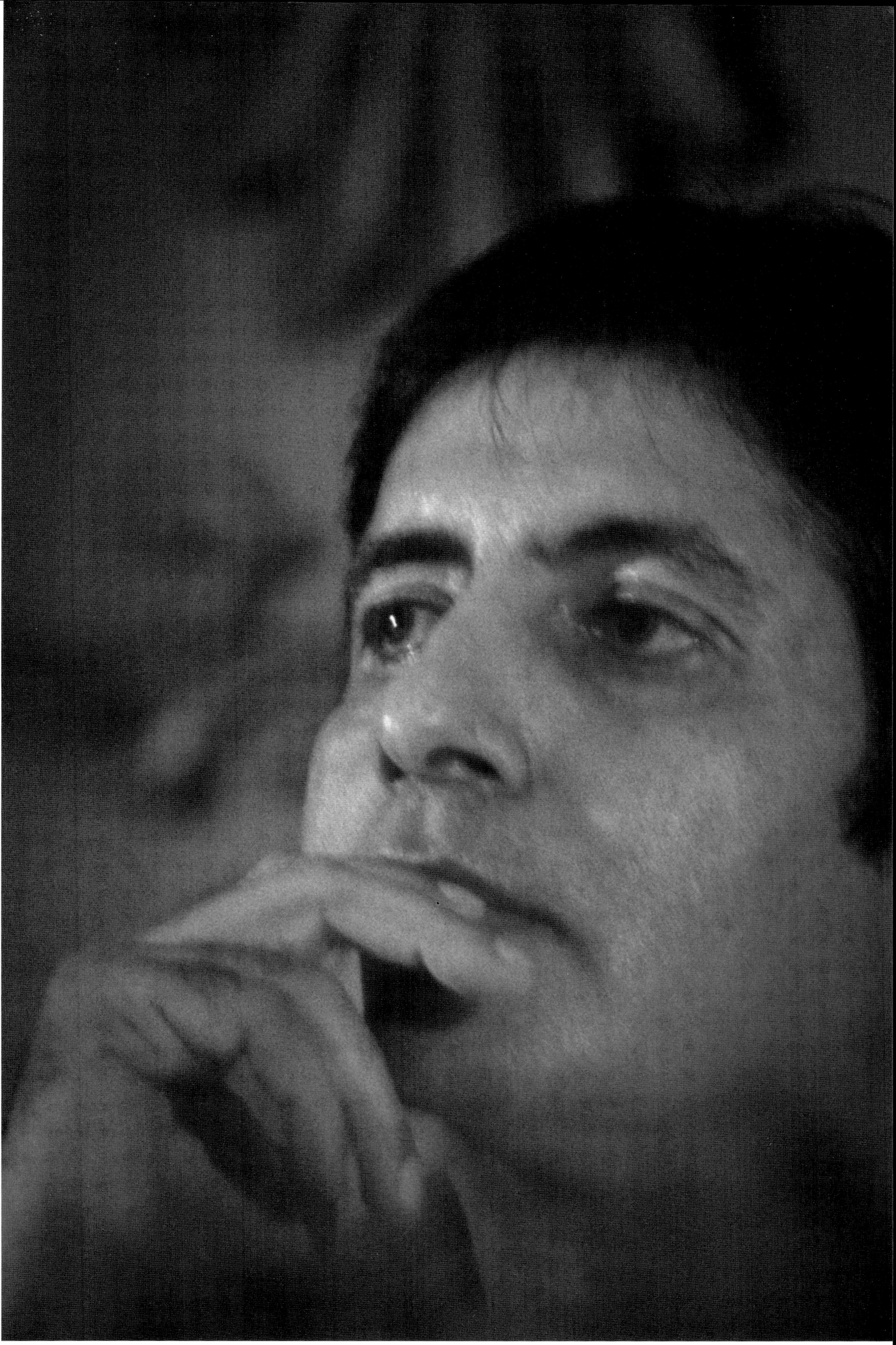

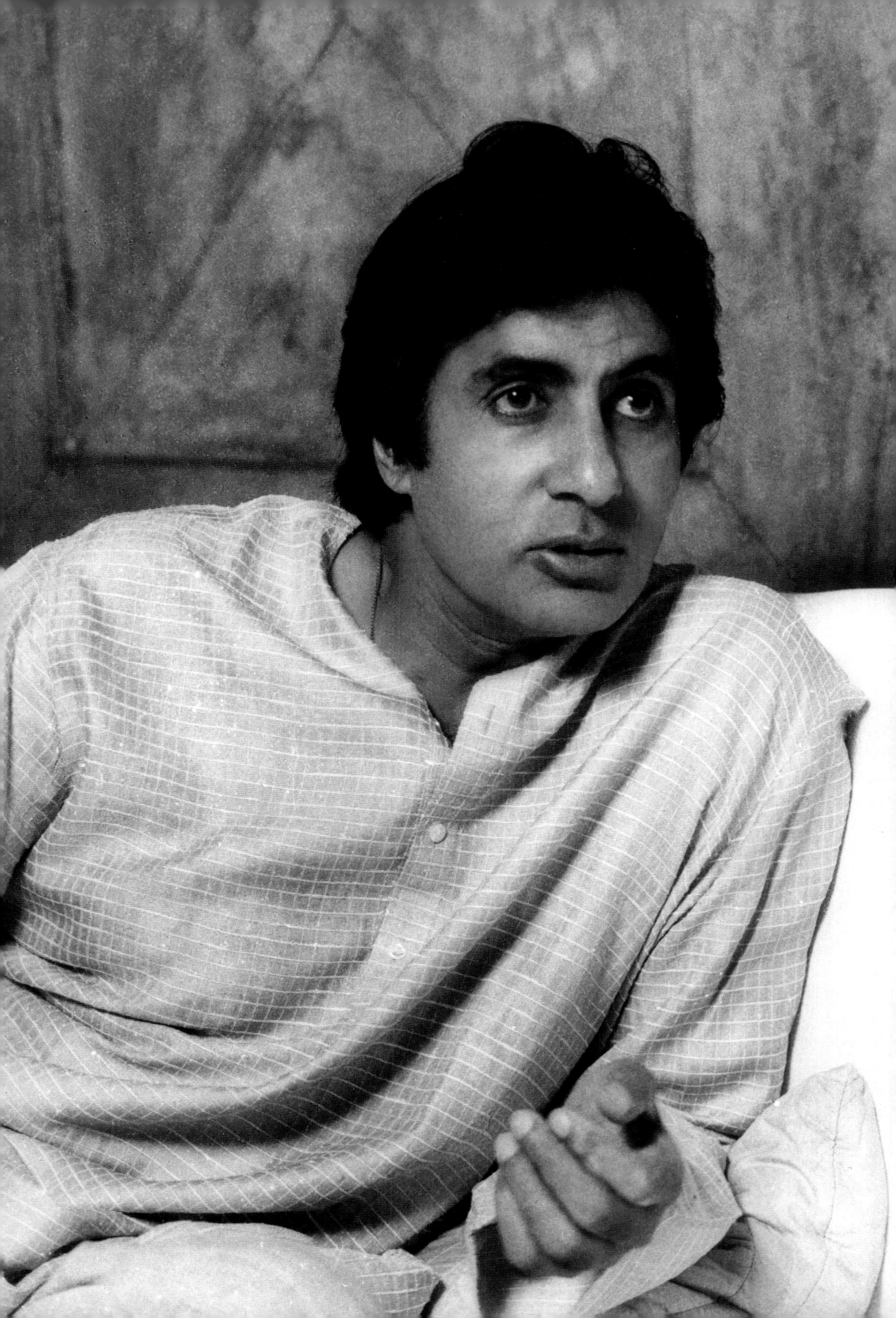

long it took to shoot the film. I met the brothers later and relayed the news. Both of them looked at each other perturbed. Amitabh said that the amount was two months' salary for him. Then Ajitabh asked me if it was possible to have another meeting with Abbas *sahab*. Eventually they met and finalised the contract.

'Amitabh was chosen and we used to go for rehearsals together. At that time I got a call from Calcutta, where I had applied for apprenticeship with Satyajit Ray. He said that he was starting a movie, and that I should come down immediately. I had to decide between acting and directing. I definitely wanted to be a director and I wanted to learn under the best person.

'I left *Saat Hindustani*. The movie hadn't started filming. The role that I was supposed to do was finally transferred to Amitabh. And Amitabh's vacant slot was filled up by Anwar Ali.'

Says director Abbas, 'I was looking for someone to play a Muslim poet and he looked poetic enough to me. He had the one qualification for the role:

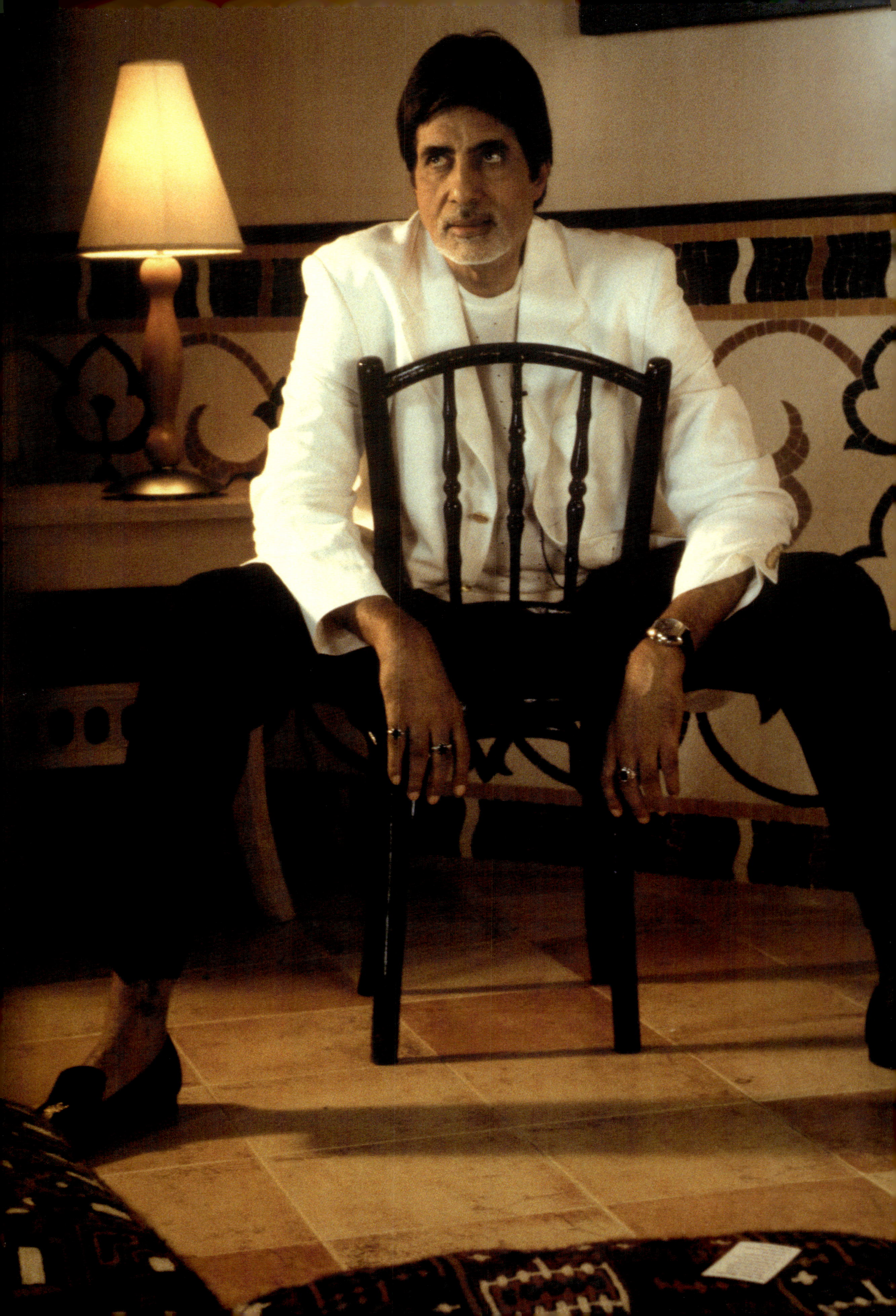

he was not a Muslim. I wanted a scrambled cast, with a Muslim playing a Hindu bigot, a Bengali playing a Punjabi.'

He did not regret his decision. In a later interview, Abbas reminisced about the flurry of attention that Amitabh's later success garnered him. 'All kinds of young men ring my door-bell (though my door is always open). They come to me because they are star-struck and think that since Amitabh Bachchan first appeared in one of my films, *Saat Hindustani,* I have the capacity (which I simply don't) to produce many more Amitabh Bachchans.'

The Writer

Bachchan is a gifted writer. Reproduced below is an article written by Amitabh Bachchan, which first appeared in the December 1963 issue of the ***Sherwoodian***, Bachchan's school magazine. In it, Amitabh describes his visit to his old school on Founder's Day, five years after he passed out.

The afternoon of 3rd June saw me climbing up the stairs to the new Infirmary Block with a feeling of elation — wonder who all have landed up? Awfully quiet up there… I hope they…

A bare hall confronted me. Elation took a step back to disappointment, as I saw just 3 occupied beds in one corner — the only signs of OSS [Old Sherwoodians Society] inhabitation!

As the evening wore on, however, things (they sure looked things) began to show up. Amongst the first was Wali Khan, a well trimmed fungus now adorning his smiling face; then came Ajit Mukherjee (Muko), Jahota, Chimni, Arora, Siddiqui, Charlie Dhawan, Sabharwal and Baby Bach, everyone looked changed, but still very much a Sherwoodian.

The first night almost turned out to be a near riot. Muko, returning late from the night show, suddenly realised, just before turning in that both his blankets were missing! Dhawan, evidently exhausted by the long walk home, flopped into bed with a bang, but within a second was seen out of it, holding onto his head. 'Who's zacked my pillow?' he groaned. There was an uneasy silence for a moment. Then Sabharwal's meek voice was heard: 'I say fellows, have you seen my, er…pyjamas?' A frantic search followed. Everyone was out of bed, turning things over. I said everyone. It should have been almost everyone, for one heap on a particular bed remained unperturbed. A rhythmic but quiet snore, the type one acquires after a good two to three hours sleep, was emerging from under the blankets.

Blankets! Muko's eyes blinked. He grabbed at them and pulled them off, and there, comfortably trousseaued in Sabharwal's night pants, resting his head on Charlie's dunlopillow, was Birendra Singh, the latest addition to the OSS group! Thus began the Founders Week for the 'Past'.

The traditional matches this year were restricted, unfortunately, to just one match, hockey, the main problem being lack of players. On the fifth evening however, a fairly competent and colourful OSS XI turned out on the field. The whistle for bully-off sounded at 4 pm sharp, and within minutes, much to our surprise the ball was seen in the Present's D, with an aggressive Rekhari behind it, and just three objects in sight before it, the two legs of the goal and a bewildered goal keeper, Puri, in between them. Rekhari swung hard and missed and the Past had lost their only hope of a secure start.

The incident seemed to have spurred the Present into action, for a fierce attack followed and at 4.10, Wali Khan heard the familiar sound of the board from behind him. A good bit of combining by the Present and Tewari did the needful, the Present were one up.

Two minutes later, the Present were back in the OSS 'D'. Off a lovely centre from left out C.S. Gill, Misra had inflicted the second blow. I don't think the Past ever really came out of this one, and their game lost punch. Birendra and Rekhari, as backs, were putting in a good performance and Raza in the forward line was making numerous solo attempts at equalising but with no one to assist him he was invariably outnumbered.

The game drifted from side to side. A little before halftime, the ball was making headway for the OSS goal. The sound of the stick and the board almost intermingled, and smiling Ken Khan was running back to his position, with the rest of the team bestowing their shabash on his back. Wali Khan, dexterously stroking his fungi, was left wondering as to how it had all happened.

Revived somewhat by the Panamas and Cools that fumed during the break, the Past were back, still looking a hostile lot. The game was settling down and the OSS were getting the hang of things. Wali was back in his 1956 form and Birendra and Mr Miller were doing well as backs. Up ahead Raza was trying to do justice to the numerous passes he was getting, Sahota, Bhargava and Rekhari now assisting him, but nothing materialised. The Present very nearly added another to their score, off a penalty bully, but Rekhari avoided further trouble. The match ended in favour of the Present and I think they deserved every one of the three they put in.

The OSS Dance on the 7th was a grand affair. Our sincere thanks to Mr Llewelyn, Mr Thompson, Mr and Mrs Bentinck and Mr and Mrs Duckett, under whose help the evening turned out to be a memorable occasion. This marked the end of week full of joyous excitement.

Chapter TWO

The Struggle

Work. Keep digging your well.
Don't think about getting off from work.
Water is there somewhere.
Submit to a daily practice.
Your loyalty to that
Is a ring on the door.
Keep knocking, and the joy inside
Will eventually open a window
And look out to see who is there

—Jalalludin Rumi[1]

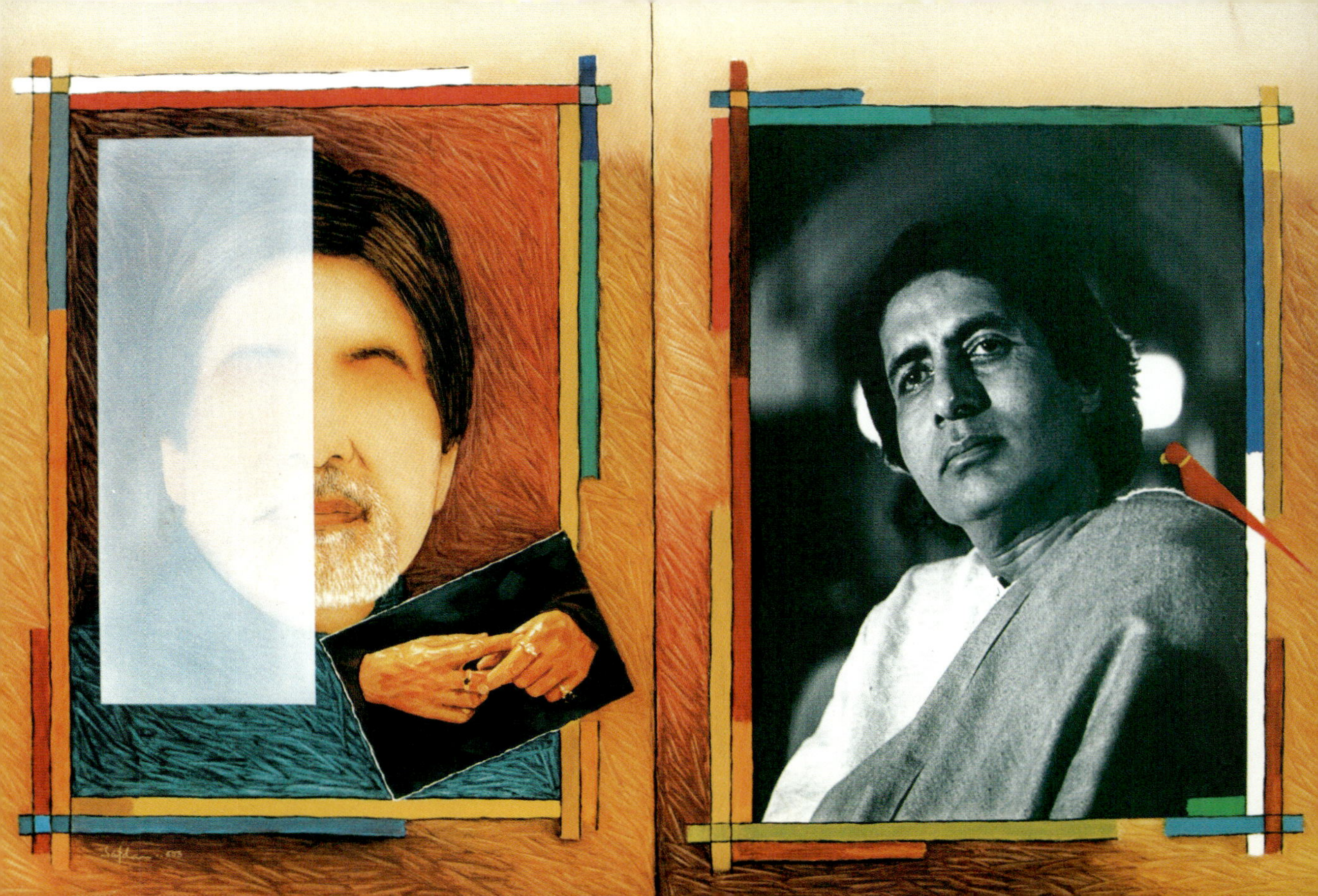

They have a saying in the Hindi film industry, that an actor whose first film is a flop is definitely going to make it big. The bigger the flop, the greater the eventual success. Bachchan, with his long wait for Dame Fortune, must have definitely stretched this rule to the limit.

The road to his first film was itself a hard one. Bachchan's photos had reached Sunil Dutt's office as early as 1967. Dutt was impressed by them, and asked everyone around him what they thought of this newcomer. The responses he got varied.

'Yes, he is okay, but not fit for a big role.'

'He's too tall to be a hero.'

'He looks more like a poet than an actor.'

Such were the contrary responses to Dutt's queries. He, however, believed that there was potential in the newcomer and persisted in looking for a suitable role for him.

There were a couple of reasons for this interest, according to Raj Grover, a close aide of Dutt. 'One, that the boy's personality had impressed Sunil, and the other, that Mrs Nargis Dutt had met Amitabh's mother at Delhi some time ago, and had come to know through her that Amitabh wanted to join films.'

It was incomprehensible to many why Bachchan wanted to give up a steady job, which came with comfortable amenities like a car, a flat and a good salary, to enter such an uncertain profession. After all, let alone success, even earning a living in films was a dicey proposition.

A few days later, after looking at Bachchan's pictures, director B.R. Chopra suggested that the aspirant be called over from Calcutta for a screen test. Bachchan arrived in Bombay after getting four days off from work. It was mutually agreed that the screen test would take place on the sets of producer-director Mohan Sehgal's film *Sajan,* then under production at Roop Tara Studios in Dadar.

'On the second day of Amitabh's arrival from

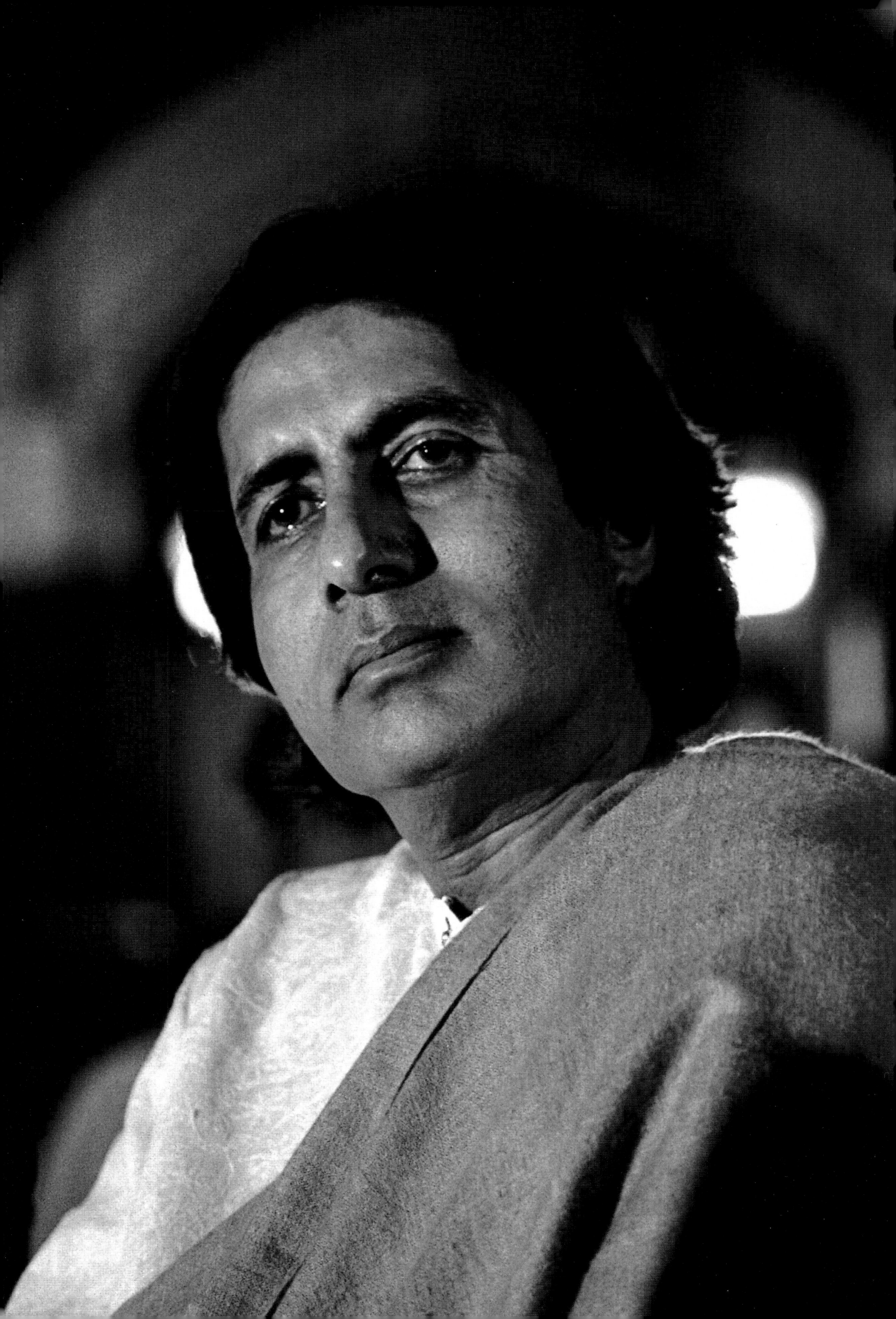

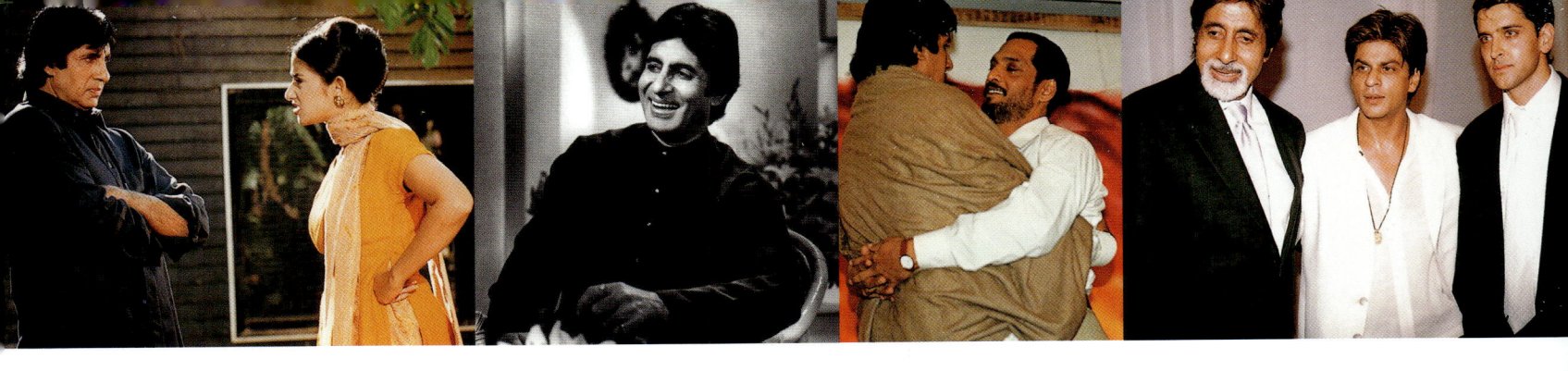

Calcutta, I took him to Roop Tara Studio at the appointed time and introduced him to Mohan Sehgal,' remembers Raj Grover. 'He only said, "Oh yes, Mr B.R. Chopra had asked me to take your screen test". The two were then asked to sit in hero Manoj Kumar's make-up room till they were called for the test. Around four in the evening, Manoj Kumar came to his make-up room and I could see that he liked Amitabh. At five I went on the sets alone and Sehgal asked me to write some dialogues for Amitabh's screen test. Bachchan spoke those lines in his first ever performance before a movie camera.'

On the third day of Bachchan's visit, Nargis Dutt fixed an appointment for him with a leading producer. 'We walked into the producer's office,' says Grover. 'Without preliminaries, the producer began: "No heroine would like to work with you, you are too tall. Why don't you take to writing? You look like a writer, and then since you are the son of a reputed poet, it should not be difficult for you…." We were there for exactly eleven minutes,' Grover remembers. 'For four of these, he spoke to Amitabh, and

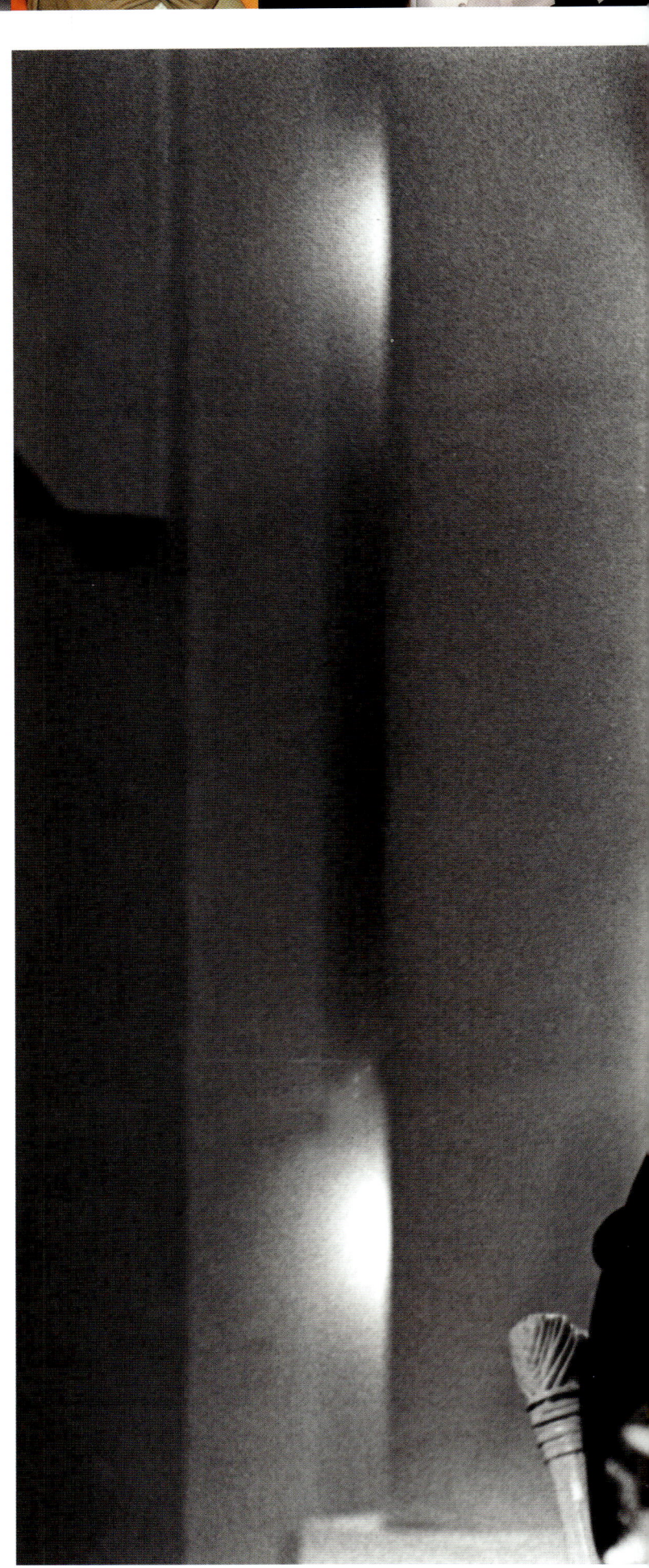

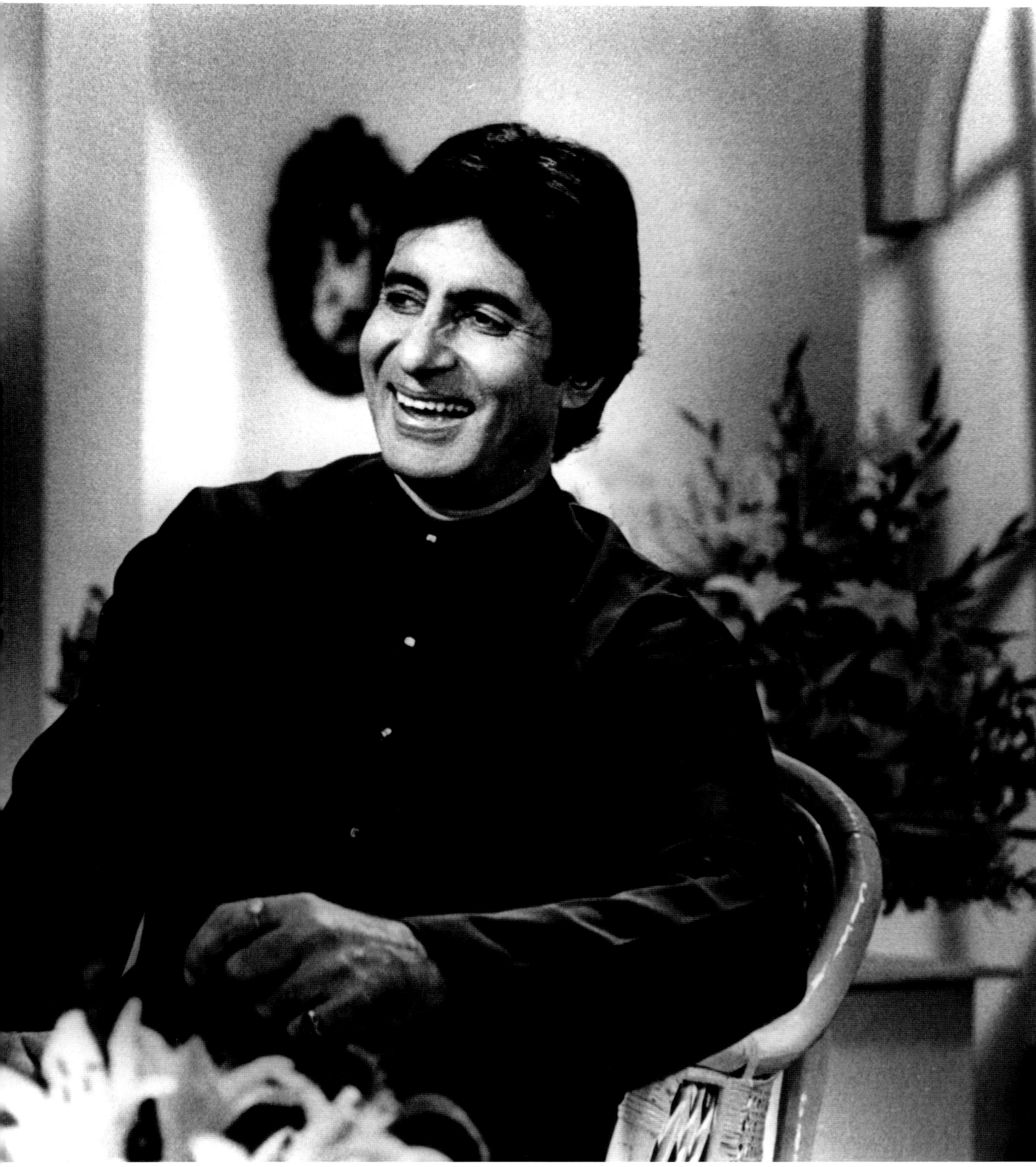

for the other four, he spoke to me, followed by a three-minute silence.'

Thereafter, Bachchan was advised by well-wishers to keep trying, but under no circumstances leave his job in Calcutta. By then, Bachchan's leave had run out and he had to return to his job. Before he left, however, Sunil Dutt promised him a role in his next film.

Two weeks after his visit to Bombay, Grover got a call from Manoj Kumar. He wanted Bachchan to do a small role in his film *Yaadgar*. He needed him immediately, as the shooting was to start within five days at Filmistan Studio. 'I called Amitabh in Calcutta and spoke about the offer, spurring off a spate of calls. Amitabh rang his parents in Delhi asking for their advice. The same night they called Nargis Dutt in Bombay and asked for her advice,' recalls Grover.

In the end, Bachchan rejected the offer, partly because it was such a small role, and partly because he would not have got leave at such short notice. The role finally went to another actor.

The decision turned out to be a good one,

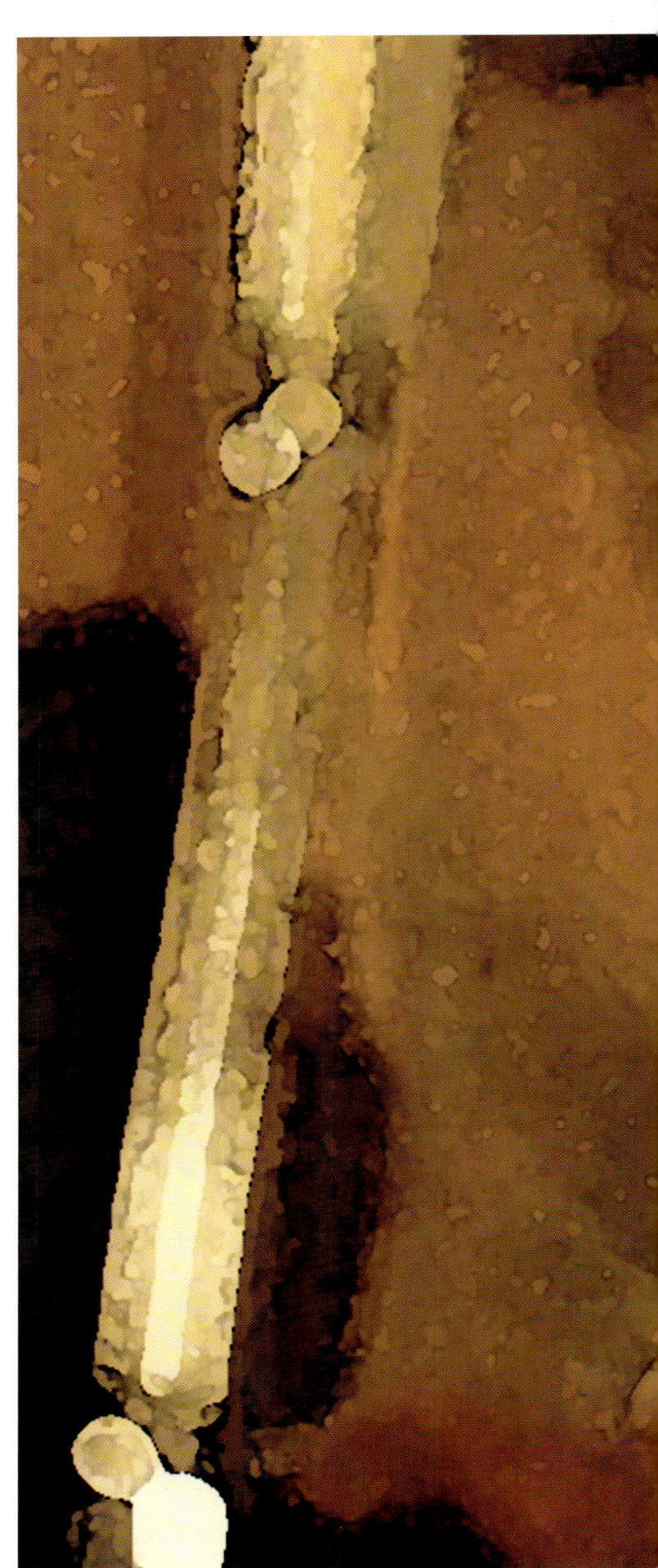

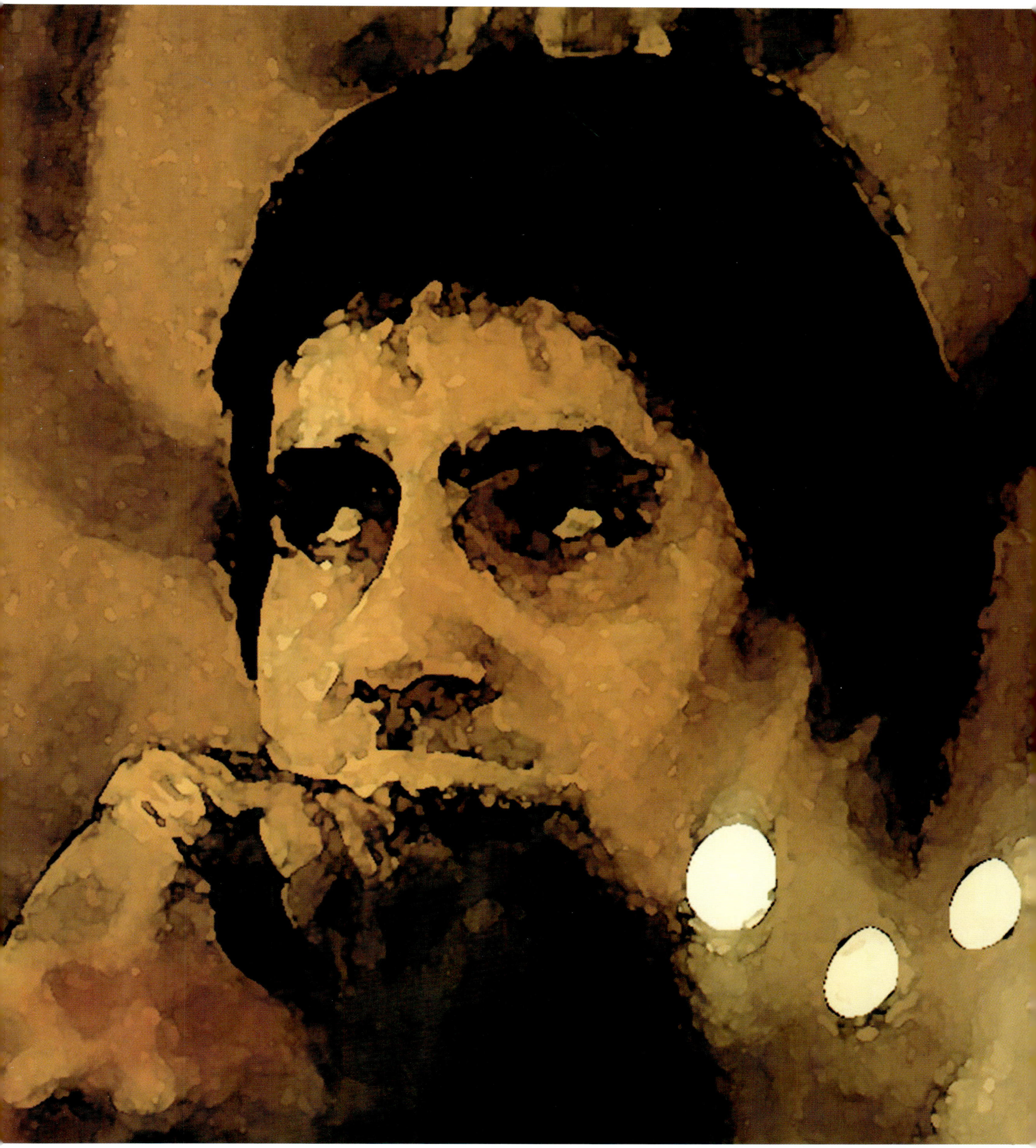

because it was after this that Bachchan was offered *Saat Hindustani.* Bachchan put his soul into his work in the film. The experience was unlike anything he had ever gone through before, but Bachchan never held back.

Shooting for the last scene of the film — where the seven Hindustanis of the title are traversing a steep hill — was as dangerous as it appeared to the audience. But Bachchan would not agree to a stunt double. In the scene, the seven actors are tied to each other like mountaineers, with Bachchan's character bringing up the rear. His boot slips and a loose rock comes free and crashes down the wet incline of a waterfall into the thousand-foot abyss. Bachchan dangles in the air while the other six attempt to pull him up. If any one of them had not been able to hold on, Bachchan would have fallen down the slope. 'With a duplicate I would have had to take a long shot,' says Abbas[2], 'but since it was him I could zoom in and show the agony on the character's face.'

After giving the shot, a weary Bachchan crawled up the incline with scraped shins. A professional

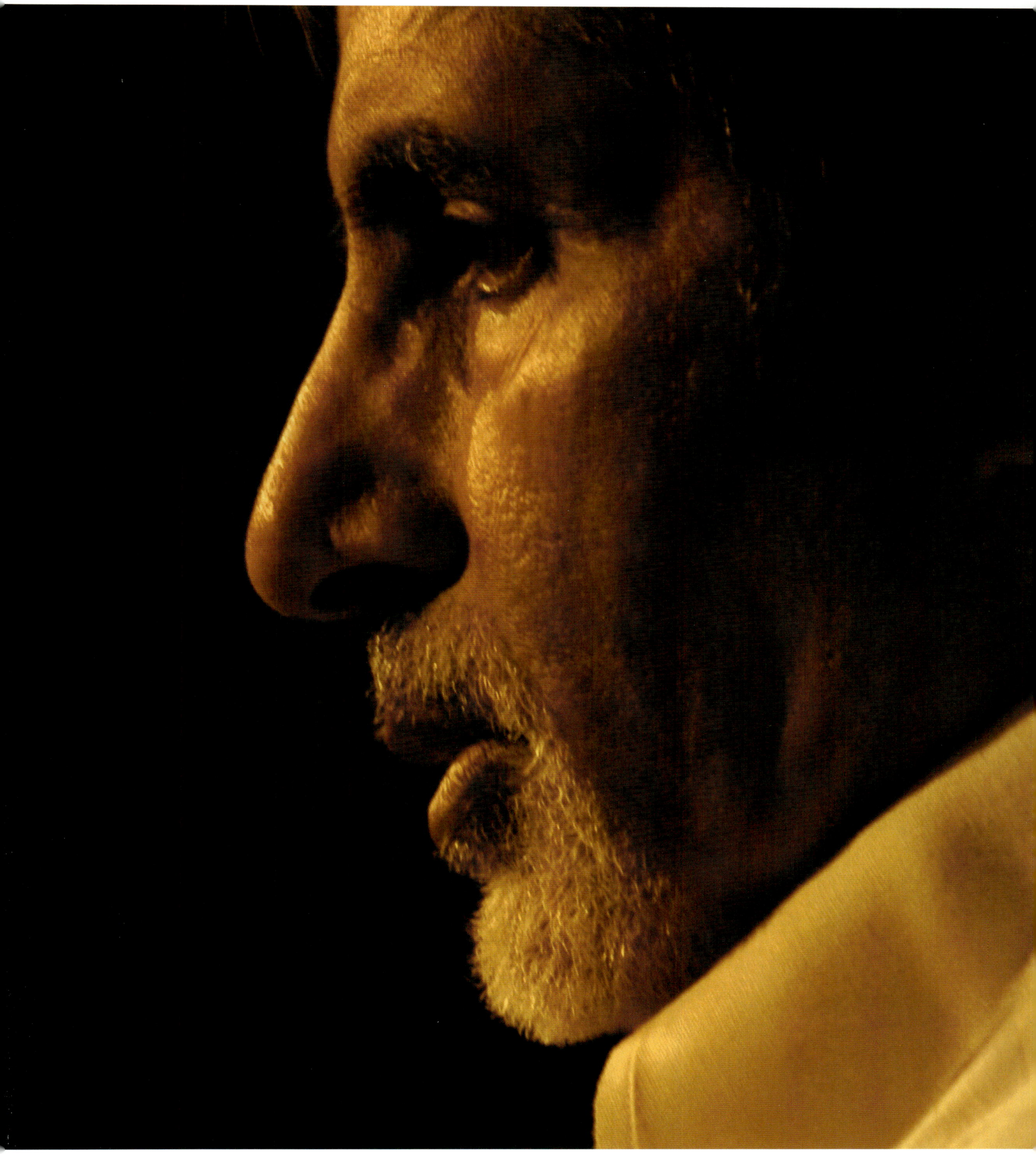

stuntman would have come out unhurt. 'We were standing with the camera two hundred feet away, drenched by the spray from the waterfall,' Abbas remembers. 'The whole unit of technicians, who normally take such emotions in their stride, burst out clapping when Amitabh clambered over the top.'

During a six-week shoot in Goa, Abbas had hired a big hall where the actors could stay. Bachchan met the film crew at Dadar station with 'the biggest trunk I've seen in my life'.

'We slept on the ground floor of a big hall,' the director recalls. 'Each one of us had our suitcases against the wall with the bedding spread alongside. Except Amitabh. Every night he would open the trunk to take out his bedding and pack it back in, in the morning.'

Other than physical courage and personal order, the late Jalal Agha[3], actor, TV personality and Amitabh's co-star in *Saat Hindustani*, remembered him for his tremendous will power and temperance.

'Abbas *sahab* makes films on a very low budget,' Agha remembered. 'But once in a while he would give fifty bucks to one of us for a bash.' On one such occasion, it was Bachchan who got the funding. Anwar Ali, Agha and Bachchan went out to celebrate at the Hotel Mandovi in Goa. They fooled around the whole night and got very drunk. The day after the revelry, Anwar Ali went over to speak to Bachchan. Himself having sworn off drinks, he told Bachchan, 'In this industry at every step you will find a drink waiting for you. I advise you as a brother and friend don't touch drinks till you make it.' To that Amitabh said, *'Beedoo, chhod diya maine.'* (Friend, I've quit [drinking].)

'And he kept his word,' said Anwar Ali. 'He didn't drink till the day his brother got married, years later. Amitabh has tremendous will power.'

After *Saat Hindustani*, Bachchan decided to stay on in Bombay. He was lonely, but he rarely complained. Says Manmohan Saral, former Assistant Editor, *Dharmyug*, 'I was an associate of Dr Dharmaveer Bharati, who happened to be a close friend of the Bachchans. He used to stay at

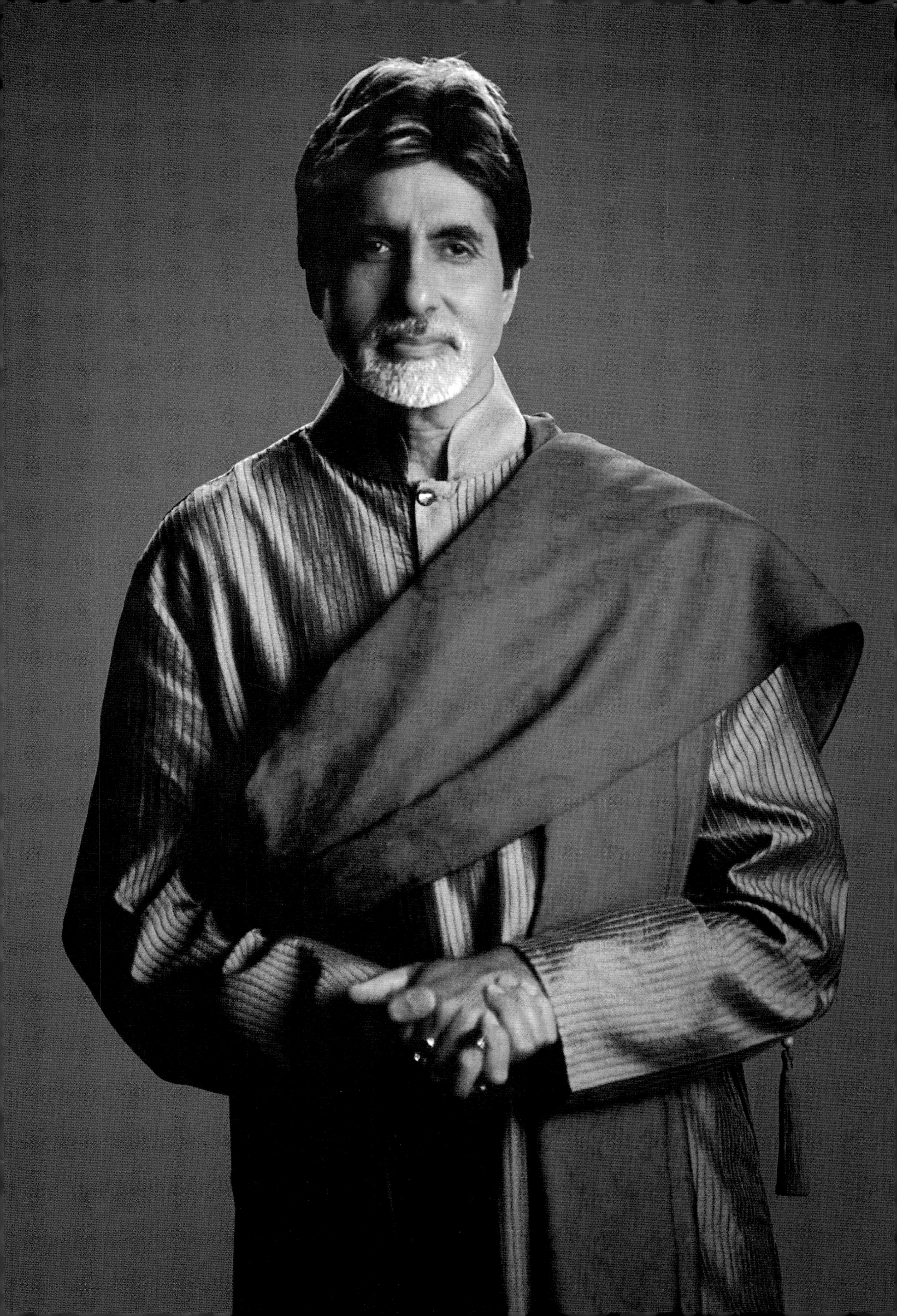

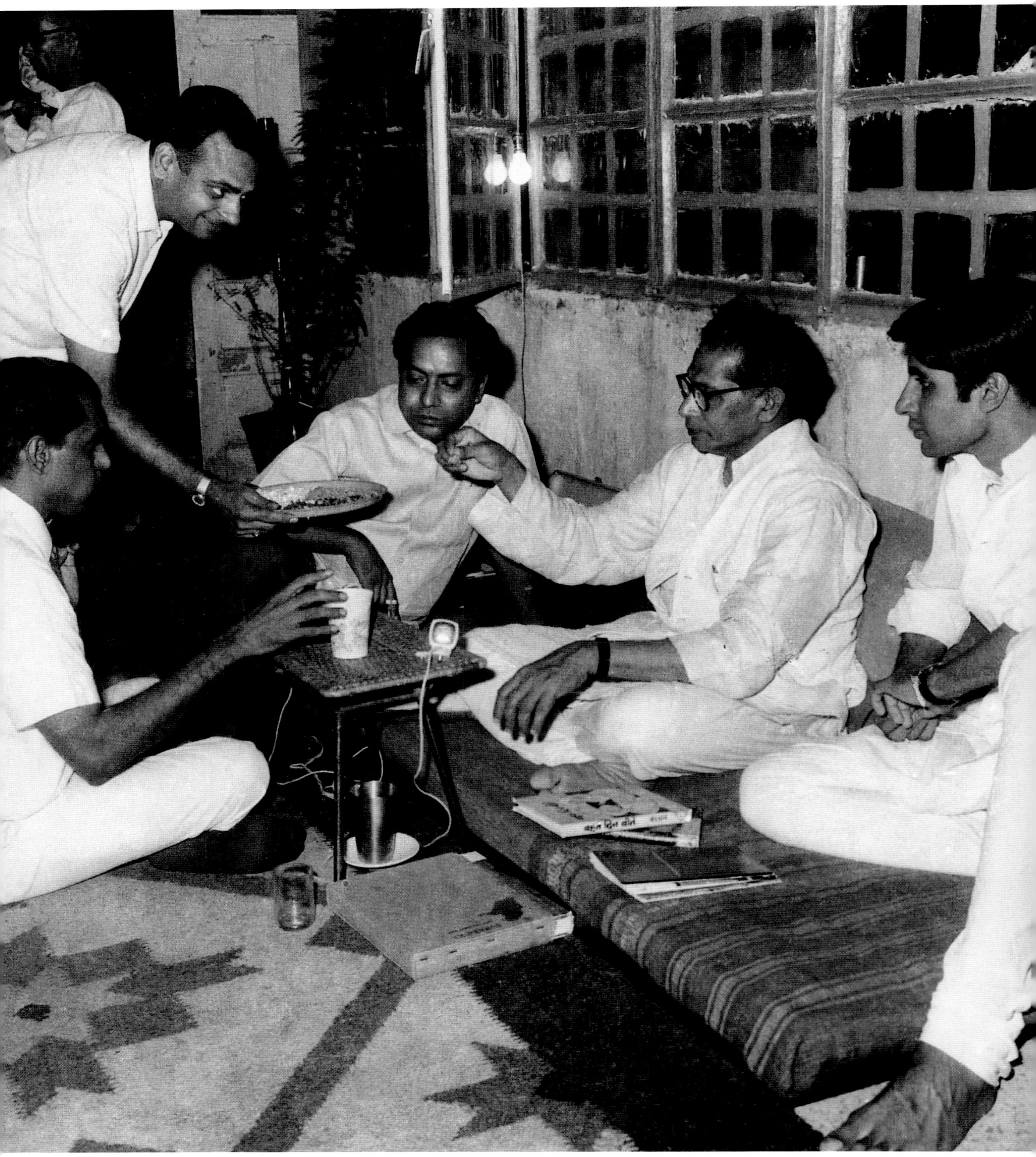
बहुत दिन बीते

Warden Road and his penthouse boasted of a big terrace. One evening he invited Dr Bachchan and other literary people for a poetry session. Amitabh had accompanied his father. He was looking very sad that evening and was very quiet. He never talked much in those days anyway.'

Later Dr Bharti mentioned to Saral how Bachchan *ji* had told him that Amitabh was very disillusioned with Bombay; he was unhappy and felt lonely in the city.

Soon Dr Bachchan started reciting poems; suddenly the host, Dr Bharti, surprised the gathering by announcing that now Amitabh would recite a poem. Amitabh could not refuse in the presence of his father and others, so he recited a couple of poems. 'He recited some couplets from *Madhushala* [one of Harivanshrai's most famous compositions] also. He was visibly more relaxed, and even Dr Bachchan realised that Amitabh was looking more animated. Then Dr Bachchan recited his last poem *Raat aadhi ho gayee* and left.'

After wrapping up *Saat Hindustani,* Bachchan and Anwar Ali, who by now was his inseparable friend, started doing the rounds of producers. Meanwhile, the photos of himself that he had circulated earlier were generating a lot of interest. Bachchan was signed on for several films after *Saat Hindustani,* but none of them worked at the box office, despite having other big names in the cast. Bachchan was lucky in terms of his co-stars. He made *Reshma aur Shera* with Sunil Dutt (who held good his promise to Bachchan); *Bandhe Haath* with Mumtaz; *Bansi Birju* with Jaya Bhaduri, who was a popular star already; *Parvana,* with Navin Nischol in the lead and stalwart Om Prakash; *Bombay to Goa* with Mehmood Ali; and *Anand* with superstar Rajesh Khanna. Of all these, only one film was a hit — *Anand.*

Bachchan was taking a chance when he accepted *Anand:* he could either make a name for himself as a competent actor because of the potential the role offered, or he could be buried under the adulation and attention that Khanna was bound to get, because, undoubtedly, the

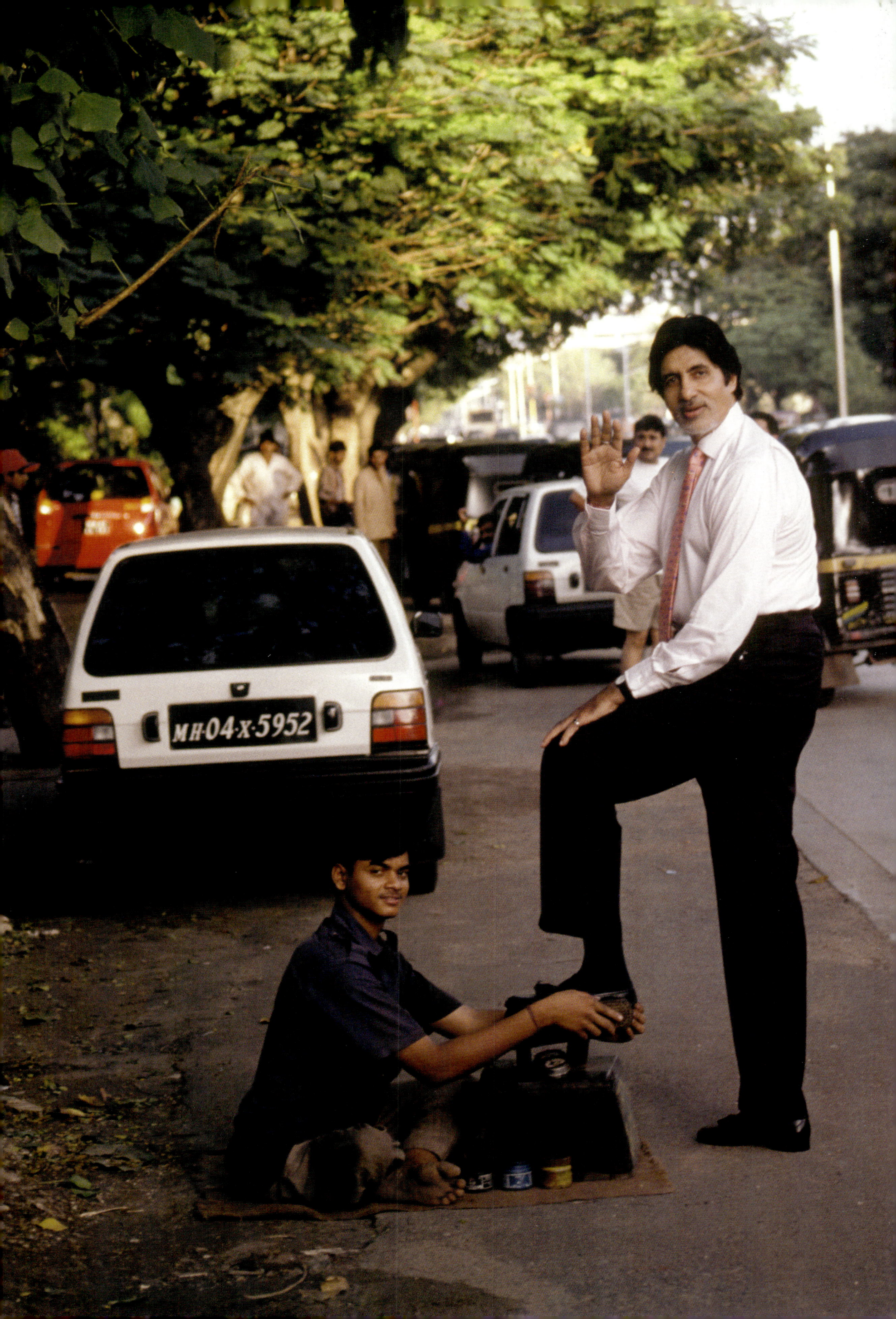
MH-04-X-5952

film revolved around Khanna's eponymous role as *Anand*.

According to James Joyce, 'Pity is the feeling which arrests the mind in the presence of whatsoever is grave and constant in human sufferings and unites it with the human sufferer. Terror is the feeling which arrests the mind in the presence of whatsoever is grave and constant in human sufferings and unites it with the secret cause….The tragic emotion, in fact, is a face looking two ways, towards terror and towards pity, both of which are phases of it.'

Bachchan carefully underplayed his role, making sure he didn't detract from or clash with Khanna's character on screen. Bachchan's Dr Bhaskar has a simmering animosity which turns into grudging pity and finally precipitates into the final cry of anguish that struck a chord with millions of filmgoers across India.

Bachchan's gamble had paid off. After *Anand*, Bachchan gained recognition in the industry. With the film's release, people in the trade were forced to admit that he was a fine actor with a good personality and a very rich voice. Bachchan's social star also rose as people suddenly started wanting to speak to him. People who had barely exchanged greetings with him earlier, now suddenly started to align themselves with him.

Although Bachchan's popularity was clearly rising after *Anand*, the one thing that still eluded him was a hit as a solo hero. Even though this was not his fault, he lacked confidence. He longed for a hit film. The siren song of success seemed to dance just beyond his grasp.

While Bachchan was struggling, he met Jaya Bhaduri, a bubbly young actress who had studied at the Film and Television Institute of India (FTII). Director Hrishikesh Mukherjee had plans to cast him opposite this talented young girl in the film *Guddi*. However, midway into the project, Mukherjee decided to cast someone else in the role he had initially thought of for Bachchan. Both actors were heartbroken, as their mutual admiration had ripened into love by then. Later, they were both approached for a new film titled *Ek Nazar* by maverick director B.R. Ishara.

Ishara had just finished his film *Chetana*, when Dinanath Shastri, Dharmendra's secretary, approached him for a new project. Ishara wasn't too keen, but agreed to consider the offer after hearing about the plans to cast big stars. 'I said okay thinking that Jaya *ji,* who was a big star, will listen to the script and say *"bhai yeh kaam ki nahi hai"* [bhai, this won't work].' Ishara hoped that once Jaya Bhaduri refused the project, it would die a natural death.

When he met both actors at the producer's house for a script-reading session, he thought they were bored and uninterested in the film. Assuming that they would refuse the project, he happily assented to it. The next day he got a call from Khanna, the producer, saying that both stars had agreed to the project. Now Ishara felt trapped; he sat down and rewrote the script extensively to suit his taste.

'Amitabh and Jaya *ka naya naya* [new] romance *thabhi chal raha tha* [was going on then]. They were in love with each other. So seeing them together on screen made people feel good. However Jaya and Amitabh were thorough professionals on the sets and I enjoyed working with them.' Unfortunately, the film wasn't a box-office success.

Despite his flops, Bachchan's co-actors were all convinced of his talent. Once, on the sets of *Parvana,* when he was shooting with Om Prakash, the veteran was clearly impressed. When Bachchan delivered his lines, 'Uncle Om called, "Cut",' recalls Anwar Ali. 'He sat down on the sofa looking a little bushed and then said, "From where has this Paul Muni come?" ' Very prophetic words, as Bachchan's star was to rise as high, if not higher, than that of this former film luminary.

Bachchan's performances kept improving with every film that he did, but still, success was elusive. Veteran actor Asrani remembers the time when *Bandhe Haath* was due for release. 'Amitabh was shooting at Mohan Studio. He was very apprehensive and Mumtaz came to cheer him up. "No hero has flopped with me", she reassured him.'

However, the film was not received well; neither were the others.

As hard as his days were, further humiliations were to follow for Bachchan. The late Kundan Kumar had shot six reels with him, when his distributors said they wanted Bachchan out of the film. Not only that, they also wanted him to return

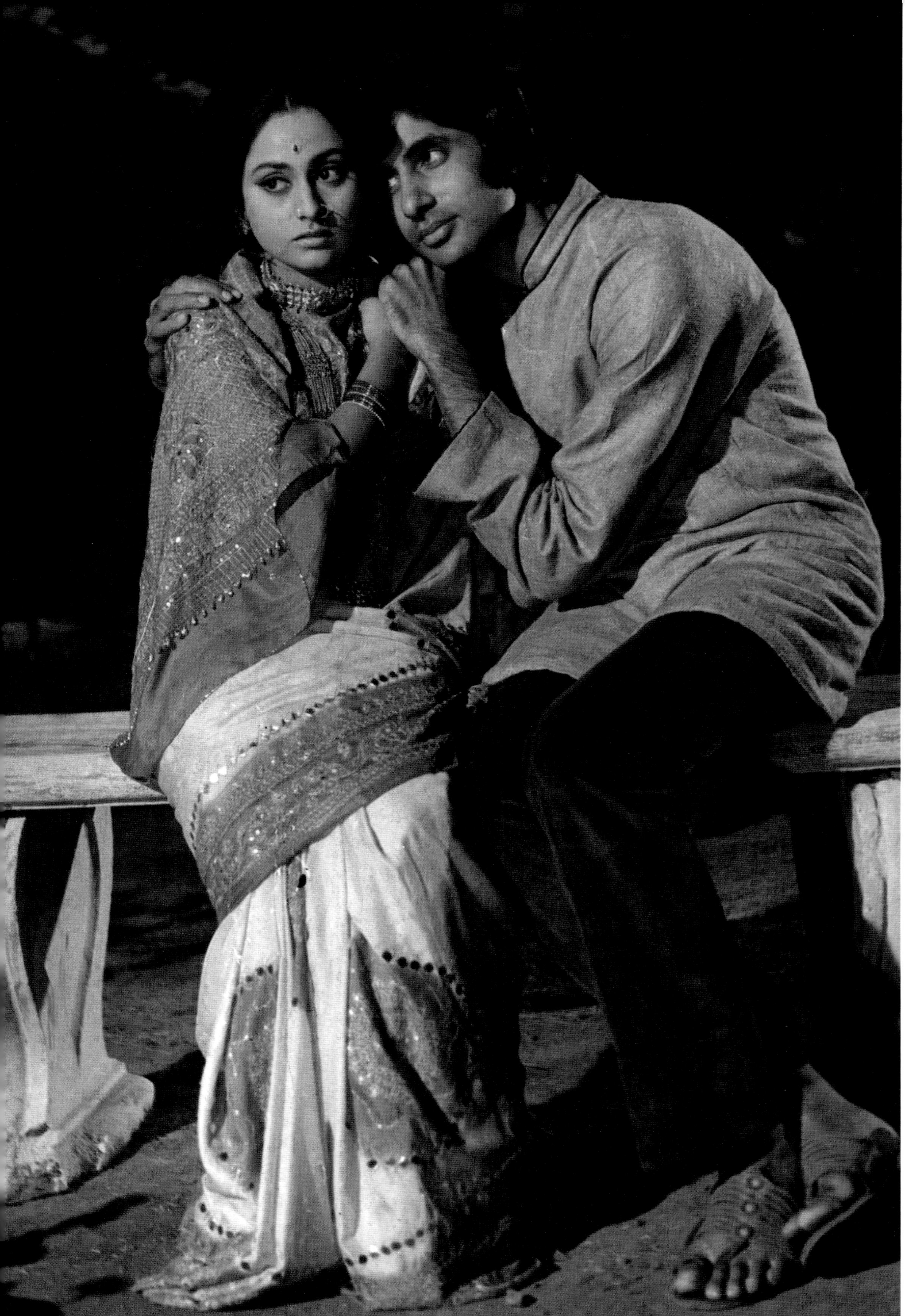

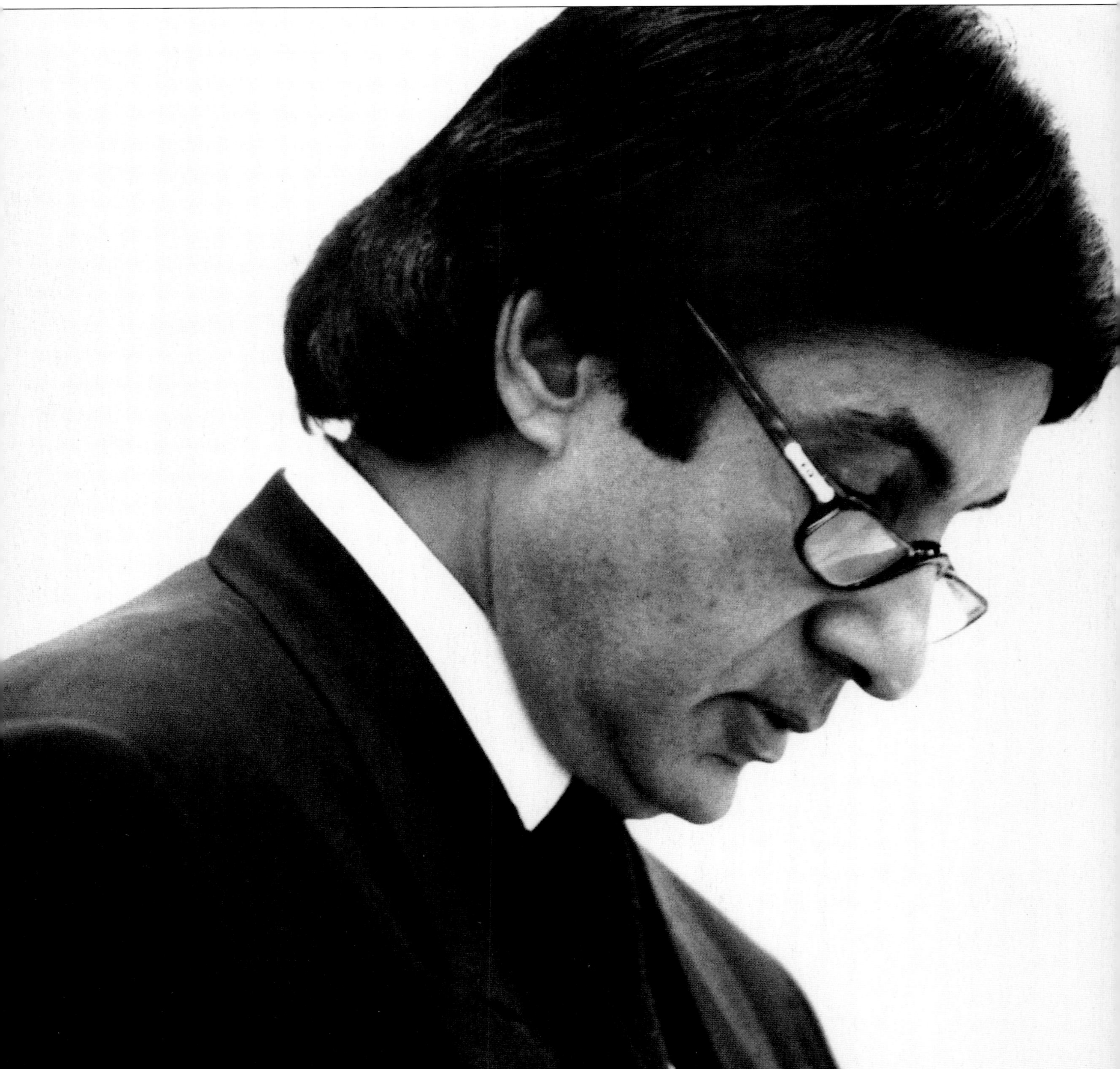

the signing amount that he had been paid at the start of the project. He could have protested, but Bachchan complied and bowed out graciously. Asrani says he too left the film then as what had been done was ethically wrong.

It was when Bachchan was shooting for *Namak Haram*, that Raakesh Kumar, then Prakash Mehra's assistant, called him for *Zanjeer*. Hrishikesh Mukherjee chided Bachchan saying, *'Yeh kya?* [What is this?] Now you are doing stunt films?'

'I was introduced to Amitabh when he was shooting on the opposite floor for *Anand,*' says screenwriter Javed Akhtar, one half of the screenwriting duo Salim–Javed. 'There was something about this man that interested me a lot. Then *Zanjeer* happened. No hero was available, or rather, too keen to act in it. Dev Anand and Raj Kumar had refused it. Somehow, I was sure Amitabh was the right man for the role. I called him, explained the role and asked if he wanted to do it. Amitabh called me over right away.

'However, Amitabh was sceptical initially, not about the role but about whether he could do it. "Do you think I can pull it off?" he asked me. You see till then he had played rather gentle characters.' But Akhtar reassured him on that count.

Zanjeer was completed at last. Bachchan, still very low on confidence, would go around with the film's cans in his car and show it to everyone he thought would give him an honest opinion. One day he came to Mohan Studio and showed it to Asrani and Nitin Mukesh. Asrani had taught Jaya Bhaduri at the FTII and Bachchan had come to trust his judgement. Nitin Mukesh was also known to be a straightforward person who could be trusted to call a spade a spade.

'After the film screening was over he took us home,' Asrani recalled. 'His mother and Jaya were waiting for us.' The Bachchans needed a lot of reassuring; they had waited a long time. '*Beta sach sach batao* [Son, tell the truth],' said Mrs Bachchan. Both Asrani and Mukesh had liked the film and told her as much, but none of those present realised what a massive success the film was to be.

Zanjeer was a blockbuster. Dame Fortune had finally embraced Amitabh Bachchan, but not before he learnt that success, already precarious, does not bestow her blessings continually. As Grover said, 'Today I am really proud of the fact that I had known him when he was new. And if he had not met with this success after the release of *Zanjeer,* I would have probably said on the mention of his name, "Oh yes, I know him. I had told him not to leave that job in Calcutta".'

However, Dame Fortune was to stay with Bachchan for the next twenty years at least. Like Rushdie's Saleem Sinai, he was to become 'public property'.

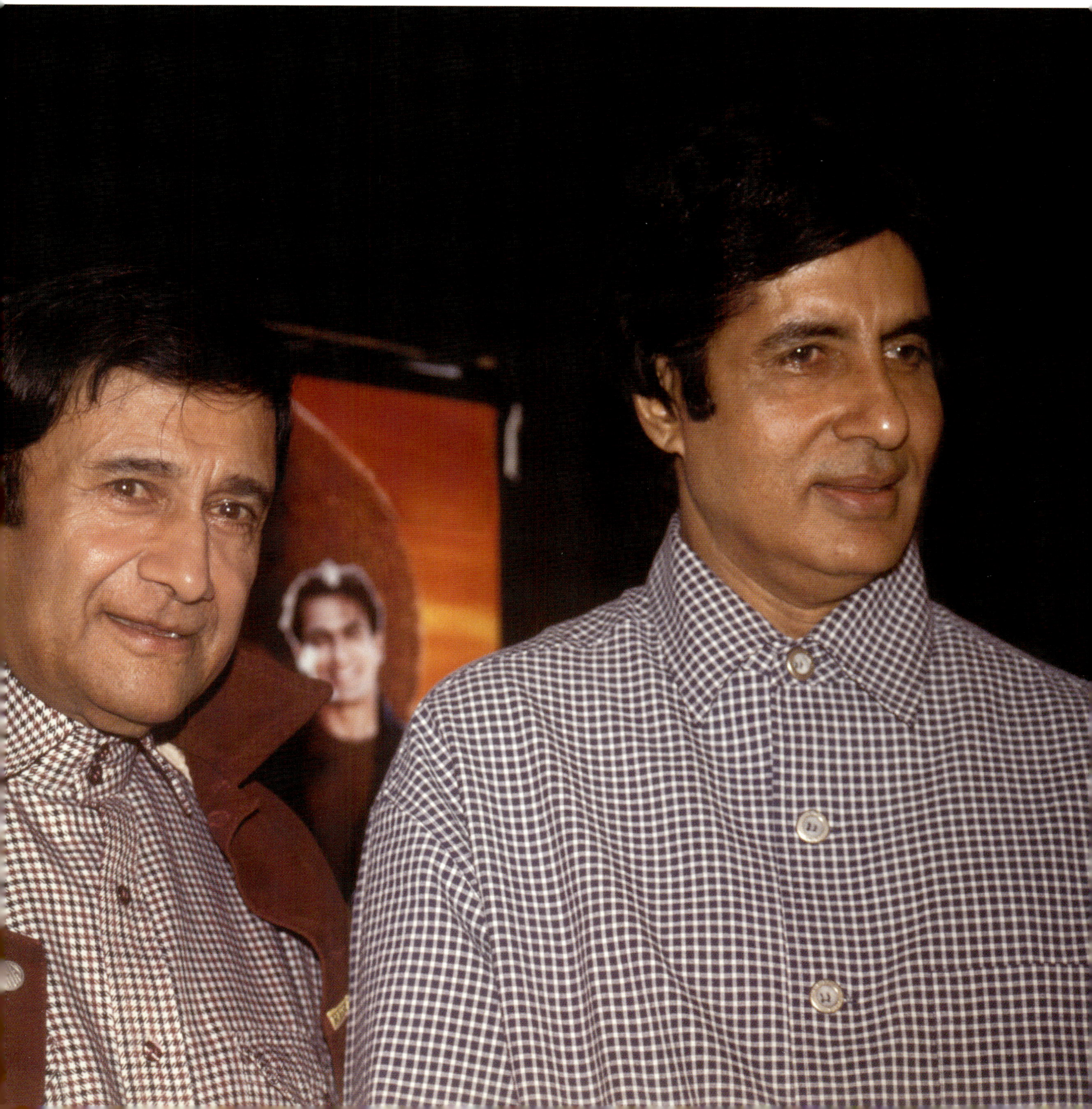

Guest Writer

The Bachchan Phenomenon

Rauf Ahmed

Believe it or not, for the first few days of his life, the first born of Teji and Harivanshrai Bachchan was called Inquilaab Rai.

It was 1942. A critical year in India's freedom struggle. There were cries of 'Inquilaab Zindabaad!' all over Allahabad. And the Bachchans thought it appropriate to call their newborn Inquilaab Rai. But the name lasted only a few days. They decided, on second thoughts, that their son needed a more conventional name, and Inquilaab gave way to Amitabh, meaning eternal light.

The revolutionary streak, however, didn't leave Amitabh. His contributions to Hindi cinema and then Indian television have been revolutionary!

In a dramatic decade (from 1975 to 1985) he not only redefined the profile of the hero in Hindi cinema, but rewrote the rules of stardom. Towards the end of the 1970s, Hindi cinema was seen as a one-man industry. Nobody could have imagined that a tall, gawky guy with deep-set brooding eyes would rule the marquee for more than two decades. This phenomenon — the Bachchan Phenomenon — not just defied convention and logic, but bent the very flow of time. And when Bachchan bowed out of the arc lights for an innings in politics, an unsettled industry went in search of clones.

His return from a brief fling with politics wasn't spectacular. The rules of the game had changed, so had the filmmakers. Old faithfuls like Manmohan Desai and Prakash Mehra were not in tune with the changing times. Starting with Mansoor Khan *(Qayamat Se Qayamat Tak),* a new breed of filmmakers had begun to make their presence felt, and in their scheme of things, 'love' was the dominant factor.

However, more than inability, reluctance (read uncertainty) made Bachchan resist taking chances and going for an image makeover. During that stage, only the late Mukul Anand tried to wean Bachchan away from his histrionic predilections. For the rest he was a god. Whom they wouldn't mess around with. The result was a disturbing vacuum.

Then someone convinced Bachchan about the possibilities on the small screen. It was like breaking a wall — to squeeze the mammoth Bachchan persona into a few inches. But when he finally agreed, it was the event of a lifetime for television in India. Star Plus — which was poised precariously at an insignificant third slot — soared to the top of the heap! Once again, Bachchan was into redefining the rules — this time of the small screen. The outcome was a new facade to the famous persona. This time it had its echo in the man behind the mask: the real Amitabh Bachchan, shorn of the seductive veneer of violence-ridden pontification.

This new, natural, avtaar of the celebrated megastar, who had held a nation of passionate filmgoers to thraldom in the 1970s and a major part of the 1980s, provided the clue to a new generation of filmmakers. From Sanjay Gupta to Sanjay Bhansali, these directors recast the Bachchan charisma. And the Bachchan mystique is at work again. And how! He is rocking all over again…on television, in commercials…and in what he is unbeatable at: on the big screen.

What is it that made an actor with an unconventional demeanour — unconventional in the sense that he wasn't among the Greek Gods emerging from the wheat fields of Punjab — scale awesome heights? In one word — talent. A supremely gifted performer, Bachchan could make even the most bizarre scene watchable.

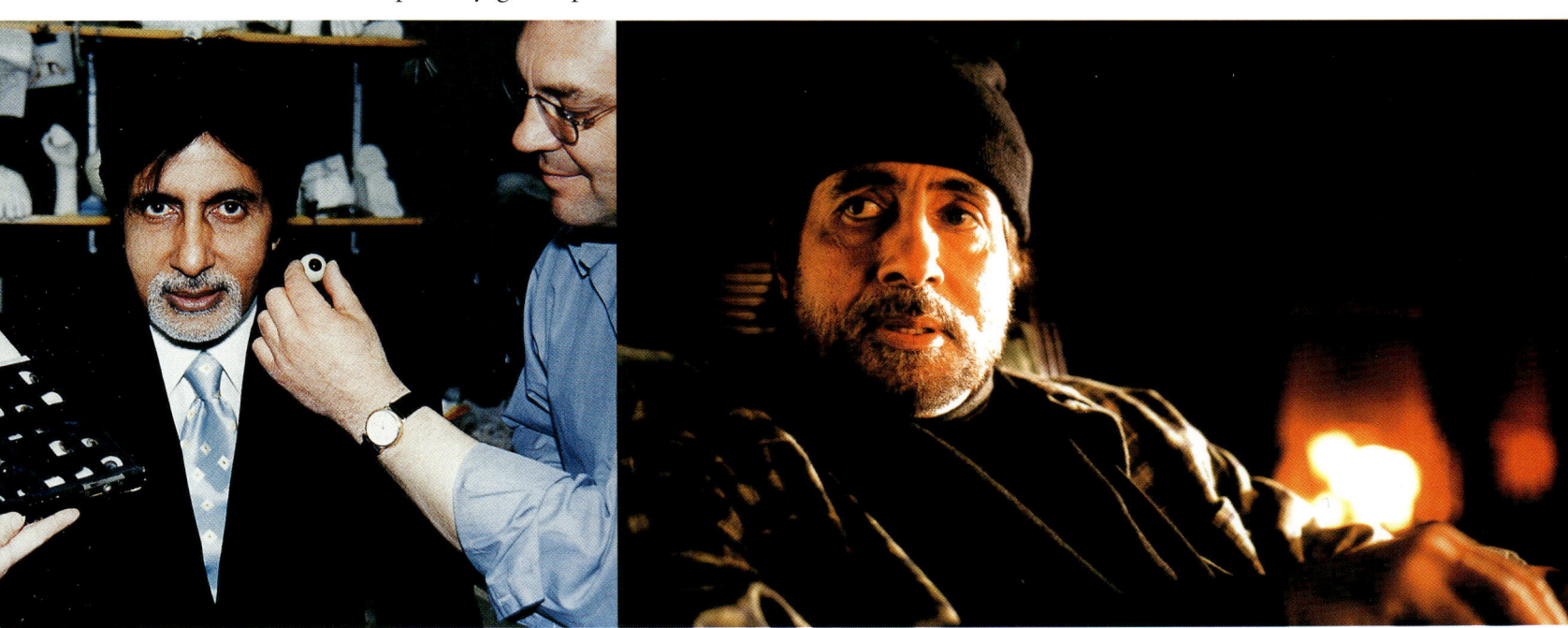

His appeal transcended all barriers. From the masses to the mandarins, they rooted for him in frenzy.

It wasn't easy, however, for the man adjudged The Star of the Millennium in a worldwide BBC poll, to find a foothold in the slippery terrain of stardom.

His first signed film *Saat Hindustani,* directed by one of his father's acquaintances K.A. Abbas, was a damp squib at the box office. But it did fetch him a National Award. His next ten films were duds too, including *Parvana,* where, out of sheer desperation, he tried to play a villain (Navin Nischol was the hero of the film). However, his performance in it did stand out, as did the brooding character he played in Rajshri's *Saudagar* opposite Nutan. But they led him nowhere. There was just one hit in that dismal first phase:

Hrishikesh Mukherjee's *Anand,* where he played second fiddle to then superstar Rajesh Khanna.

Anand had happened by a stroke of luck. Amitabh had accompanied K.A. Abbas when the latter visited Hrishikesh Mukherjee. Hrishida was then casting for *Anand,* a film inspired by his own friendship with Raj Kapoor. 'I was paranoid about something terrible happening to Raj,' Hrishida recalls. 'And I wanted to make a film to get over that persistent feeling of fear.' In Amitabh, he saw his Babu Moshai, which was himself. 'It was his voice and the intense, brooding eyes that clinched it,' remembers Hrishida. 'I instantly changed my decision to cast Uttam Kumar as Babu Moshai. It was a risky decision, because in the film, Amitabh, a rank newcomer, had to stand up to Rajesh Khanna, who was a rage in those days.' But the gamble paid off.

The intense deep-set eyes and the brooding look led Hrishida to cast him in his next film as well. *Namak Haram* was based on *Becket*, and Bachchan played Peter O'Toole's role. It was this character — with its violent shades — that did the trick. *Namak Haram* was released at a time when public protests were growing in the social milieu. A distraught generation was seeking a means of expressing its frustration and disorientation. It was just the right time for a larger than life character, who could look out for himself and fight his own battles.

Amitabh was the man for the moment. The Angry Young Man. Amitabh believed in his ability to play the angry young man. The one who took on the establishment. 'There seems to be a strong sense of revolt within me,' he admitted. 'Perhaps it's in my genes. I have seen rebellion in my father's early writing. It had a deep influence on me. When I tried to express anger on screen, it seemed to happen so naturally.'

Hrishida saw a glimpse of this anger in a brief scene in *Anand,* where Amitabh chides an over-exuberant Rajesh Khanna. 'That's when I realised the power and strength he could exude through a mere glance and his voice,' he recalled. 'And I cast him as an angry young man in *Namak Haram.*'

Javed Akhtar saw that anger simmer in a fight sequence in *Bombay to Goa.* It was the scene where Shatrughan Sinha punches him and Amitabh falls to the ground. 'As he was getting back on his feet, he kept chewing at a piece of sandwich he had in his mouth,' recalls Javed. 'It was dramatic the way he was doing it, simply fascinating. I went back and told Salim *saab* that I had found the hero of *Zanjeer.*'

Amitabh himself, however, was a bit sceptical about pulling off the crusading police officer in *Zanjeer,* according to Salim. 'Essentially because it was in total contrast to the introvert Babu Moshai-like characters he had been playing. Besides, *Zanjeer* had been declined by stalwarts like Dilip Kumar, Dev Anand, Raj Kumar and Dharmendra.' At the same time, Amitabh didn't want to let go of the film, because 'he saw the immense potential in the script'. His ability to judge a script, the duo agree, was amazing even at that early stage in his career.

Zanjeer, incidentally, was Amitabh's thirteenth film. For the next thirteen years, right up to *Aakhree Raasta* (1986) he had only three (*Imman Dharam*, *Aalap* and *Faraar*) real failures out of the sixty-one films released. An unprecedented record! At one stage in 1979, eight of his films — *Amar Akbar Anthony*; *Parvarish*; *Don*; *Kasme Vaade*; *Besharam*; *Muqaddar Ka Sikandar*, *Ganga Ki Saugandh* and *Trishul* were simultaneously celebrating their Silver Jubilee run in Mumbai! It's a record not likely to be overtaken.

Zanjeer, Deewar, Trishul. They established an archetype peculiar to Indian audiences: the die-hard rebel who rises in anger against a cold-blooded establishment. He was no paragon of virtue either, like earlier protagonists. He even resorted to violence to achieve what he thought was justified. His conflicts were not romantic, like the ones faced by the heroes of an earlier generation. They were by and large social. Romance was not an essential part of the Angry Young Man's existence. His girlfriends invariably stayed in the background like Raakhee's character in *Trishul*. His macho image was always in command, like in *Laawaris* or *Dostana*, where he subjugated his women, at times crudely. The masses seemed to lap it up though! They seemed to readily accept the 'functional existence' of the woman.

Beneath the veneer of anger, however, there did exist soft spots, generally reserved for the 'mother' and the 'child'. In some films he did everything for the mother (*Deewar*) in some others he went all out to woo the child (*Natwarlal*). In the midst of all the mayhem he let loose, there have been several moments of tenderness and emotion which brought huge lumps to sensitive throats. Like those eloquent moments of silence in *Sholay*, the dramatic capers in *Muqaddar ka Sikandar* and the emotional interludes in *Kabhi Kabhi*.

The awesome phase not only changed the face of the hero in Hindi films, but changed the very pattern of filmmaking. Amitabh did almost everything in his films except play the heroine. The comedian became redundant. So did many other ingredients. For a while even music lost its importance in a Hindi film. *Deewaar* and *Sholay*, two of Bollywood's biggest hits, had no great music in them. A Bachchan film, as Ramesh Sippy once said, ended up being a one-man variety show! And those who didn't get Amitabh Bachchan to star in their films looked for clones. It virtually became a 'one-man industry' as a cover story in *India Today* chose to call it.

It was an incredible achievement for a man who had wondered how he would ever do the kind of things a Hindi film hero did before the camera. 'I used to spend most of my time watching film shootings at various studios. Once I watched Manoj Kumar shooting a dance number for a film called *Pehchan* at the Sun 'n Sand Hotel. I felt perturbed just looking at him do those strange movements! That night I kept asking myself, "Will I ever be able to do all this? Will I be able to prance uninhibitedly in front of so many people?" That night I even contemplated returning home. But I stayed on…'

The inhibitions did show in his earlier films. He almost got thrown out of *Parvana* because dance master Suresh Bhatt got very impatient with him. And the late Kamal Master, who choreographed some of Amitabh's most successful numbers, actually got him replaced by Sanjay Khan in a film because he found his movements clumsy. 'That day I decided that it wouldn't happen again. I would give my all to dances. During *Don,* I rehearsed at least twenty times for each shot and I re-did each shot again and again,' he once said. The *Khaike pan Banaraswala* number from the film went on to become a chartbuster.

There were hiccups, such as Amitabh's run-in with the Press. It had begun as a collective move of the film industry stalwarts to curb yellow journalism indulged in by a section of the film Press, through non-cooperation. But, after the initial eagerness, most actors developed cold feet and backed out. They even 'exposed' those who were 'plotting' against the Press! But Amitabh stood his ground. And the 'cold war' between him and the Press lasted more than a decade. 'I stuck to my principles even though the others decided to back out. Because, in giving in, my integrity was at stake,' he clarified later.

The ice was finally broken on the sets of *Ajooba*. Shashi Kapoor, who produced and directed the film, persuaded Amitabh to forget the past in an attempt to get *Ajooba* publicised. But the fifty-odd journalists who landed on the sets went back and wrote about Amitabh's face-off with V.P. Singh and the Bofors row. There was almost nothing about *Ajooba*. If it served any purpose, it gave Amitabh an opportunity to give his side of the story. The Press, which had no access to him, had been getting at him with speculative stories.

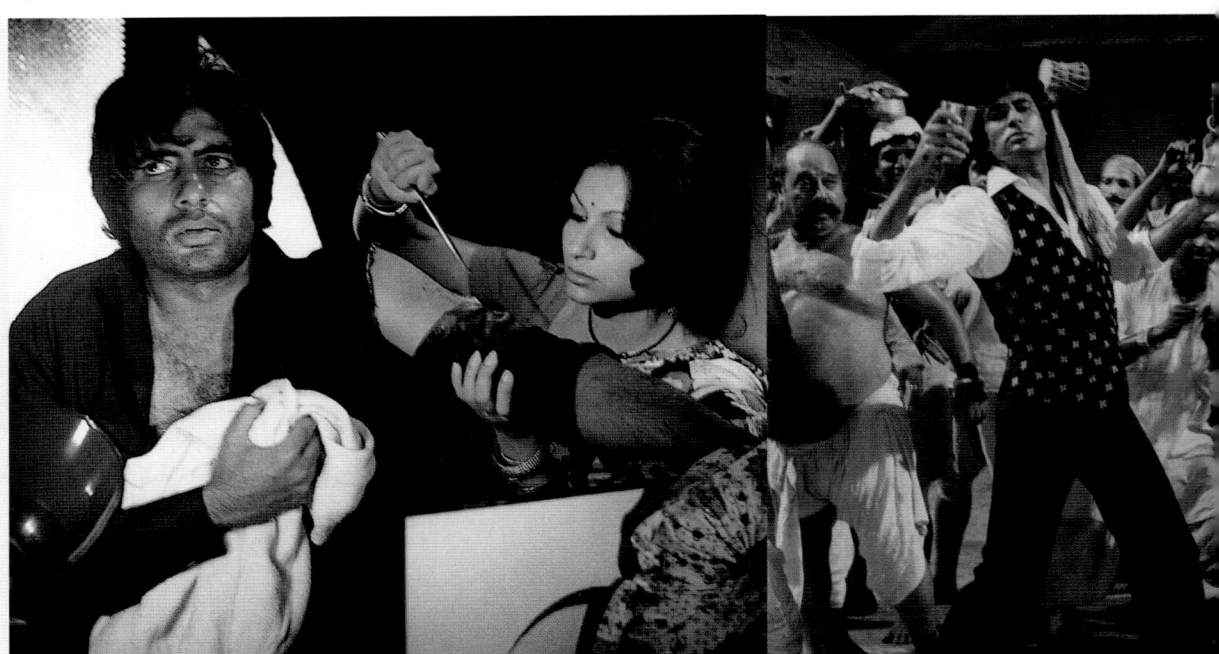

The second hiccup was his reluctant foray into politics. Today, Amitabh dismisses the episode as a bad dream. A blunder he will never commit again. It certainly was a nightmare, but not a blunder. He was done in by an inability to play ball, rather than an inability to do justice to the new role. I remember accompanying him to Allahabad to do a feature for *Filmfare,* the magazine I was then editing. It was a few months after he had become an MP. We were struck by the rapport he had struck up with the locals and their appreciation of the work he was beginning to do for him. His proximity to Rajiv Gandhi seemed to fuel their hope. But then, it's not good work that always matters in politics, as he was quick to learn. It's your ability to manipulate things and create perceptions. Amitabh seemed a bit too naïve to understand this at that time. The twenty-four-hour access he had to the PM seemed to do him in, in a way. There were four hundred-odd others waiting for their turn. They could not digest the privilege he was enjoying.

The failure of the films he made after 1986 — the post-politics phase — had little to do with the perceived public outrage against him. The assumption that it does is naïve and simplistic. *Shahenshah* did face trouble engineered by self-appointed social activists, but that could hardly be seen as a public outcry. The truth was, both Manmohan Desai (*Ganga Jamuna Saraswati* and *Toofan*) and Prakash Mehra (*Jaadugar*) were on a downslide by the time Amitabh returned from his political adventure. They were clearly out of fresh ideas. The old formula had worn thin. It was too much to expect Amitabh to keep pulling off the kind of one-man extravaganzas most of his regular directors had been churning out. Sensing this, Amitabh resorted to a new age director, Mukul Anand, who was making waves as a 'wiz kid'. But things didn't work. Mukul, obsessed as he was with form, couldn't reinvent the Bachchan persona. He did help him win a National Award for *Agneepath* however, and raised Amitabh's screen-age to the fifties in *Hum*, but couldn't move him away from the anger-action-dance routine by any significant extent.

For almost five years Amitabh made tentative attempts to reinvent himself without really shedding the image that had once swept the nation off its feet. He did not meet with much success. The fault was not his really. None of the directors he worked with during that critical phase in his career had the guts to break the Bachchan mould although it had outlived its utility. They weren't big enough to command Bachchan and do something drastic to erase the vestiges of a fading image. It was the small screen eventually, which managed to do this at the turn of new millennium.

Kaun Banega Crorepati might have been a stroke of fortune, but the outcome was staggering. Emerging as himself, he turned the television industry on its head. It was like recreating the magic of the 1970s. He had finally rediscovered himself, giving in to the dictates of Time.

KBC went on to redefine the rules of the business of entertainment. It transcended the mere reinvention of the Amitabh Bachchan persona and giving a new dimension to his acting career. It catapulted the Star network to the top slot, something no one had really anticipated. It edged Zee TV out of its secure citadel. But the miracle didn't end there. Its reverberations echoed on the big screen, marking the beginning of a sensational new innings for the Big B.

It led to a marked change in the way Bachchan looked at his own image on the big screen. He was no longer hung up on sustaining the Action Hero role, which had once sky-rocketed him to unbelievable heights of superstardom. *Baghbaan* was a glaring example of this. The newfound sense of self-belief opened up new vistas before the actor in Bachchan. *Dev, Black, Bunty Aur Babli, Sarkaar, Viruddh* …these films brought out a range and depth which would have eluded an actor trapped in the legacy of being a megastar.

The journey, for Amitabh Bachchan, seems to have just begun…

— *Rauf Ahmed is former editor of* Filmfare *and* Screen

Chapter Three

The Angry Young Man

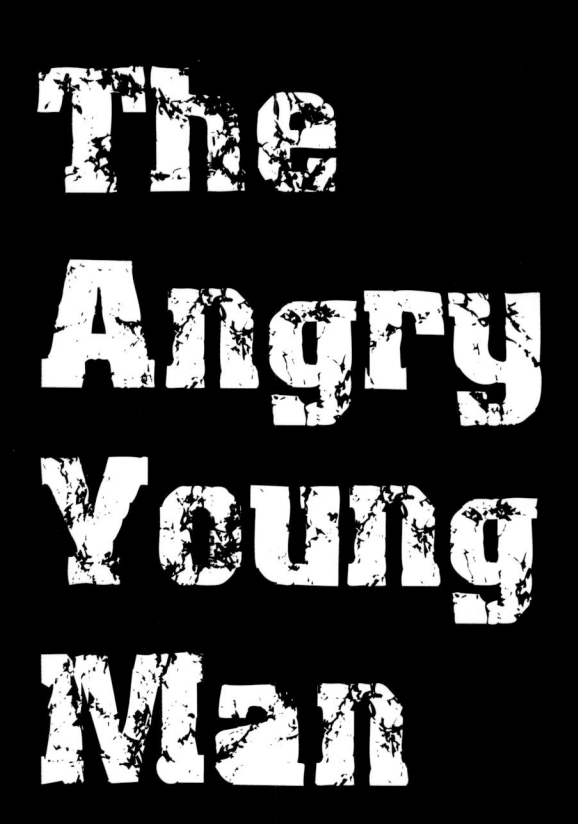

'Hindi films provide poetic justice in just three hours — a feat that none of us can achieve in a lifetime, or in several lifetimes.'

–Amitabh Bachchan

50

INDIA

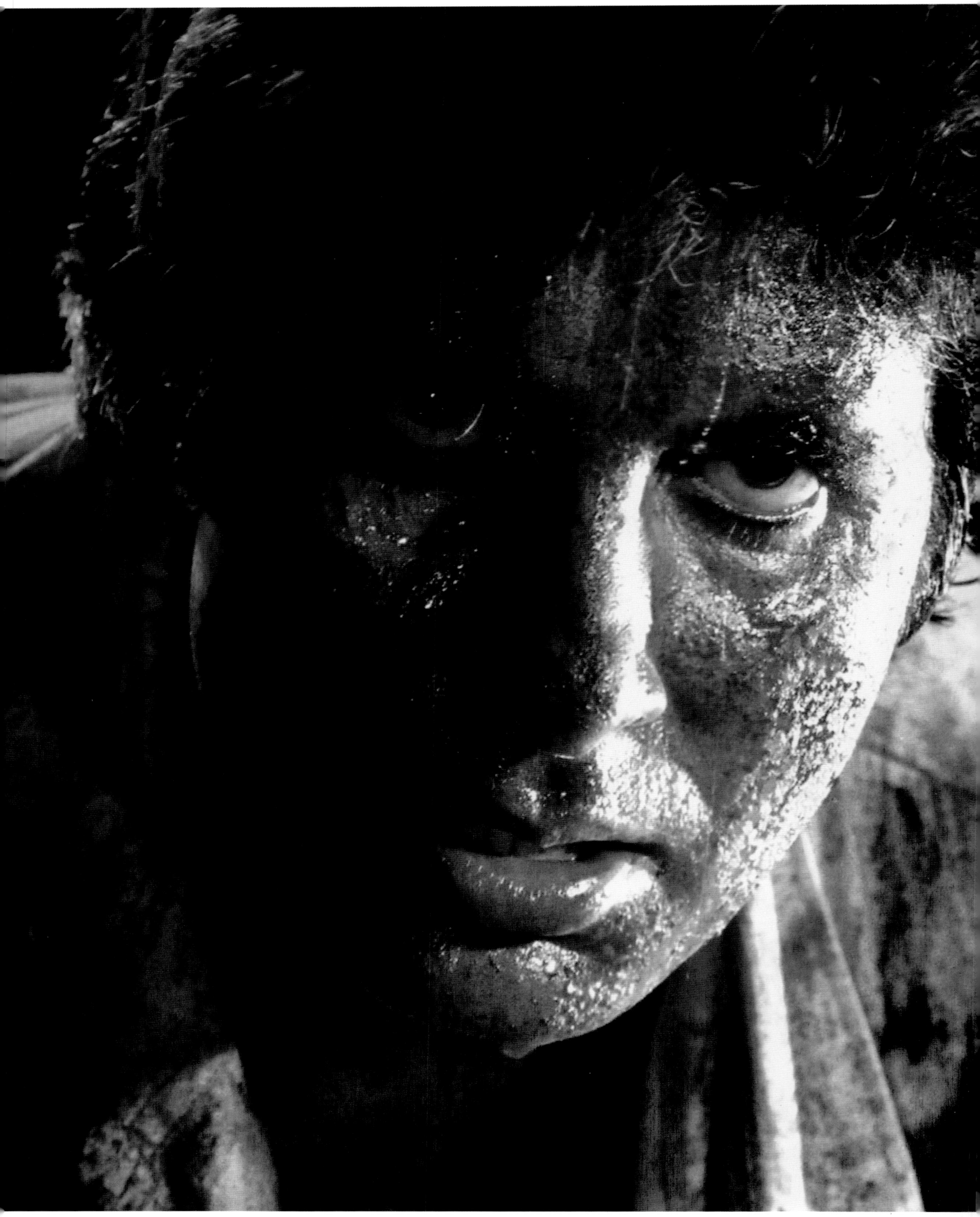

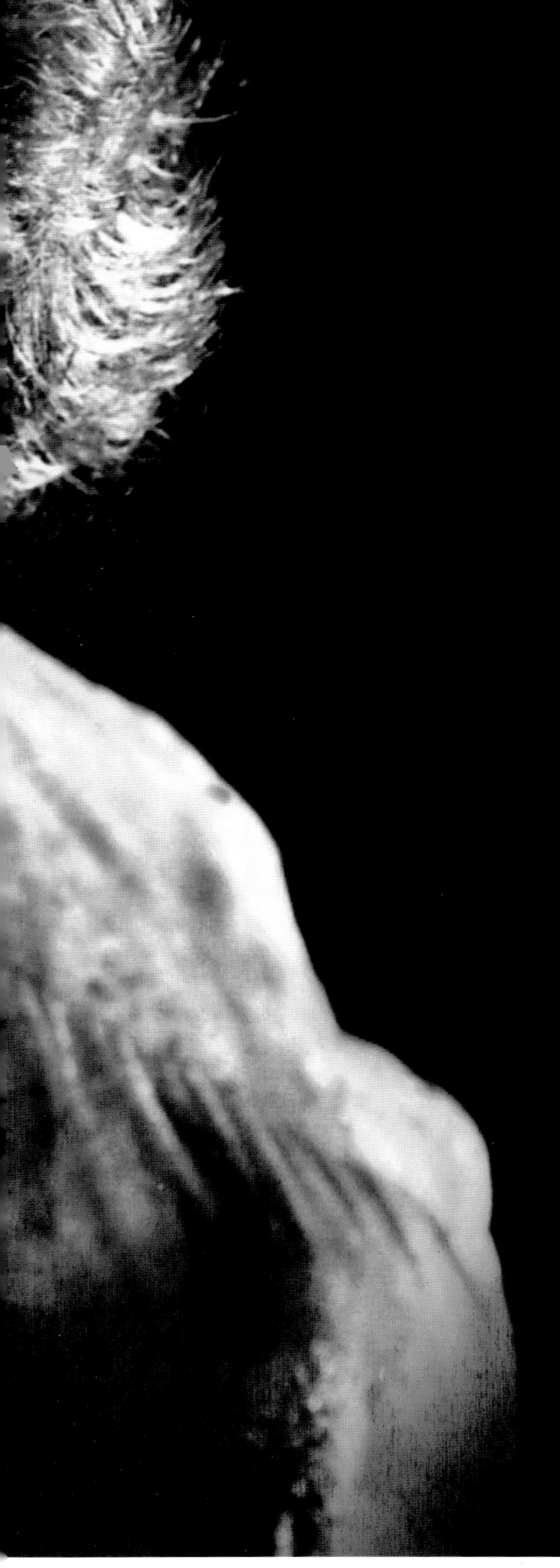

$\mathcal{B}$achchan's role in *Zanjeer* marked a watershed point in his career. The film made Amitabh Bachchan an icon for the masses. The Angry Young Man phase, as it came to be called, captured and held the imagination of the country for over two decades.

The 'Angry Young Man' was essentially a good person, usually the better endowed of two siblings, or rivals, who is suddenly dispossessed and made to struggle back into the mainstream. Amidst the prevailing social and political conditions, the persona touched a chord with the average Indian. Examining this phenomenon gives us an insight into how much Hindi cinema reflects the reality of life in India; how close their paths lie. Says filmmaker Govind Nihalani, 'Any kind of image attributed to an actor, like the Angry Young Man (in the Seventies), concerns not only that actor, but also the environment that prevails in that period of history in which people are functioning. If there is a certain anger in the minds of the people, against certain kinds of systems or against some kind of governmental policies or social norms, or taboos, and if somebody expresses it...if the actor is able to convey that anger effectively, then he's actually expressing the collective anger of the pent up emotions of his own generation.'

Bachchan himself had been floundering to find

his groove in the industry. *Anand* had given him a toe-hold, but he still needed to establish himself. The current trend when he started out was for soft, reflective or repressed characters. Bachchan played them all, but no one noticed that the trend was playing out. In the Seventies, the masses had that inner angst which they had suppressed for so long. They needed an outlet to vent it. Only, they didn't know how. This is where Bachchan came in. 'Bachchan conveyed the Indian people's disillusion and angst that followed the honeymoon period after independence to the period of betrayal,' says ad filmmaker, Prahlad Kakkar. '[His] character went against the establishment and created social justice. He followed the course of natural justice in all his films, conveying that "I'm not worried about the means, just the results". He became a folk hero.'

The 'Angry Young Man' character was created by screenplay writers Salim Khan and Javed Akhtar. Says Akhtar, 'There was something about the man. I even saw his flops as his intensity always came through.' According to Khan, 'His personality inspired the kind of films we wrote for him. We kept his personality, his talent and his acting ability in mind and wrote films around these criteria. …For instance, I have observed since the days of *Zanjeer* that when he used a gun, it conveyed…that he meant business. If anyone else held it, I would feel like telling him, "What are you doing, it'll go off!".'

'For the first time, there was this Hindi movie hero who wasn't a toffee-nosed sweet boy, but a man. It worked very well with his roles,' says Kakkar. 'He created relevance in all his characters, whatever he played.'

Says Nihalani, 'The time at which these roles were being written, was the time, you must remember, that parallel cinema was also happening. There also, anger was being expressed in films like *Aakrosh, Ardh Satya* of mine, Shyam babu *ke Ankur, Nishant* and *Bhumika,* Ketan Mehta's films. Several people were making films and all of them had such kind of anger or tension against the system at the time. Various forms of anger were being expressed, so you know people were thinking along similar lines. But because of the talent and the intensity he brought to those roles, Bachchan became something that the whole nation identified with.'

In the mid-Seventies, domestic politics was in great turmoil, student unrest was high and the employment prospects for educated young men in their twenties and thirties were bleak at best. As a wry Bachchan remarks in *Shakti*, '*Hamare desh mein kaam dhoondhna bhi ek kaam hai.* [In our country, finding work is also a job.]' Indians felt wronged during and after the Emergency; the social balance was tilted against the populace. They had very little to believe in, just like the young Amitabh in his films. When the villain gets his deliverance, the people got theirs too, in collective.

'He was the hope of the frustrated common man in that at least he got something done,' says Kakkar. 'The Angry Young Man was anti-establishment, and the Empire was the system. Bachchan was the force that went after them.'

The Legend

The Angry Young Man usually started off as a person who is good at heart and is capable of giving much love and being loved in return. However, due to circumstances beyond his control, he loses everything and is thrust into adverse circumstances and made to traverse life the hard way.

The character, usually a child at the start of the movie, grows up in a social wilderness. This man, already bitter, is hardened further as he is unable to give or receive any form of love or trust in the unforgiving wilderness that he is in. He surrounds himself by facsimiles of comfort and security to give himself love, a palatial home to imitate the loving environment he recalls vaguely from his youth, but they are not enough.

This enigmatic loner is attractive to plenty of women, who seek to find out if they can penetrate the lonely aura which surrounds him. However, so hardened is our hero that he frequently self-destructs his relationships.

Even friendship doesn't come easy to our hero in his dog-eat-dog world. Friendship is earned after trust is gained, and that comes after a conflict which also functions as a trial by fire. The woman he loves, too, must pass the test to join the hero's inner echelons.

Bachchan gave this decidedly negative typecast a very identifiable pathos which couldn't be ignored. Bachchan's first portrayal of the angst-ridden hero as Inspector Vijay Khanna in *Zanjeer* is relatively less misanthropic. Vijay Khanna's idealism is a result of more than the personal tragedy that he has suffered. Vijay's parents are killed by a man wearing a horse pendant. As an adult, he is continuously plagued by

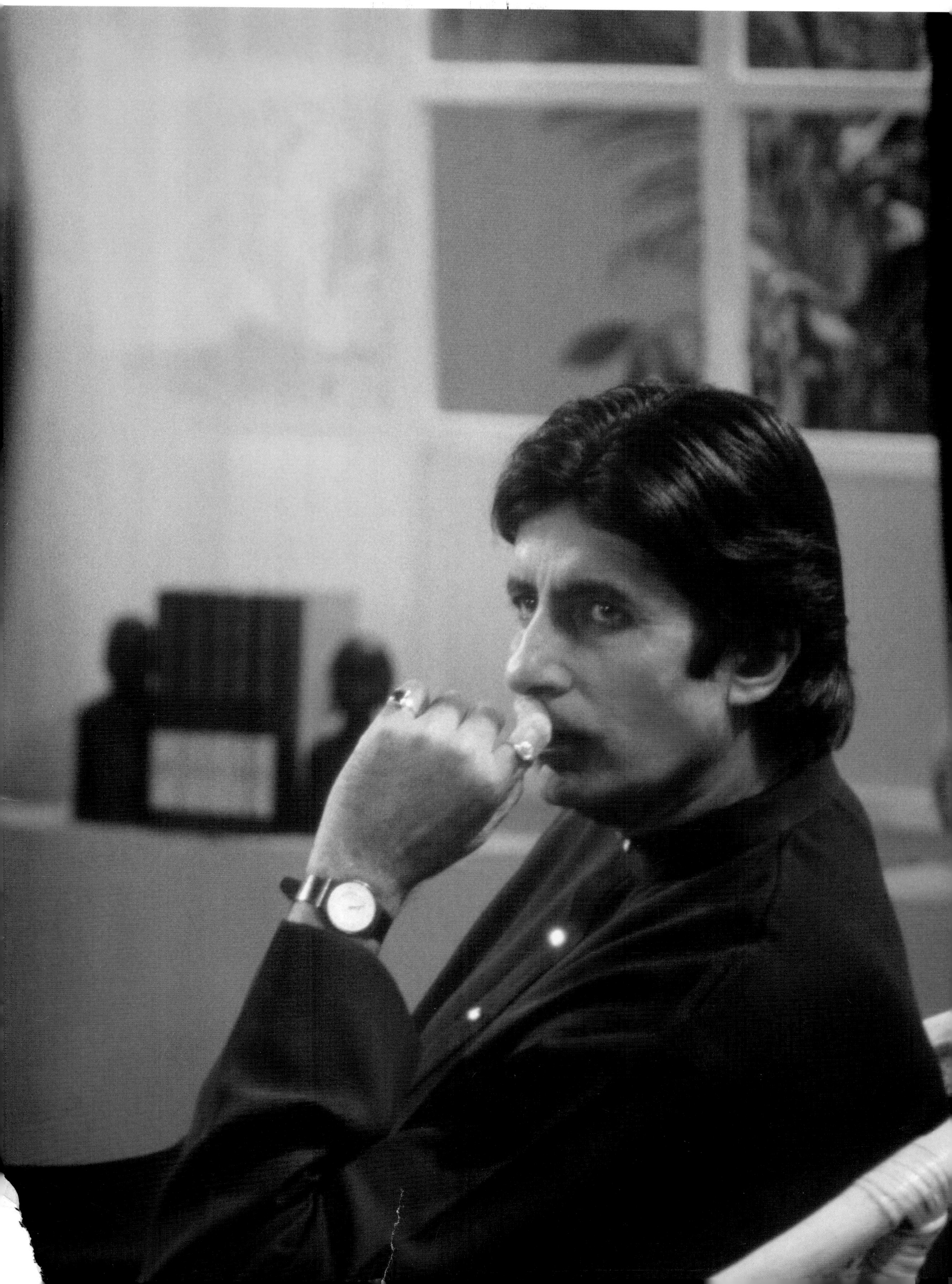

nightmares about a masked rider on a horse, and his anger is also a grown man's disquiet at having to confront his nightmares. The man on the horse represents his psychological foe, his subconscious longing to find and bring his parent's killers to book. Eventually, the hero confronts the villain and slays him, consequently finding catharsis from his childhood bête noire.

Bachchan went on to play some classic roles: the mafia don and smuggler whose brother is a policeman in *Deewar;* the son of a strict police commissioner, who takes to a life of crime and smuggling in *Shakti;* the masochistic miner trying to bury his demons in *Kaala Pathar.*

In most of these films, the force that holds the hero together is his mother, that primary source of love that promises him the nurture and security of the womb. The mother is an important figure in the history of Indian cinema. Very little is beyond her ken. She is the pivot around which the entire family revolves. Joseph Cambell, in his *The Hero with a Thousand Faces*, which examines the archetype of the hero and his journey, writes: 'Having responded to his own call, and continuing to follow courageously as the consequences unfold, the hero finds all the forces of the unconscious at his side. Mother Nature herself supports the mighty task. And in so far as act coincides with that for which his society itself is ready, he seems to ride on the great rhythm of the historical process.'

Mehboob Khan, in his *Mother India,* immortalised on film the 'mother' as the matriarch of a new nation. Bachchan himself has acknowledged that if there hadn't been a *Mother India,* there would

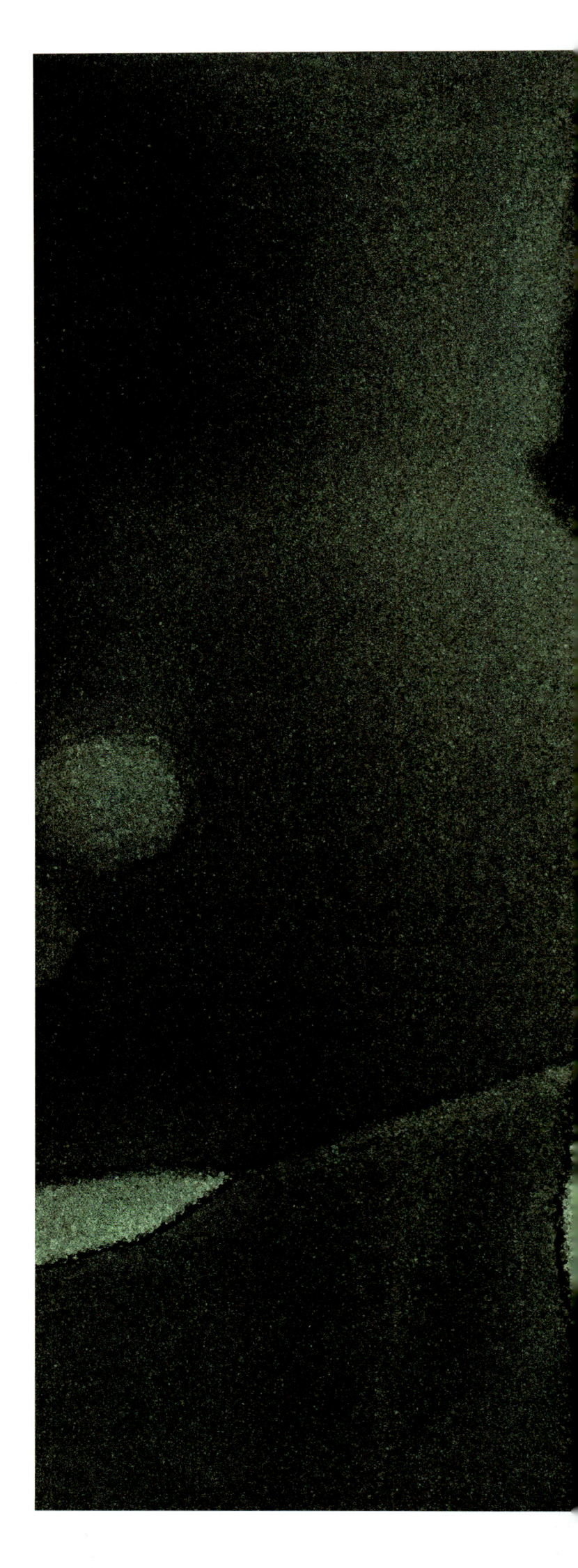

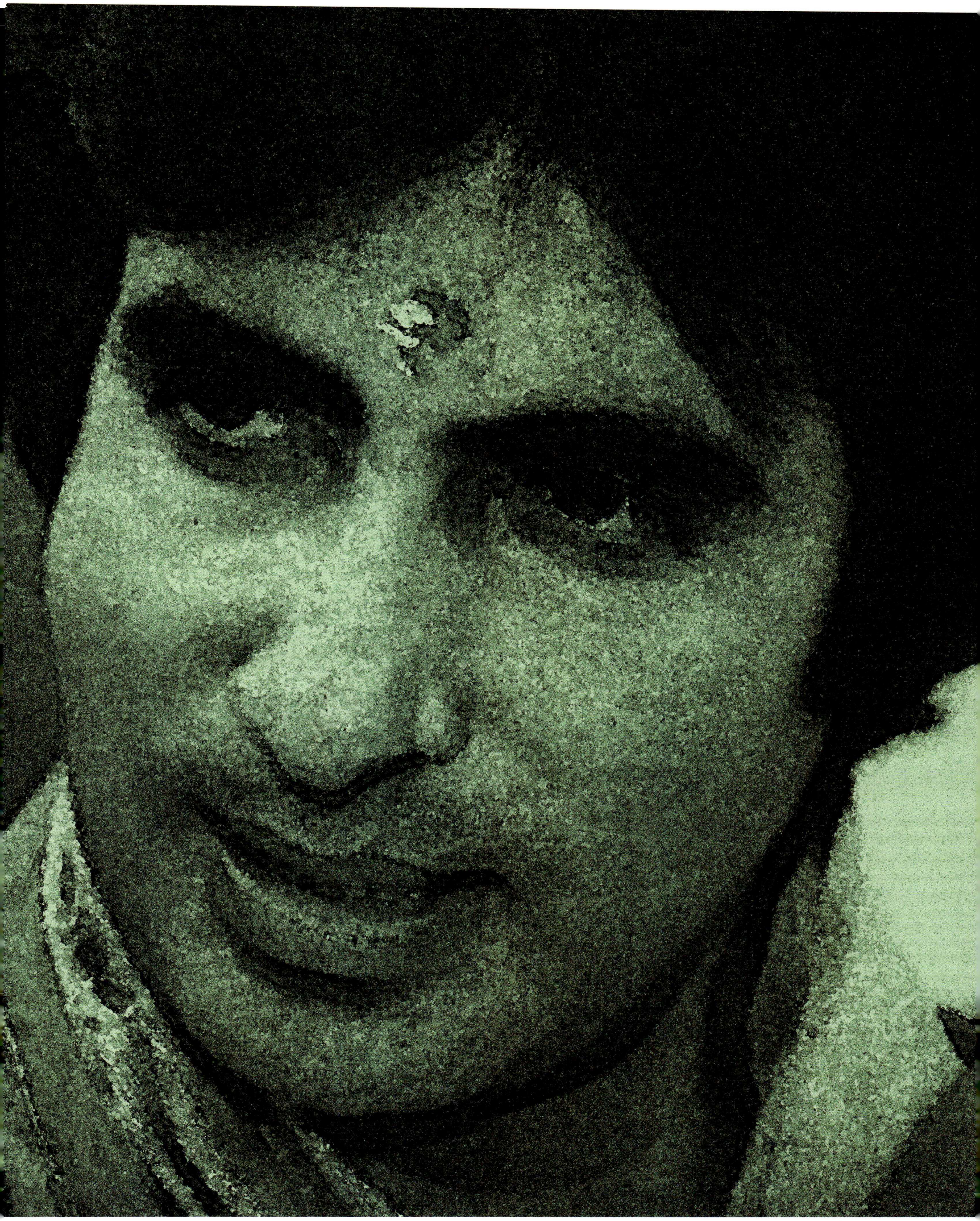

have been no *Deewar*. However, there was a difference in how the character of the son in each of these films was received. When *Mother India* was released, the public empathised with the 'good' brother, played by Rajendra Kumar. They agreed with the mother's decision to discard the 'bad' son played by Sunil Dutt. In a newly independent country, there was no room for individual weakness and sentiment: righteousness prevailed.

However, when *Deewar* was released, India was going through a different, and difficult political period. Was the government's position as an authoritarian big brother right? Didn't everyone have the right of individual choice?

Bachchan's character, Vijay, in *Deewar* is unapologetically in the wrong. '*Uf tumhare usul, tumhare adarsh! Kis kaam ke hai tumhare usul, jo ek waqt ki roti tak nahi bana sakta?* [Oh, your principles, your beliefs! What good are your principles, which can't even provide food?]' he demanded in *Deewar*. And all of India's youth agreed with him.

But, whereas the universal hero flows in harmony with the sacred feminine, Bachchan's angst-ridden young man in *Deewar* runs parallel, and even counter to it, in the end. It is his most caustic role as the 'Angry Young Man'. Where *Zanjeer's* hero was tempered by righteous idealism, *Deewar's* protagonist has an open war with society and the 'right' side.

Bachchan's hero in *Deewar* is a survivor; whatever be the cost required to survive, Bachchan's angry young man would pay the price. However, the hero's yearning for legitimacy simmers underneath. It flashes briefly in his longing for his mother and in his

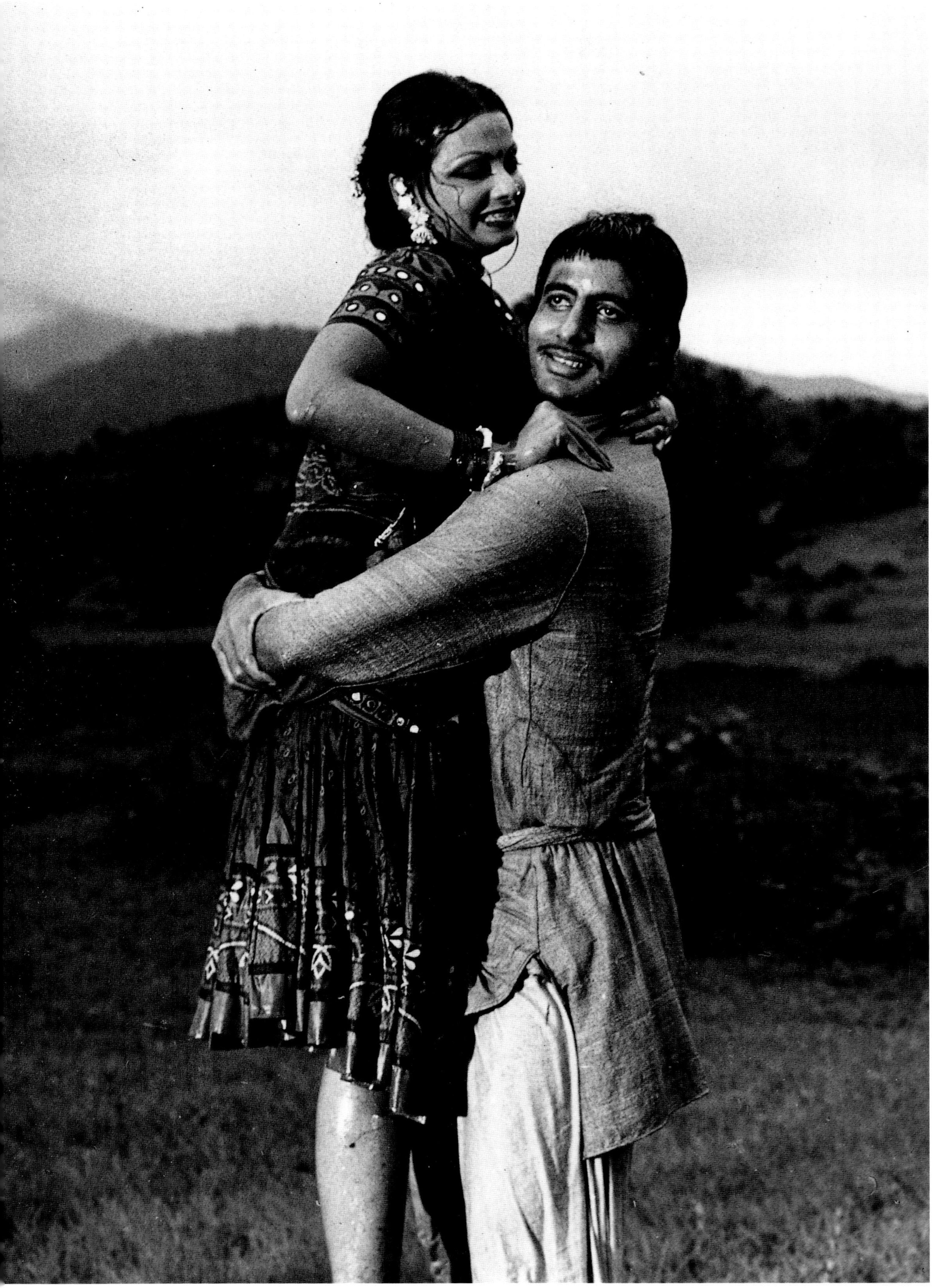

tenderness towards the woman he loves, who believes in him.

The long-suffering Nirupa Roy was by this time the veritable symbol of virtuous Hindu motherhood. Her most enduring screen partnerships were with Bachchan in their mother-son castings. Bachchan, it was said, touched her feet and sought her blessings even when they met in real life.

Many sociologists and film critics agree that Amitabh Bahchan's portrayal of the son gone wrong can be compared with Karna in the Mahabharata.

Karna's father was a god, his mother a princess. However, he is abandoned as a baby as the princess fears the social stigma of being an unwed mother. The god who impregnates her makes sure she remains a virgin even after the birth of the baby, evoking the theory of immaculate conception, the Cosmic Mother, who gives birth, yet is unattainable. Campbell, in *The Hero with a Thousand Faces*, writes: 'Whatever in the world has lured, whatever has seemed to promise joy, has been the premonitory of her existence —in the deep of sleep, if not in the cities and forest of the world. For she is the incarnation of the promise of perfection; the soul's assurance that, at the conclusion of its exile in a world of organized inadequacies, the bliss that once was known will be known again: the comforting, the nourishing, the "good" mother — young and beautiful — who was known to us, and even tasted, in the remotest past[1].'

Karna is adopted by a charioteer and his wife and goes on to be a sterling young man. He is aware that he is probably of a higher caste than his parents, but the boy is so dependent and grateful for his foster

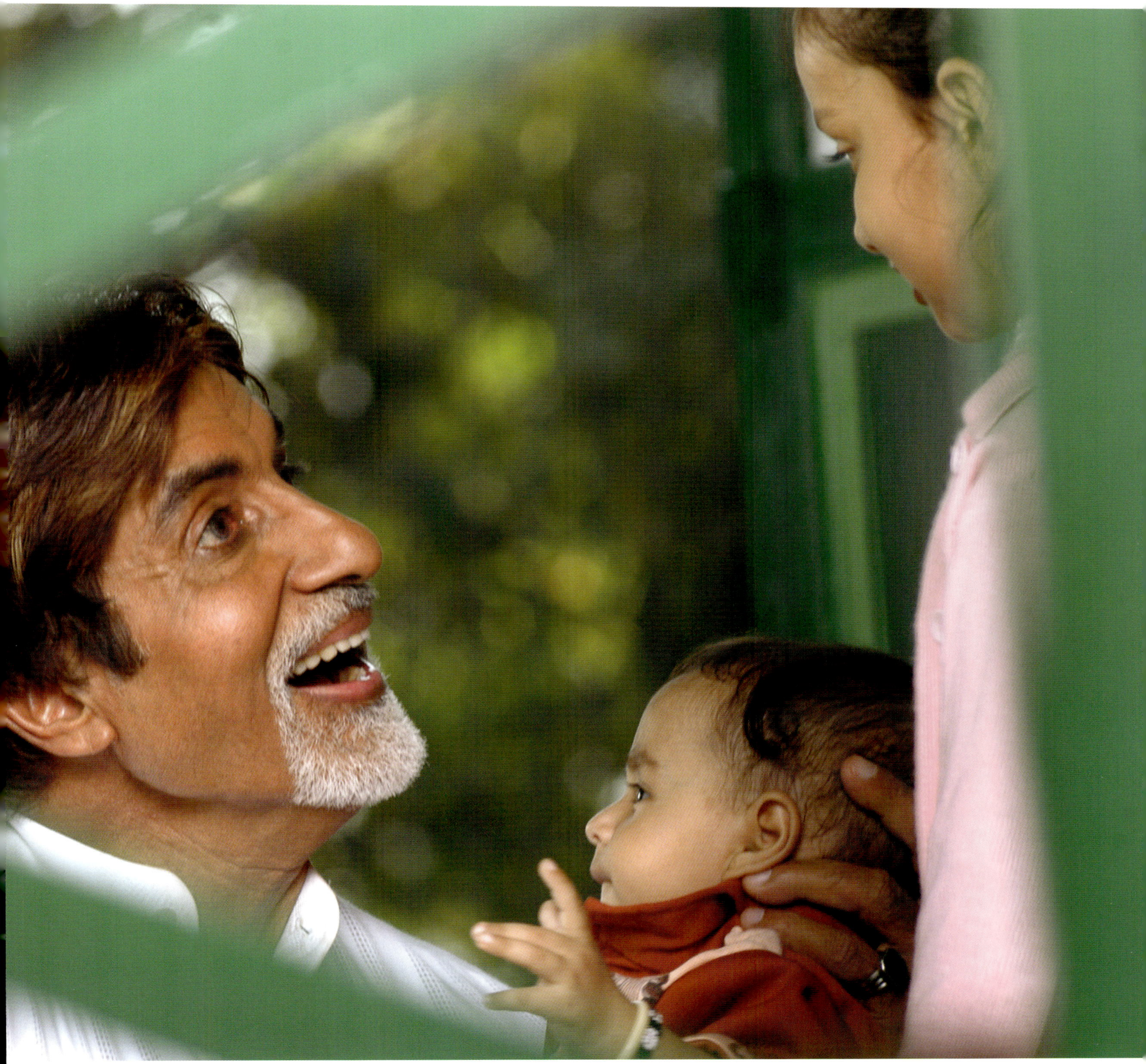

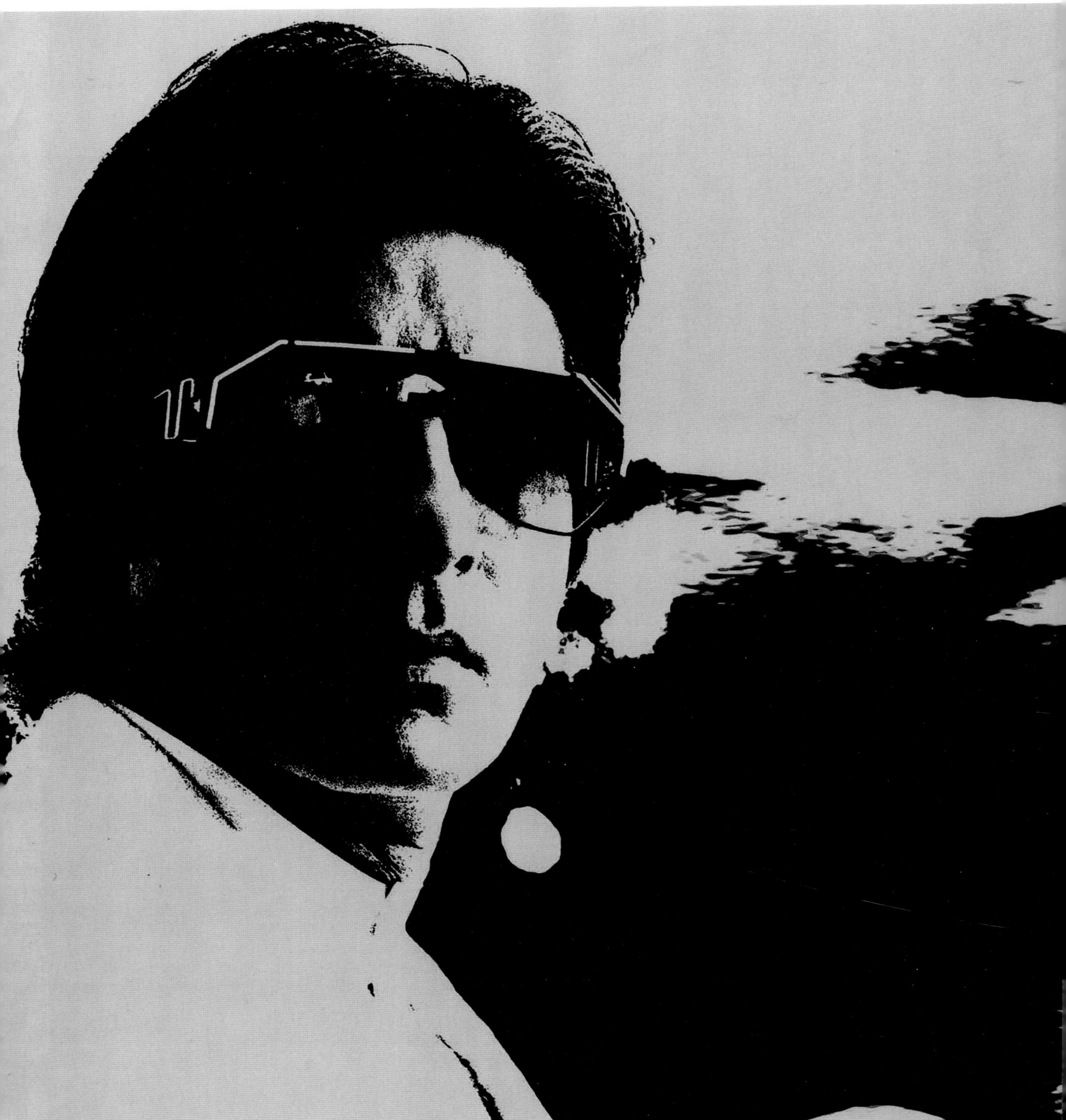

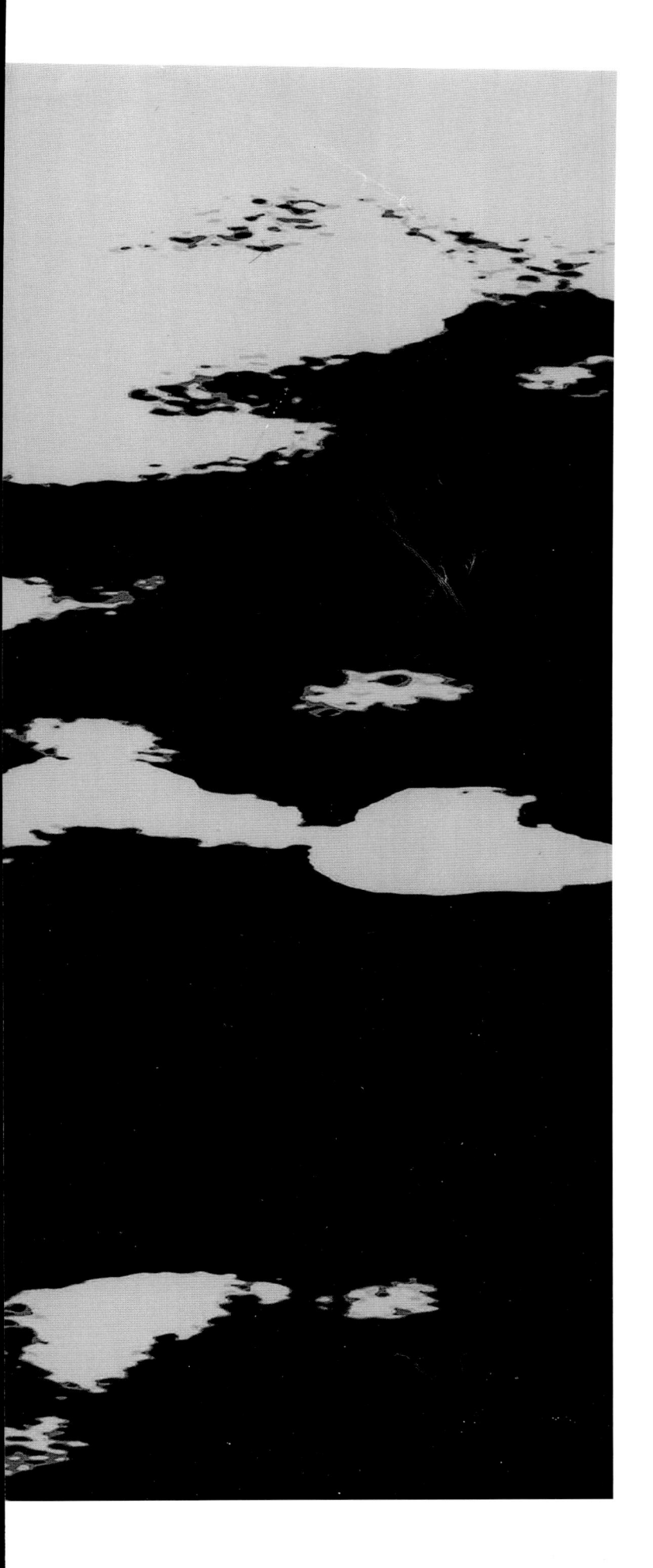

mother's love that he calls himself Radheya, after her name. At the same time he can't forget the other woman.

The princess Pritha, meanwhile, becomes Queen Kunti after marriage, and begets five more sons, of whom Arjuna emerges as the finest warrior in the land. Karna challenges him in an open tournament and wins.

Like Karna, who believed that knowing his mother would make his destiny clearer to him, *Deewar's* hero equated social acceptance with his mother's approval. Prince Arjuna trounced Karna without arrows or armed combat in the end merely by asking him to state his father's name, while Queen Kunti quailed unseen in the pavilion. Similarly, the policeman brother in *Deewar,* who maintains his harmony with the sacred feminine, crushes the smuggler hero's braggadocio with his simple statement: '*Mere paas maa hai.* [I have Mother.]'

Karna loves his mother though he knows she sides with his brothers. He accepts the injustice of it all, but doesn't nurse a grudge. In *Deewar,* Vijay too, pays homage to his mother's memories and effort when he buys a building at several times its actual value. When laughed at and told that he doesn't know how to do business, he remarks, '*Business to aap ko karna nahi aata, sethji. Is building ke aapne paanch lakh zyaada maange hote, tabh bhi mai ise le leta. Kyonki is building mein meri maa kaam kiya karti thi.* [It is you who don't know how to do business, sethji. Even if you had asked for five lakh more for the building, I would have still bought it. Because my mother used to work in this building.]'

Vijay is always anxious about his mother. Similarly, when Kunti comes to Karna before the war begins, asking him to spare Arjuna's life, Karna tells her that he cannot grant her that wish, but he tells her he will not harm his other brothers. The tenderness with which he tells her to leave, is as palpable in Bachchan's Vijay when, after his mother moves into her younger son's house, he asks her gently, *'Maa, tu khush to hai na...?* [Ma, you're happy, aren't you?]'

Vijay's desire to reform emerges after he finds out about his mother's illness, which threatens his life force because her death would mean the loss of his own hopes of acceptance and redemption.

As an individual, Vijay is separate from society, he has been separated from his guardians at an early age and he is cast into the wilderness. He grows up on the wild side. There comes a time, however, that he is offered a chance at justice and fairness, and he is given a chance to judge and sentence a perpetrator — perhaps the same perpetrator who wounded him once — by the same standards that he was judged by. This is his final reckoning, the moment of truth. And sometimes, he is destroyed in accomplishing it.

As Karna explains to Lord Krishna when he realises who he is and that he is fighting a lost cause: 'But Krishna, unsuccessful life, like love unreturned, has its own rainbow. You cannot have a rainbow in life unless there are tears to be lit up by the setting sun. Mine is such a life. I am hoping for this rainbow to light up the last few days of my life and illuminate my path to dusty death[2].'

Vijay too dies after being gunned down by his police officer brother, but he obtains his redemption

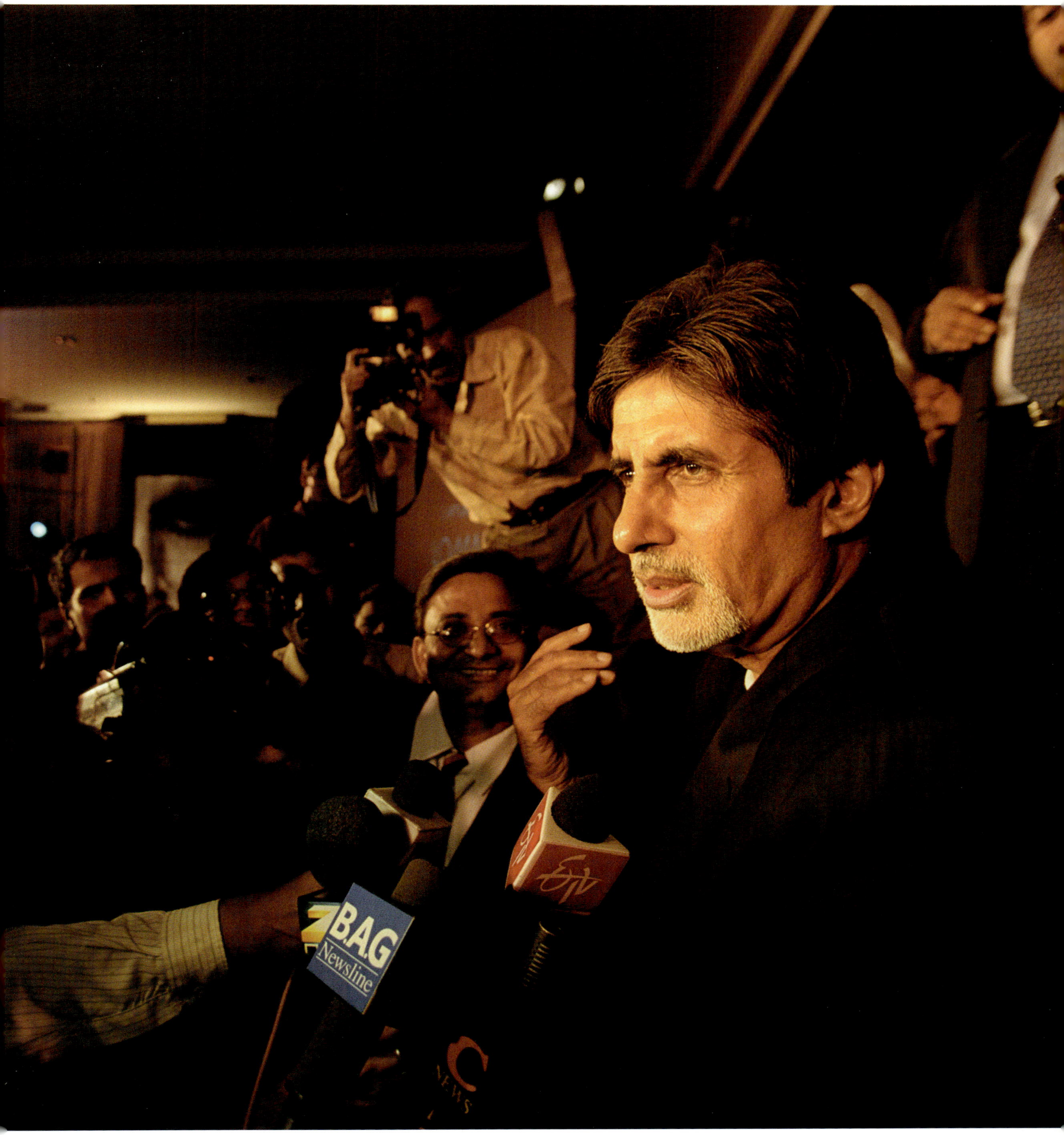
BAG
Newsline

from his mother and dies happy, with his head cradled tenderly by her, in a sense reverting back to his lost innocence.

In 1979's *Kaala Pathar* — director Yash Chopra's adaptation of Joseph Conrad's *Lord Jim* — Bachchan plays a young naval officer who deserts his ship's passengers to save his own life during a storm. He is afterwards discredited and removed from service, but eventually finds work as a shaft operator in a coal mine.

The subject of the film is of particular interest to young people. Everybody wants to prove that they are heroes, and not cowards. But the truth is, sometimes we encounter situations that can destroy this idea of ourselves. This is something that everybody fears, and this fear is lived out through the protagonist of this film.

This young man is angry all right, but for a change, he is angry at himself. His rage is internalised. He despises himself and cannot reconcile with the fact that he let himself down. He despises his act of cowardice and subsequently, during his work in the coal mine, he frequently puts himself in danger, doing things that are fraught with risk. He not only tries to negate his earlier act of cowardice through this, but also exorcises the hatred he feels for himself.

His deeds make him admired; he is like a pillar of strength to the fellow miners who are constantly fighting a battle with the elements in the mines' black wilderness. In a way he is the leader of the band of miners, living in semi-exile. However, Bachchan's character is playing a constant mind game with himself. He wants to die with a bang, something that

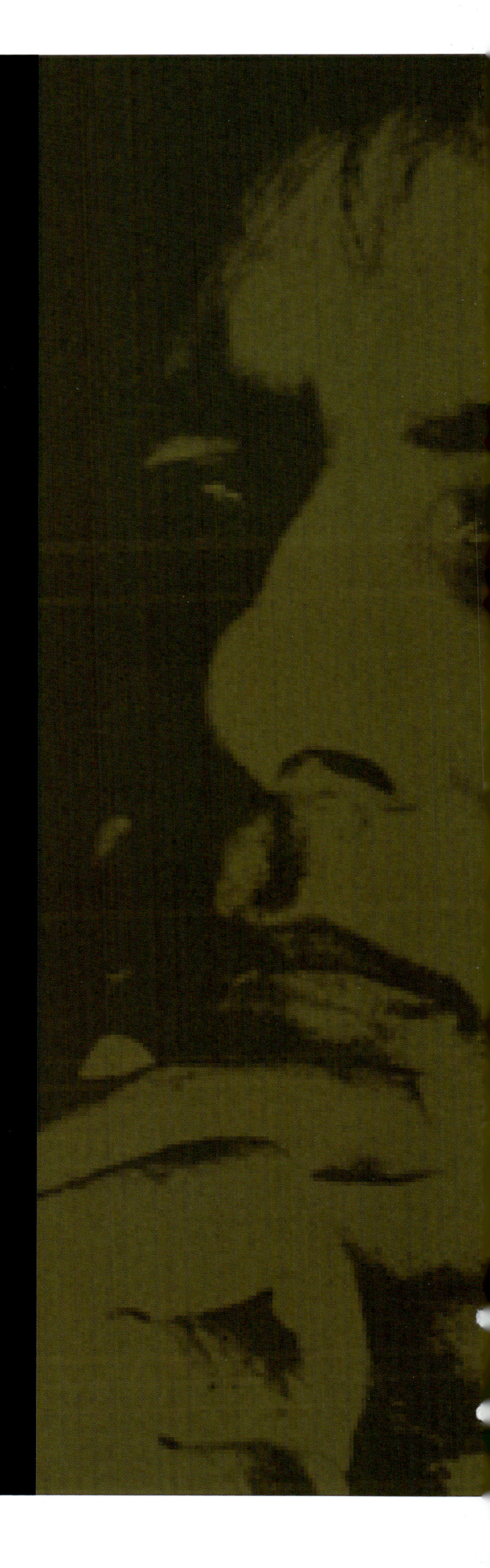

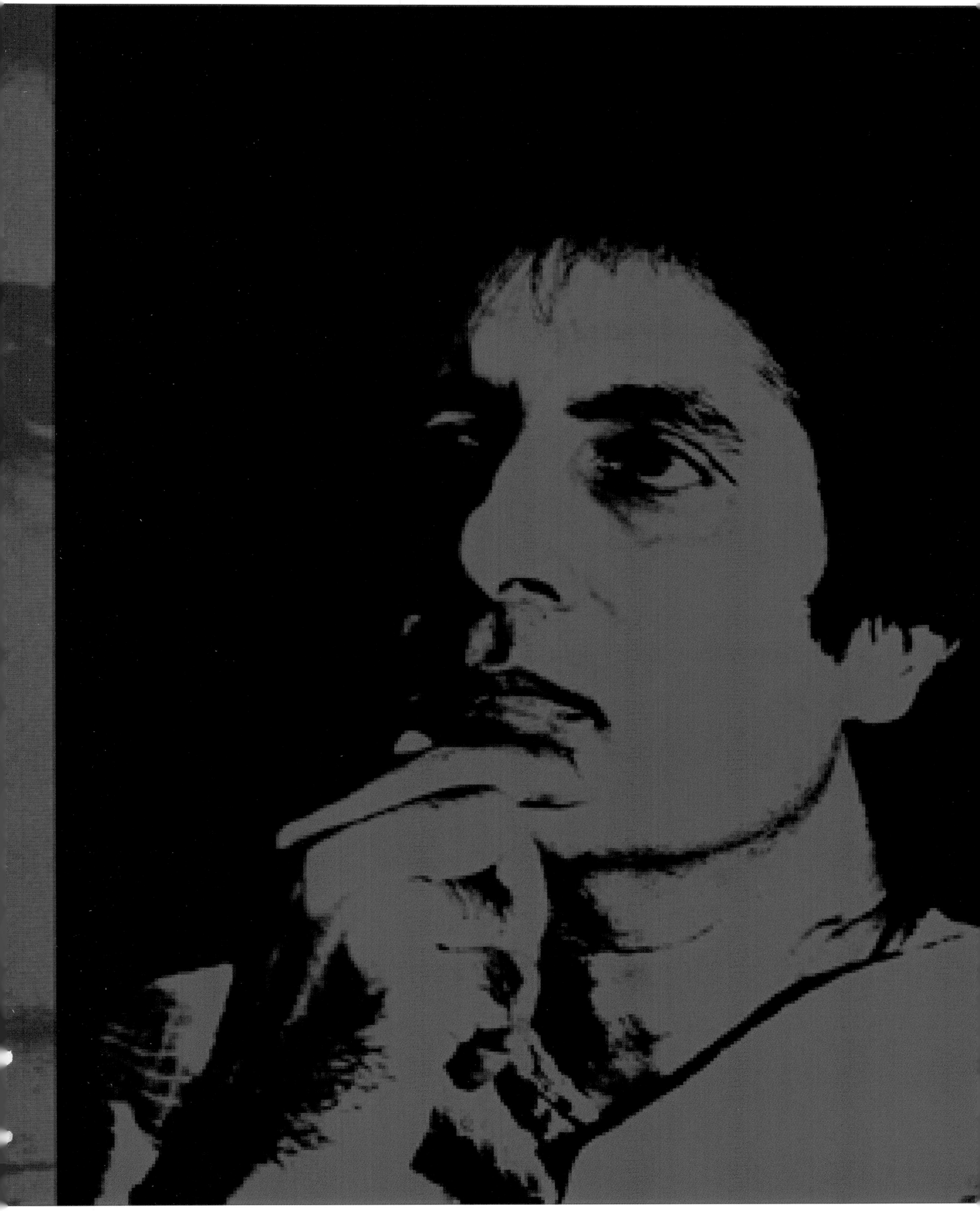

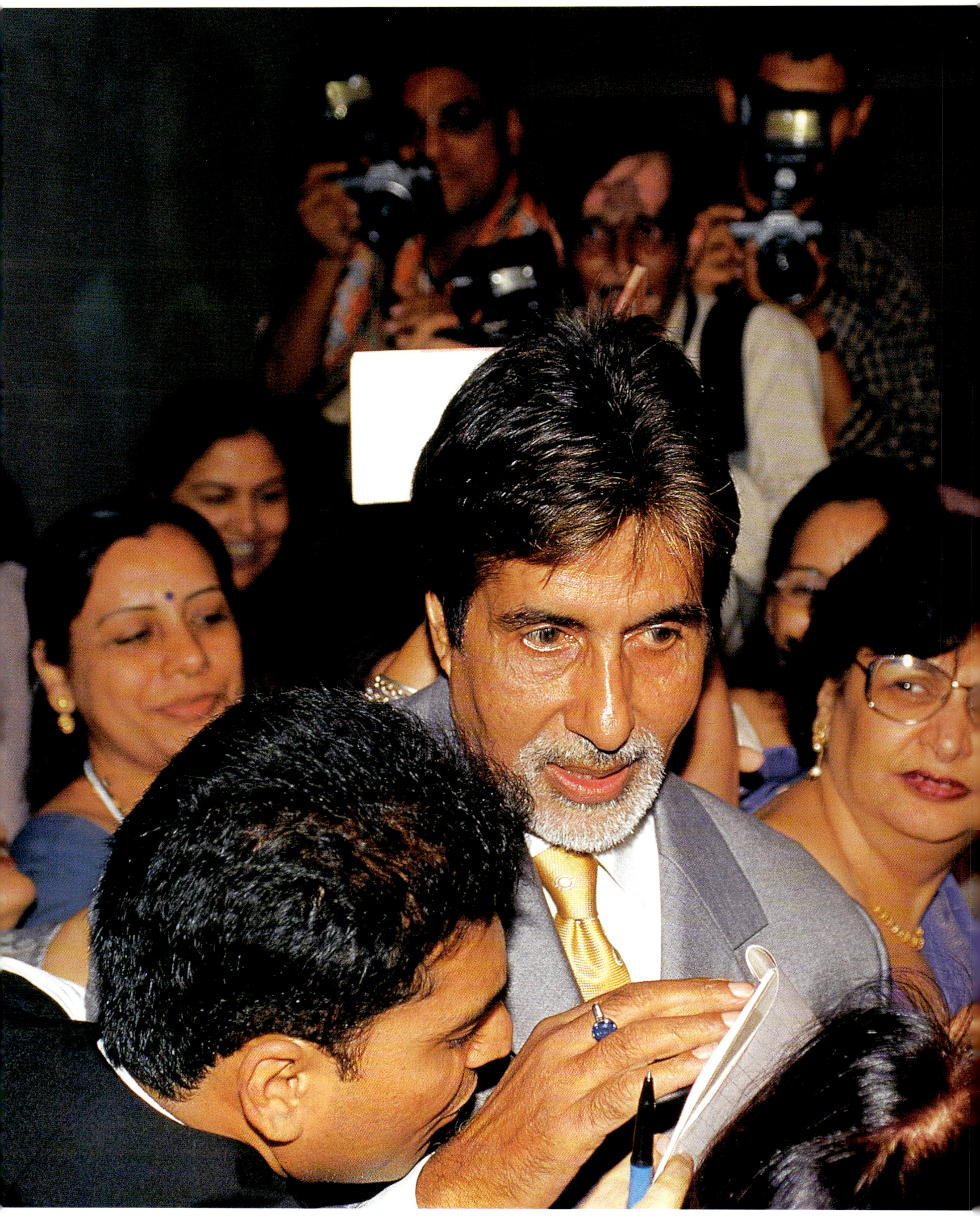

will erase his previous act of cowardice. If one were to look at the actual act dispassionately, it is probably something that he could have put behind him. But the coal miner cannot accept what he has done. When he starts working at the mine, he is at once the strongest and yet the weakest of all the men there.

Since he lacks the will to kill himself, he walks on a parallel plane with the rest of humanity. He is supremely indifferent to his exploits at the mine. Instead he craves pain as a branding catharsis to his shameful memory. He believes in nothing and no one to help him with redemption, sparing himself absolutely nothing by way of hope.

Unlike the survival instinct prevalent in the young man of *Deewar*, *Kaala Pathar's* coal miner is in self-destruct mode, his angst is internalised. And unlike the young man in *Zanjeer*, whose pain stems from reasons beyond his control, the self-loathing coal miner spirals down because of his own actions. He has fully set himself up for a thorough self scourge, but doesn't see a way to finish the circle to complete catharsis. He is still stuck in a rut. The reason is his self-conscience and his ego. When he puts himself at risk, he does so not out of a concern for others, but for the selfish goal of proving to his conscience that he is not the coward the world thinks him to be. So his incomplete catharsis is because his conscience recognises that something is missing. Something else is required to set him free. The pain of the world's contempt he carries like a cross, unflinching. 'My pain is my destiny and I can't avoid it,' he says.

Kaala Pathar's coal miner finds his redemption when he saves several miners from certain death in a massive flooding deep inside the mines. 'As the rising smoke of an offering through the sun door, so goes the hero released from ego through the walls of the world...' Joseph Campbell writes in his *The Hero with a Thousand Faces*.

For the average man, who is young and filled with self-doubt, what message could be more powerful than the opportunity for second chances in life, even if one does make horrible mistakes along the way?

In the end, the miner's conscience is satisfied and lets him dump his emotional baggage because of one overwhelming flow of feeling. As American writer James Lane Allen defines heroism in his short stories *King Solomon of Kentucky, Great Short Stories of the World*, 'It was not grief; it was not gratitude, nor any sense of making reparation for the past. It was the softening influence of an act of heroism, which makes every man feel himself a brother hand in hand with every other — such power has a single act of moral greatness to reverse the relations of men, lifting up one, and bringing up all others to do him homage[3].'

Bachchan, however, feels that the Angry Young Man character began not with *Zanjeer*, but with Hrishikesh Mukherjee's *Namak Haram*, as it was in this film that he first explored the persona's characteristic emotions.

Namak Haram brought Bachchan and Rajesh Khanna together again, and this time around, Bachchan completely stole the thunder. The film got him a Filmfare Award for Best Supporting Actor.

An adaptation of Jean Anouilh's *Becket*, Bachchan's character in the film is a take off on Henry II, the Norman King. Bachchan's angry young man this time is Vicky, an industrialist's son. An apt euphemism for royalty in 1970s India. Rajesh Khanna is Somu, a young man from a middle class background, who is Vicky's best friend. Vicky's angry young man, is confused and hurt when Somu, previously his staunch supporter, starts to identify with the workers in Vicky's father's factory. He starts to think of Somu as an ingrate.

This is a story that is imbued with a natural drama as it expresses a tension that is central to humankind: how we distribute power between the influential few who disperse it, and the teeming many who receive it.

'Why do you put labels onto everything to justify your feelings?' asks King Henry of Becket, in the original play, struggling to understand someone he loves but cannot reconcile with.

'Because, without labels, the world would have no shape, my prince,' replies Becket.

'Is it so important for the world to have a shape?'

'It's essential, my prince, otherwise we can't know what we're doing[4].'

When Somu poses as an employee and joins the factory to quell worker unrest, he does so with the intention of proving that employee strength and industrialist clout could be combined into one power. This doesn't quite work out the way he planned. The two are and must be quite distinct, he soon discovers. And it is possible to respect both

The Legend

97

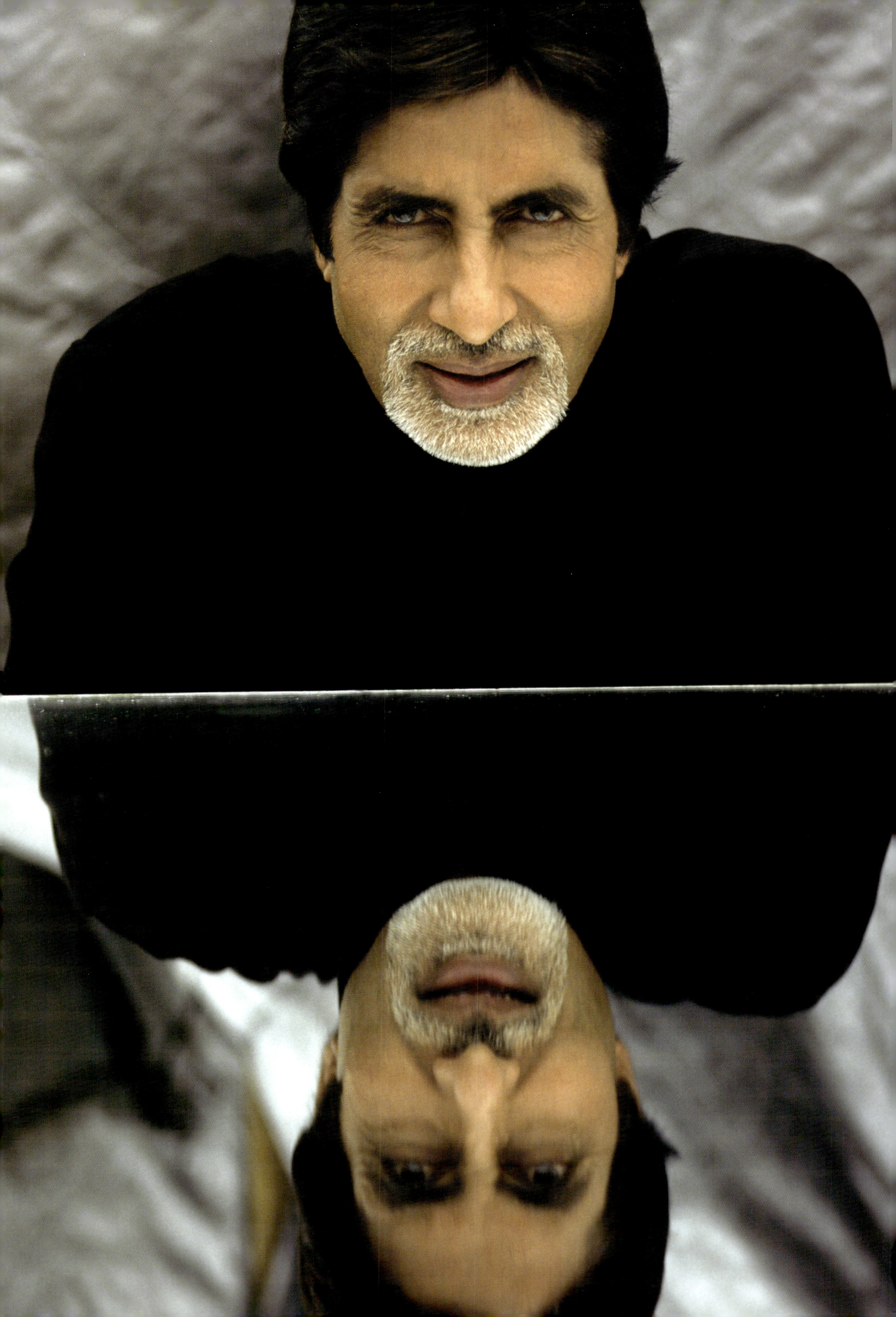

sides in the struggle between the two. It was necessary for Somu to establish the rights of the workers in civil matters — the capitalist cannot remain so far beyond the reach of civil authority that he and his son are virtually untouchable. The tension between the capitalist and the worker is healthy, though it must sometimes break and lead to disruption, even to violence and death, as becomes the case in this film.

Vicky is egged on in his misconception about Somu by his tycoon father. Eventually, the father secretly arranges for Somu to be revealed as a spy to his colleagues, who, enraged, beat him to death.

When Vicky gets to know about this, he is furious with his father for interfering. *Jo kuch bhi hua, woh mere aur uske beech mein hai, koi teesra beech main aaya toh…* [Whatever happened is between him and me, if a third person comes in the middle…]' he screams at his father.

His rage is palpable in the scene where he goes to retrieve Somu's body. He roars out to those responsible for beating his friend to death, 'Hai kisi maa ke laal mein himmat jo mere saamne aaye? [Is there courage in any mother's son to face me?]'

The film *Shakti* is especially noteworthy as here Bachchan is cast opposite another screen legend, Dilip Kumar. Bachchan's angry young man is pitted against Kumar's rigid patrician policeman. Kumar's portrayal was ironclad as the long hand of the law. Bachchan's character was as flawed and human as they come.

Bachchan is vintage angst-ridden hero as Kumar's smuggler son. In order to hurt his father, he tells him, 'Us aadmi ka toh bahut bada ehsaan hai. *Kyonki us aadmi ne to us waqt meri madat ki thi, jab mere apne baap ne mooh pher liya tha.* [I am grateful to that man. Because, he helped me at a time when my own father turned away from me.]'

The stage in the journey of the universal hero, which Campbell describes as 'Atonement with the Father[5]' happens in the death scene in *Shakti*, where father and son reconcile with each other. Kumar's policeman acknowledges his love for his son while the latter breathes his last peacefully, knowing that he has surmounted the biggest deficiency in his life's journey.

Why was the 'Angry Young Man' so successful? Yes, the political instability and increasing corruption, student unrest and high level of unemployment in the 1970s was enough to make many young men angry. Bachchan was reflecting some of their own anger and restlessness on screen. And watching him onscreen purged many of them of their own frustrations. When he remarks, '*Kyonki mujhe befizul baat karne ki aadat toh hain nahin* [Because I'm not in the habit of saying inconsequential things],' he demonstrates the mood of the entire country.

For years on end, the onscreen Amitabh was largely angry, be it in *Deewar, Trishul, Shakti* or *Sholay*. He captured the feeling of the entire mass of unquiet Indian youth for over two decades. His dialogues captivated audiences and were repeated in the nooks and corners of India by the youth who adored him. No other star in the 1970s and 80s was half as successful. And he in turn found the perfect medium for self-expression: the Hindi film.

Guest Writer

Nothing Angry About Him

T.R. Gopaalakrishnan

'My name is Amitabh Bachchan.'

I had been waiting for some time in his dressing room in one of Mumbai's studios when I was hit with that line; he walked in dressed as a Pathan, having just completed a scene with the beautiful Sridevi for *Khuda Gawa,* probably his last major hit as the angry hero.

My own introduction obviously had nowhere near the same resonance. I doubt whether any other name of that time had the same recognition quotient. In the decade since then, that recognition quotient has only gained in strength and vigour. The phenomenon, he was called then. The phenomenon he remains today.

I was as much a fan of Amitabh's as anyone else during his heyday. In those days, an Amitabh movie would be booked in advance for weeks. It was the delight of the black marketeers outside Delhi's cinema halls. Watching an Amitabh movie on the first day of its release was something of a coup. As a very junior hack in Delhi, I still remember getting to see his movie *Naseeb* on the first day. It needed a police escort from the local police station to get me that much-prized ticket. A face-to-face meeting with Amitabh was still in the realm of dreams then. And it actually happened only many, many years later.

That first meeting with Amitabh Bachchan was for a cover story we were doing on him. Till then, he had remained aloof from the media. But his brief stint with politics and his name being dragged into the Bofors controversy, I think, made him want to give his side of the story. I think that interview to me and *The Week* was the first time he really spoke his mind about his political foray and the insinuations that were being made about him and his family with regard to the gun deal and his brother's pharma company in Switzerland. He became far more accessible to the media after that. But now, as then, it was more a case of the media needing Amitabh, rather than him needing the media.

Amitabh was never the boy-next-door kind of person. And neither did he try to cultivate that image. He had the advantage of his family pedigree that got him the initial entry into Bollywood. He understood as well as anyone else how cruel and heartless the industry could be to a struggling young actor. He had his share of heartbreaks and failures. But once he made it to the top, he was obviously determined to make it last long. He had seen others shoot to stardom and fade away. A fate he knew could befall him too.

Luck or design, or a combination of both, has ensured that Amitabh has been able to grow old gracefully as an actor. It is a transition that few of his predecessors were able to make. But Amitabh has not only made the transition successfully, he has in the process managed to reinvent Bollywood's traditional formula in the kind of roles older people play. To the extent that he remains the main crowd puller for his films even today.

Fame and fortune, those most fickle and demanding of companions, sit lightly on Amitabh. He has made his share of bad life and career decisions. He has had his share of personal misfortune. But at the end of the day, he has emerged from those episodes in his life with dignity. In an industry that is either at one's feet or at one's throat, Amitabh is one of the few good guys, having somehow steered clear of Bollywood's legendary jealousies and viciousness — an icon for all age groups. Respected and admired, and no doubt envied, but in a genteel sort of way.

Life at the top cannot be easy for him or for anyone else. All the simple and small freedoms the rest of us take for granted is denied to someone in Amitabh's position. Privacy needs to be guarded fiercely. Family protected from a raucous media. His movie *Abhimaan* with wife Jaya could well have been a metaphor for one chapter in his life story. *Silsila* was generally regarded as a depiction of another story from his life. True or false has little meaning in a world of tinsel and hype. One needed to guide perception. However he did it, Amitabh did manage to make himself seen as an intensely private person, without being a recluse, and a devoted family man.

Never a Bollywood party person, Amitabh worked hard to keep away from the filmi media frenzy and, in recent years, from the Page 3 madness. He has lent his name to some public and social causes, carefully orchestrating each and every public appearance. But from the very beginning, he has made it clear that once he finished work for the day, he wanted to be left alone.

What drives Amitabh today? The busiest actor in Bollywood and probably the most expensive brand ambassador for any product, what peaks are there left for him to climb? Should he get more choosy about the kind of films he does? Should he exercise more care in selecting the brands he endorses? Is there still any life for him outside the world of cinema and advertising? Should he get into TV serials? No doubt he has asked himself these questions often in recent times. If he has found an answer to any of them, he is keeping them to himself. Not surprising that, really.

— *T.R. Gopaalakrishnan is editor-in-charge of* The Week

Chapter Four

A Search For Identity

Like the sharp edge of a razor is that path,
Difficult to cross and hard to tread — thus say the wise
–Kathopanishad 3-14

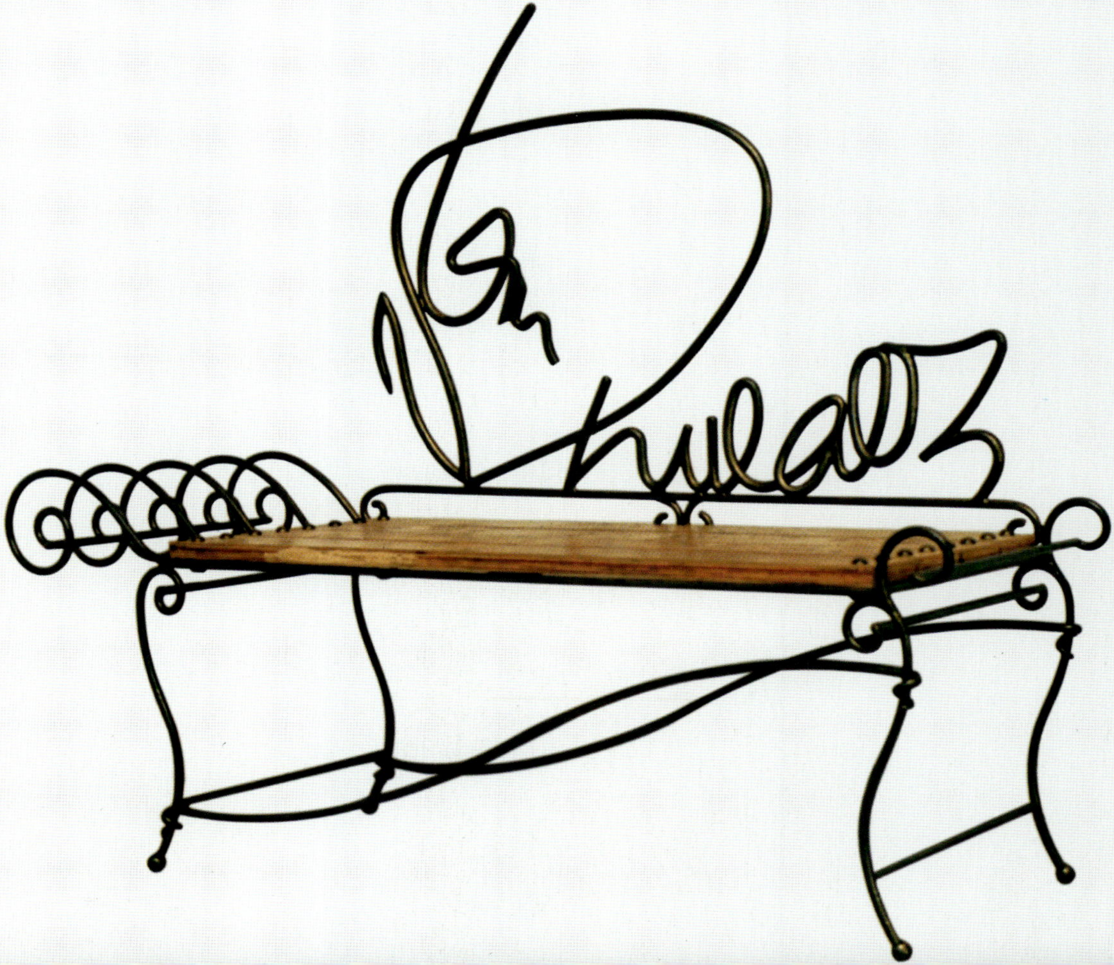

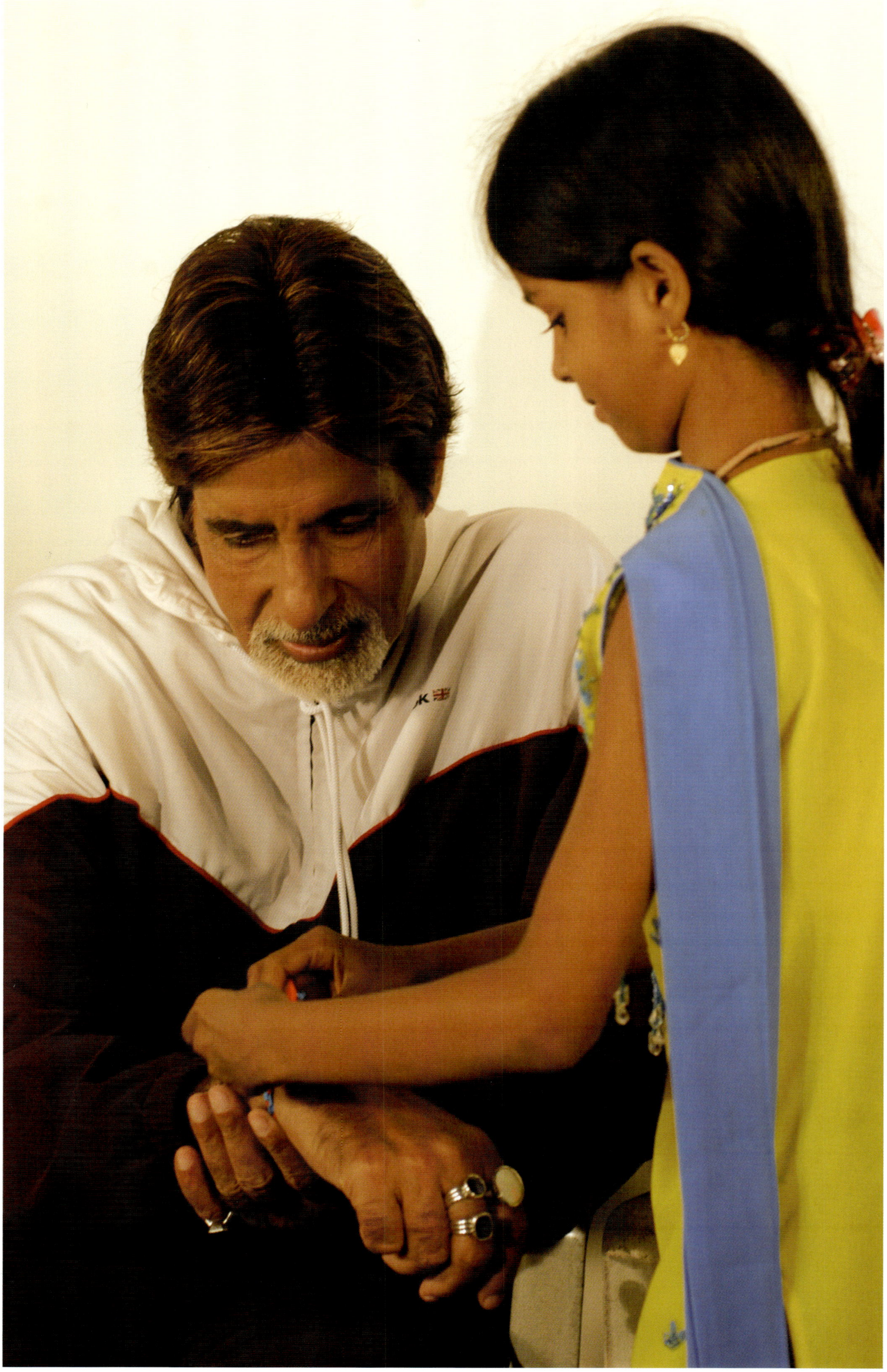

Bachchan went on to rule the box office for two decades. Though his later films didn't always hit the scale of his 'Angry Young Man' movies, they raked in money at the box office. Enough to keep him in his premier position at the box office. Films even rumoured to have his involvement found buyers immediately.

So much of an icon was he that a comic book revolving around him as a superhero came out in the market. Apart from Sunil Gavaskar, he is the only celebrity to feature in a comic book series. 'Supremo' featured Bachchan as himself, but with a secret alter ego who becomes the superhero Supremo whenever peril calls. 'Supremo', masked and resplendent in a magenta and yellow costume, came with his own private menagerie on a secret island replete with a character cast that included a yellow singing whale called Sonali.

The movies that came in the wake of his 'Angry' films were diverse, but they resulted in some famous partnerships like the one he had with filmmaker Manmohan Desai, which resulted in the unforgettable *Amar Akbar Anthony*.

Says the filmmaker's son Ketan Desai, 'Once Amitabh came into his [Manmohan Desai] life, he could not see beyond him. When Man *ji* explained the character of Anthony to Amit *ji*, he was first very awkward about the way Anthony speaks. He had some reservations about it. He said "I come from a literary

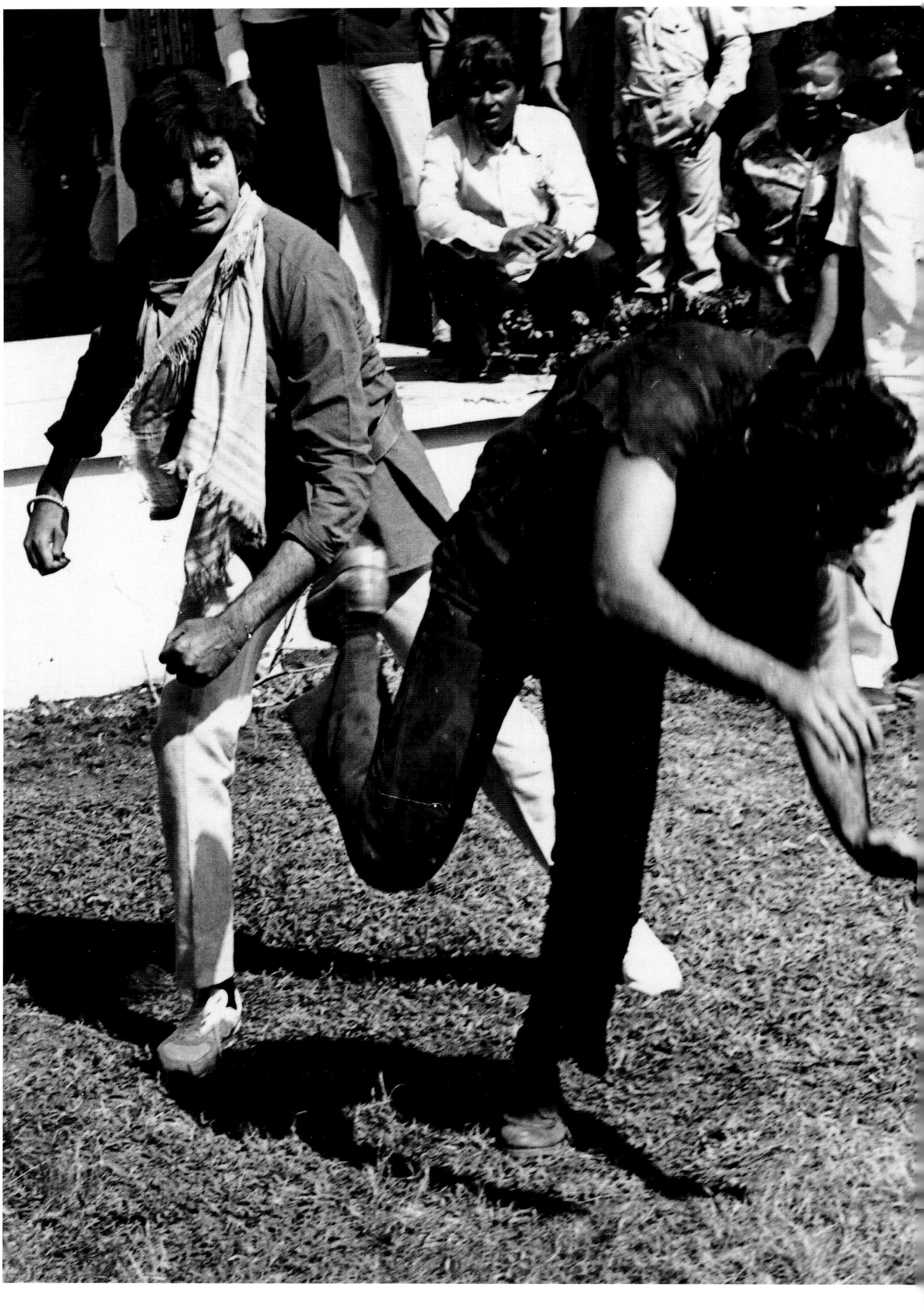

family in Allahabad". He was afraid of what his father would say after hearing the language he uses in the film. Man *ji* said, "I have a lot of conviction and faith in you. I promise that when the film is released, people will call you Anthony *bhai*".'

And then, in 1984, an invitation came from close friend and then Prime Minister Rajiv Gandhi to join the Congress party. Though not too driven about his role as a politician, he joined the party all the same and was a success wherever he went. Such was the strength of his personality, that he eventually ended up making some enduring friendships despite the quicksilver nature of political relationships.

Bachchan says his decision to enter politics was an emotional one. 'Nobody advised me. But there had been a great tragedy [Indira Gandhi's assassination]. I was known to the family and I just thought that I should stand beside the young man who wanted to lead the country[1].'

Things looked good for Bachchan. He divided his time between acting in films and the rallies that he had to attend while contesting his political seat. Such was his popularity that he beat a senior leader like H.N. Bahuguna for the Allahabad seat. The win took him back to the city of his youth. 'When I went back to campaign, all the childhood spots were there in an almost unchanged condition, which is very nice, but also very sad because it shows that Allahabad has not developed at all[2].'

But Bachchan had more to be grateful for than his success in politics and films. Only a year back, there had been an incident on the sets of *Coolie*, in which Bachhan had almost died. While shooting a fight scene for the film, Bachchan went down to a thrust by co-star Puneet Issar. The blow caught Bachchan unawares and jabbed him right in the solar plexus. He collapsed and had to be taken to a hospital immediately. The entire nation was in shock.

Issar, for no fault of his, was blacklisted by the film industry, for being the man who had injured India's favourite superstar. However, the star himself never held it against him. Issar has, since then, recovered from this professional setback and continues to enjoy Bachchan's friendship to this day.

If anything, the accident reaffirmed Bachchan's public acclaim. 'The accident effectively immortalised him in the hearts of the people,' says photographer and painter J.P. Singhal. The entire nation prayed for his life. The then Prime Minister Indira Gandhi visited him at the Breach Candy Hospital in Mumbai.

Bachchan emerged from his illness humbled by the power of mass prayer. 'It is their [the Indian public's] selfless adoration which has provided me the will to live in face of dire calamity,' he acknowledges.

Bachchan revealed his mettle the day he reported back on the sets of *Coolie*. Says Ketan Desai, 'After the accident and recovery, when he returned for the shoot, Man *ji* suggested that they start with a light scene with a song and dance, but Amitabh insisted on starting with the scene he had left off, the fight scene. It takes a lot of courage to do such a shot.'

Bachchan was about to slip off his pedestal, however. In the late Eighties, rumours began floating thick and fast about the Bachchan family's involvement in a gun deal involving Swedish arms company Bofors. Instead of protesting his innocence while still holding his seat as any other insouciant politician would have, Bachchan decided to step down and fight to clear his name. He was in uncharted waters. As H.D. Thoreau put it, 'Virtue is a bravery so hardy that it deals in what it has no

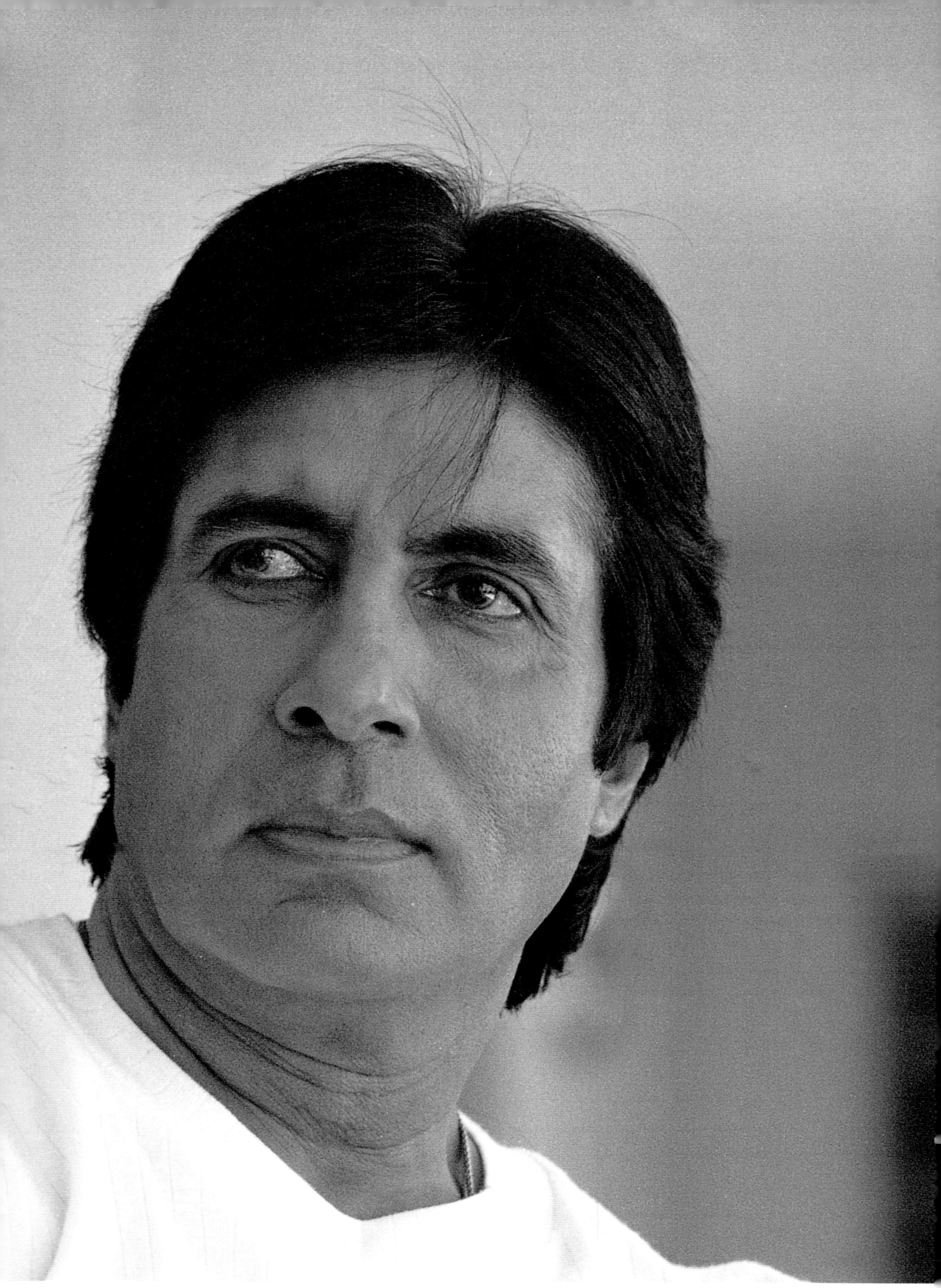

experience in.'

'I resigned on moral grounds. It was an emotional decision, I know. But then my decision to join politics was equally emotional[3]. I decided to fight to clear my name and everything but also for the sake of posterity. I was going to leave my reputation behind for my children, and I needed to tell them what the truth was. Not just my children, but the whole nation[4].'

So he single-handedly took on all his detractors and set out to prove them wrong.

It was to be a long fight. Public opinion had turned. The once reverential masses had become cynical to the point of even mocking his primary career. 'I remember during the elections, one of the allegations made was that: *"teen ghante mein to picture ban jaati hai* [A picture is made in three hours]"! It surprises me as to how ignorant people are about filmmaking. What is finally seen on the screen: do people realise how much labour, how much sweat and blood it has taken to produce that moment of entertainment? How can they take it for granted that because you have a smile on your face on the screen, everything is fine? It does not necessarily mean that your mind is not troubled or bothered by some sad experience.'

He recounts, 'There are so many times when we have gone to funerals of our colleagues…and as we are on the road carrying their body, people are still laughing and joking at us and saying *"aey, dialogue bolo* [Hey, give us a dialogue]"[5].'

To clear his name from the case, Bachchan first met the journalists who had uncovered the Bofors deal: *Hindu* editor N. Ram and reporter Chitra Subramaniam. Ram met him in Delhi. 'I have one of my reporters in Stockholm, would you mind if we ask him to go and talk to the people in Bofors about you?' he asked. Bachchan readily consented. The result was that Bofors said that they had never heard of Mr Bachchan in this connection[6].

By then, another tragedy had struck: his friend and political mentor Rajiv Gandhi was assassinated. The death of Rajiv, a close friend since they were in college, was especially hard to take.

'You forget how you react in moments like this. But you go through a sense of numbness. I tried to contact his family — which was my first reaction. I tried to contact my own family — which was my second reaction. Then, the next thing was to gather everybody and to go back home.

'I think he was a very noble, very decent human being. He was most unsuited for the profession that he eventually took up. I myself opted out of it because of these reasons. I think it was easier for me to do it than for him.

'I have known Rajiv Gandhi since the age of four. We have been friends, we have been family friends. I do admit that I had access to the Prime Minister as a friend…I was never a member of his coterie…his so-called caucus. I was never a part of his decision-making team. I was at best a Congressman. And his friend, who used to meet him informally,' he says refuting charges that he had a disproportionate access to and influence on Rajiv Gandhi.

'His commitment was more resolute and one admired him for it. But basically he was a good human being, and I don't think that politics is really a good place for good human beings,' he said[7] in a memoir to his friend.

After the release of *Khuda Gawah* and *Hum,* Bachchan decided to cut down his acting assignments and do some thinking. 'I had been working continuously at a feverish pace, and I felt that I was stagnating — I feel I've been stagnating for thirty years, but that's another issue — and I felt I had reached a stage where I needed to take a break. I just stopped signing films,' Bachchan told Vir Sanghvi in an interview.

Introspection followed, interspersed with some serious globetrotting; he divided his time between the United Kingdom, the US, and India. 'I slept when I wanted to, went out where I wanted to. That was my

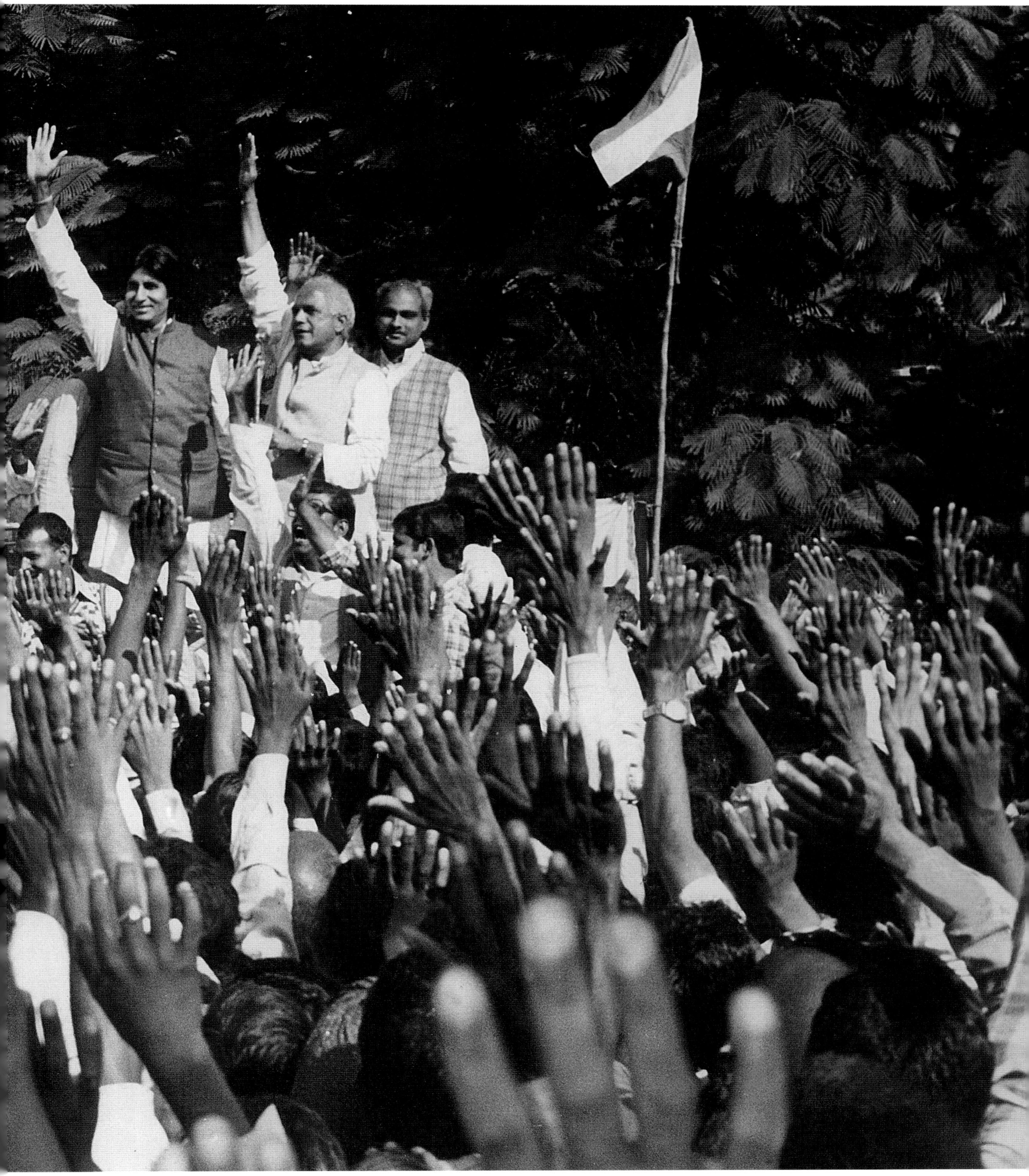

nature…' said Bachchan of this sojourn into his self.

He probably felt as Thoreau did, when the author said, 'You think I am impoverishing myself by withdrawing from men, but in my solitude I have woven for myself a silken web or chrysalis and, nymph-like, shall ere long burst forth a more perfect creature, fitted for a higher society.'

'I had roamed and seen a lot in those five years. Sometimes, I was recognised immediately, be it Egypt or the Middle East, Russia or Africa. This surprised me. This wasn't my recognition; it was a paean to the Indian film industry. People wouldn't call me by my name, but the names of the roles I had done. When they saw me on the streets, they would sing my songs and call me Vijay,' Bachchan said in an interview recently.

Indeed, even during the shooting of *Khuda Gawah* in Afghanistan, Bachchan and the rest of the film crew were received like royalty and entertained lavishly. The political situation in the country was chaotic at the time, as this was shortly after the Soviet Union had withdrawn its troops from Afghanistan. Once, just after wrapping up a shoot, the film crew

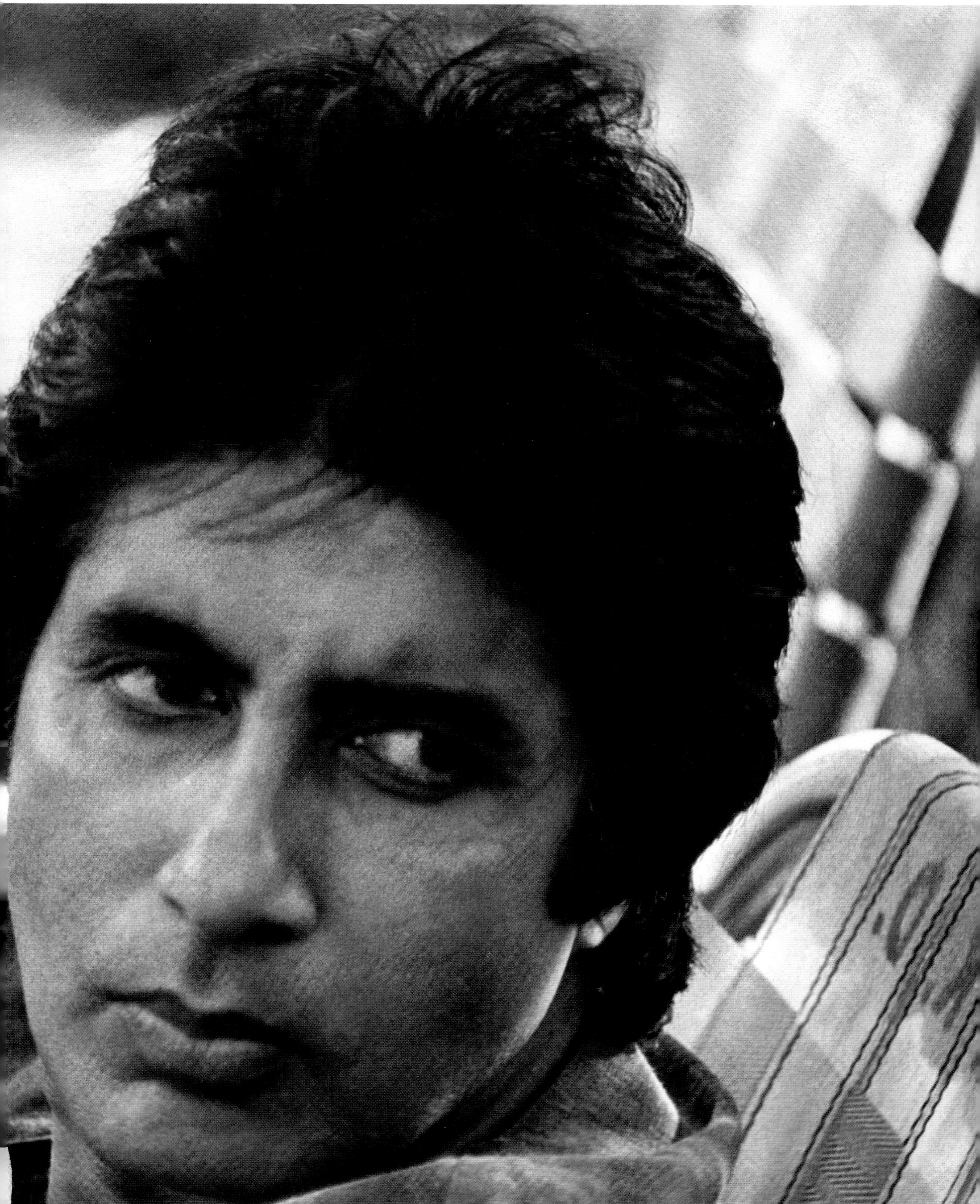

was visited on the sets by several Mujahidin horsemen. They asked the film crew about the great Amitabh Bachchan. They were led up to the actor by a frightened film technician. To their surprise, and collective relief, the horsemen led him up to their leader, who only wanted to greet the film star and personally present him with the best stallion from his stables.

After five years, Bachchan decided to return to the film industry. But he was not without a plan. He came back with a blueprint to clean up the clutter in his home ground — the Hindi film industry. The instrument was to be Bachchan's own company: Amitabh Bachchan Corporation Limited.

'During my thirty-year career, one of the accusations that used to come my way was that you've never invested back into the film industry. You've invested in pharmaceuticals, in this and that. But you've never invested your money back into the industry. But here, I felt, was one activity that was very genuine. I really was putting money back to raise the standard of working in the industry,' Bachchan said of his first corporate venture concerning the Hindi film industry.

The idea for the company germinated during his break from films, when people in different corners of the

the Legend

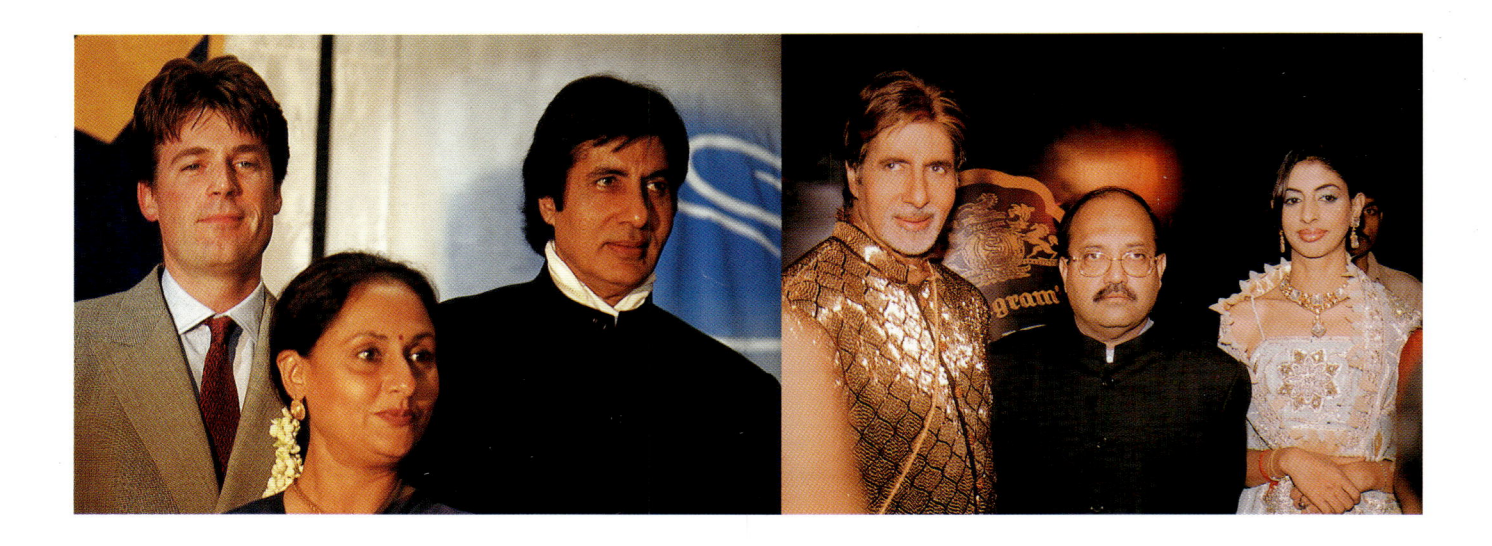

world recognised him despite his having taken time off for an extended period. Bachchan felt that, if there was so much recognition for the Hindi film industry in non-Hindi speaking regions of the world, it would definitely be worth marketing and promoting it on a much larger scale throughout the globe. Also, it would help the industry if there was an organised and professionally handled company within so much creative chaos.

It was then that he thought of forming a corporation much like international corporations worldwide, to get a semblance of professionalism and corporate attitude in the entertainment industry. 'That was the attraction. That really brought me back again,' he said[8].

Though he returned to films by contracting himself out through his company, his primary image this time was of an entrepreneur. As the face of ABCL, he was to do one film every year. He also made history by trying to introduce transparency into a film's financing. His contract with ABCL was a public document. The world now knew for sure that a Hindi film star could command millions. He was also the highest paid star in the Hindi film industry that year. ABCL's contract paid Bachchan a cool three crore rupees for each film.

But like every contract, what the big print giveth, the fine print taketh away. And so it was with a paycheque of three crore rupees. The fact was, because he was the brand ambassador and main promoter, Bachchan's earnings were always ploughed back into the business as ABCL's capital. The same was the case with all the television commercials that he did then. Ditto for the BPL and Eveready endorsements.

Bachchan made it clear that he was only the face of the enterprise and not the brains. He always painstakingly pointed out that the company was managed by professionals. 'I don't have business sense,' he said once. When pressed, he dismissed the issue saying that he was trying to find out if he had what they called business sense[9].

His superhero status, the undisputed reign over the Hindi film industry for over twenty years, all gave him and his undertaking an invincible glow. All that was needed to seal the case was for his first film with ABCL — also his first film to be shot after his five-year hiatus — to be declared a hit. This

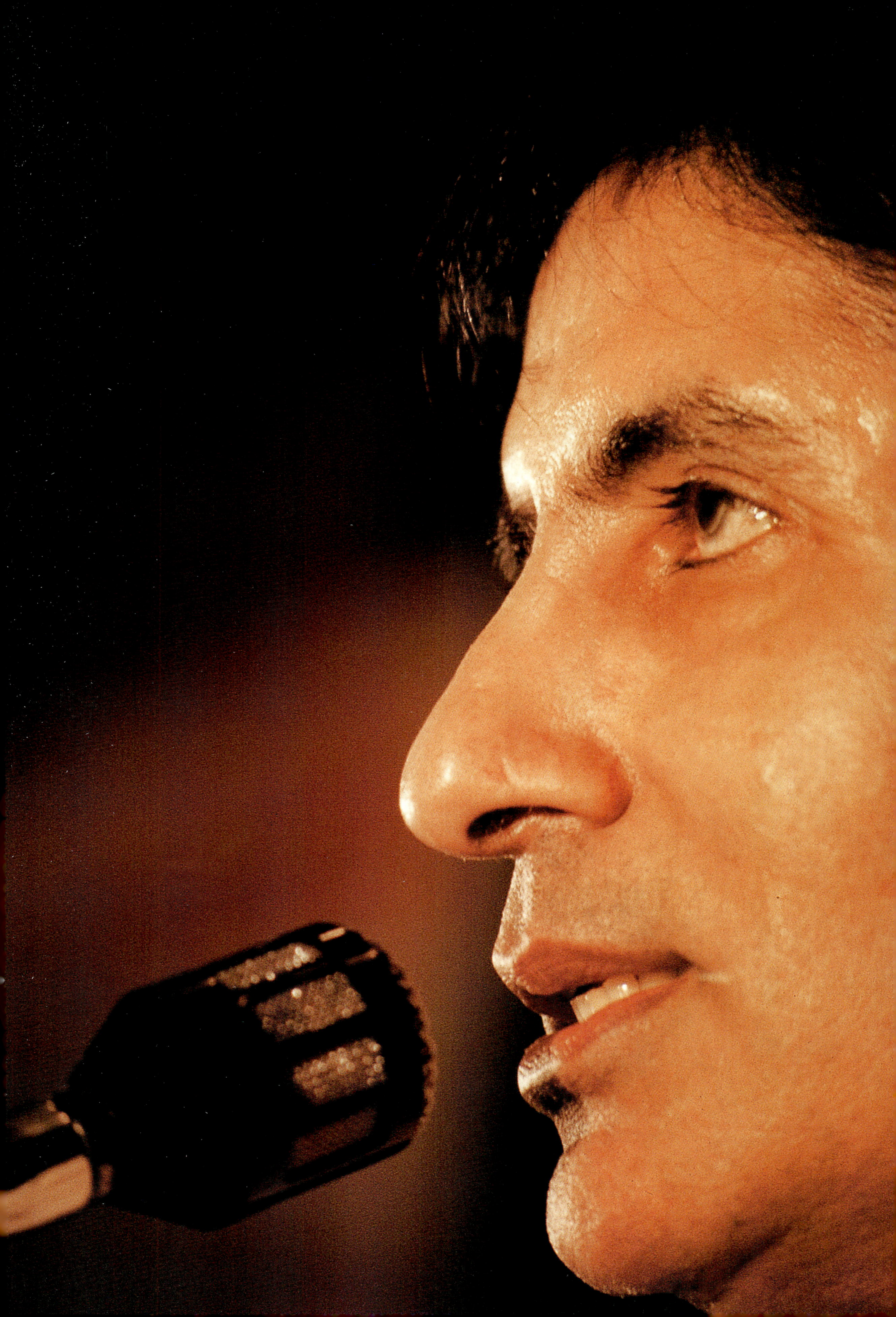

wasn't to be. *Mrityudaata* did not fare well at the box office. However, Bachchan did manage to generate waves through some clever casting and a marketing coup: singer Daler Mehndi's item number in the movie became a very popular song that year.

Though *Mrityudaata* bombed, Bachchan wasn't all at sea. There were other releases after that, including *Lal Baadshah* and good friend Tinnu Anand's *Major Saab*. Anand was a lucky director for Bachchan as his earlier movies with him, *Kaalia* and *Shahenshah,* had made box office magic.

Bachchan managed to hold his own, despite increasing public disfavour for his movies. But the money flowed in sluggishly. *Major Saab* was a hit and so was *Bade Miyan Chhote Miyan,* which paired the lanky Bachchan with Govinda. The movie went on to make over a crore. After the movie was shot, Bachchan called the producer Vashu Bhagnani to his house and told him that the amount that he charged was not the right figure and that he would reduce it. The producer was aghast. 'I was totally against it because no one else in the movie was reducing their fees, but Amitabh

The Legend

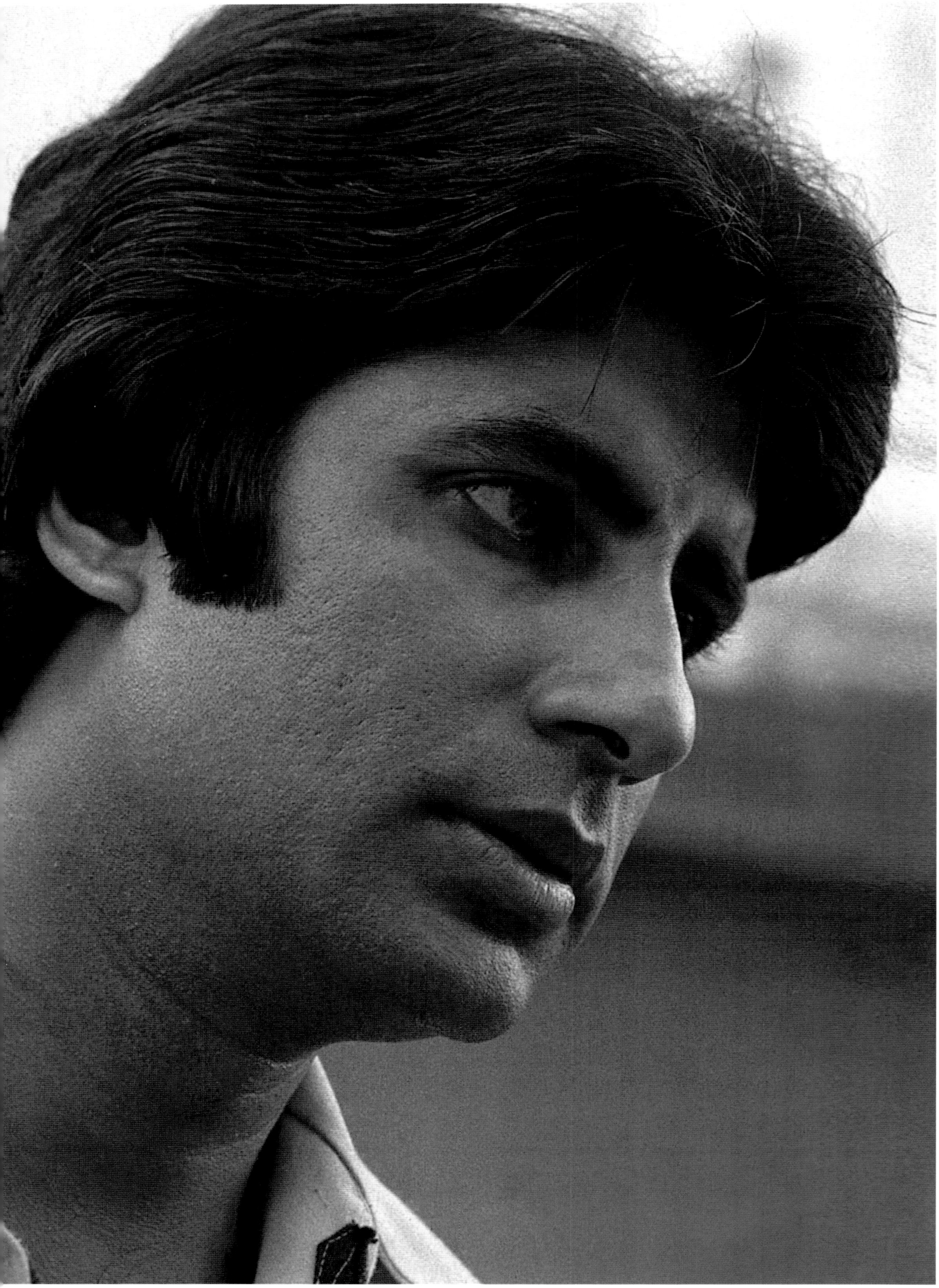

stood by his decision saying that it would hurt his conscience if he did not return his money. And all this at a time when he was in financial trouble. And let me tell you that he didn't reduce it by one or two lakh, but by as much as thirty percent. Never has this happened to me and I don't think it will ever happen that an actor will call me home and reduce his rates. I tried to convince him that it was because of him that I was getting so much for this movie. If it had been only a Govinda movie it wouldn't have gone on to make over a crore. But he was still steadfast and insisted on returning the money. He works because he has a passion for the job and not for money. We work for our money and our family but not him.'

It was obvious that, although Bachchan was in debt due to *Mrityudaata*'s failure, he was not about to abandon his values. Bhagnani was very sad to see an actor of Bachchan's stature being troubled by debt.

'After this I was shooting for another movie and I called him and said he was my lucky mascot and that he must come and shoot for me. He came graciously. He was there from seven in the morning to four at night. Everybody was surprised that Amitabh came for such a small role. While he was shooting I left some money in a briefcase with some sweets in his van and left. When I left I got a call from him. I got afraid that I had paid him less because this is how the industry works. I was afraid that he would be angry about that.'

But the phone call was for a different reason.

Bachchan told Bhagnani very firmly that he wasn't working on his film for the money and said he was returning the entire briefcase. Bhagnani tried to convince him to take it because he knew ABCL needed that money but he refused. 'I told him to at least keep the silver coins and the sweets, but he said just the sweets would be more than enough and that everything else would be returned.'

'The company collapsed owing crores,' Bachchan says of the ABCL debacle. 'I was enveloped day and night by the sheer absurdity of such a crash. The "third hand" [an allusion to Harivanshrai Bachchan's poem *Teesra Haath* which talks about support] which I trusted were nibbling me down like termites. My bank account went nil, I owed ninety crore rupees, faced several cases in court and the only house I owned was mortgaged and faced auction.'

Predictably, Bachchan did not try and place the blame for ABCL's losses on anyone else. Although admitting that the managers had perhaps not done their job well, he feels the ultimate responsibility lay with him. 'I was not practical and so could not manage the accounts very well…' he says.

It was extremely frustrating for Bachchan, as by that time, his saleability as an actor had also hit a low.

According to filmmaker Mahesh Bhatt, however, Bachchan's flops at this time were more to do with how the public perceived him, rather than a reflection of the actor's talents. 'The decline is not because of the actor. He is compelled to restrict himself to the persona that the market gives him,' he says.

'I had no films. I was dying inside, despondent and unable to face my family. I had to do something. Early in my career, when the sun broke its cloudy cover and began shining benignly I took care to continue working normally under its brilliance. I

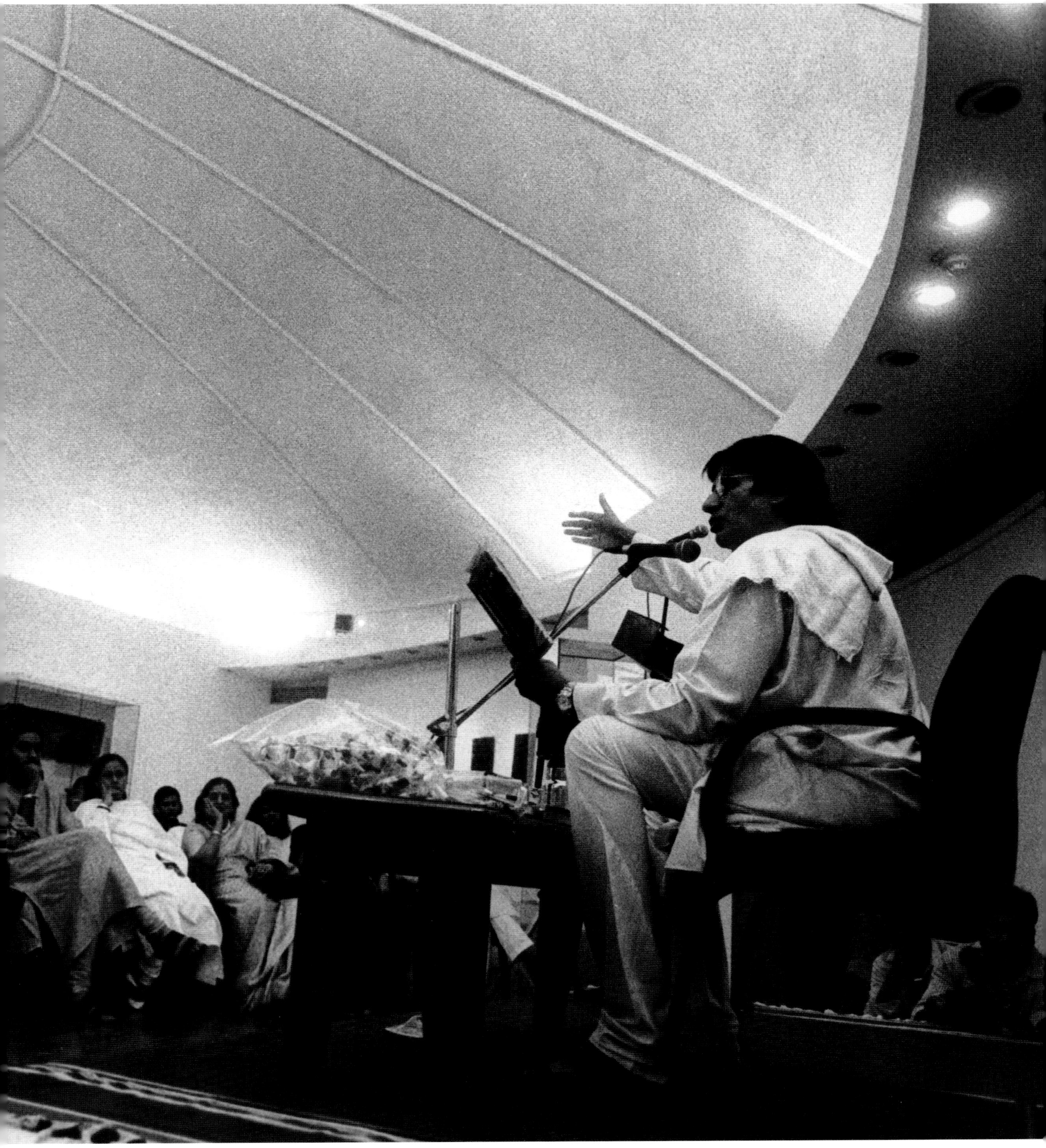

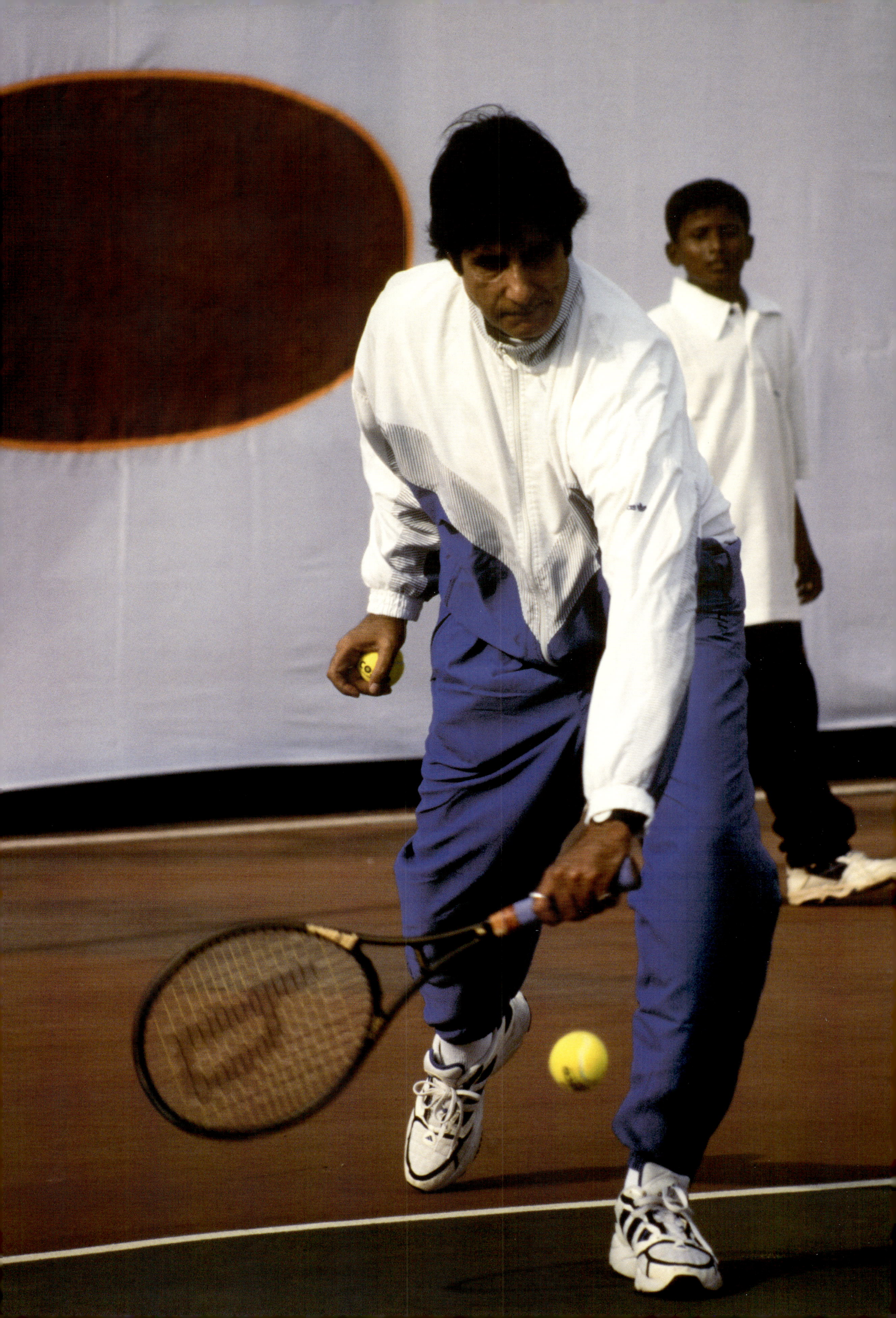

realised that while it was noon, eve would soon arrive to make way for the long darkness of night. This practice helped me during the lean period. Undeterred I spent nights trying to think of a way out.'

The days were spent in courts and offices; and Bachchan would return home to lenders gathered outside his house. Amidst promises he could not keep just then, Bachchan had to listen to a lot of people whose money he couldn't return. Yet he strove to maintain his poise.

Exercise helped him. 'I did not run away from people and problems; but I jogged to keep myself fit and dealt patiently with things as they came.' Though he had never been to a gym before, Bachchan began to exercise regularly in order to keep himself physically fit. 'While I never aspired for a flamboyant body, fitness and activity could well counter the tension and anxiety of those days.'

He trained himself in other ways as well, so that he could respond better to tough calls during this trying situation. 'Some other habits I acquired were brevity of speech, active listening, regular yoga or pranayam, never to speak ill of others, to correct the wrong, being sensitive, howsoever difficult, to contemplate calmly whenever chance permitted.'

But the calm during the day was always offset by the evenings, when he was less busy and therefore had more time to think. He spent many sleepless nights. 'A void before my eyes began its incessant haunt. Friends implored me to take recourse to bankruptcy like so many respected names in business, but my soul could never agree to such a retreat.' Bachchan took further loans to manage his household affairs in such a way that no one in his family got wind about how bad the situation really was.

His dignity took yet another beating when someone spread a rumour that his house was going to be auctioned off. This, of course, resulted in several television crews assembling outside his house. A dejected Bachchan requested them not to invade his privacy. But he was told that his house would be surveyed from the neighbour's rooftop. His response? He had the main gate changed and the boundary wall repaired. He also requested some of his friends to park their vehicles in his portico to give the impression that

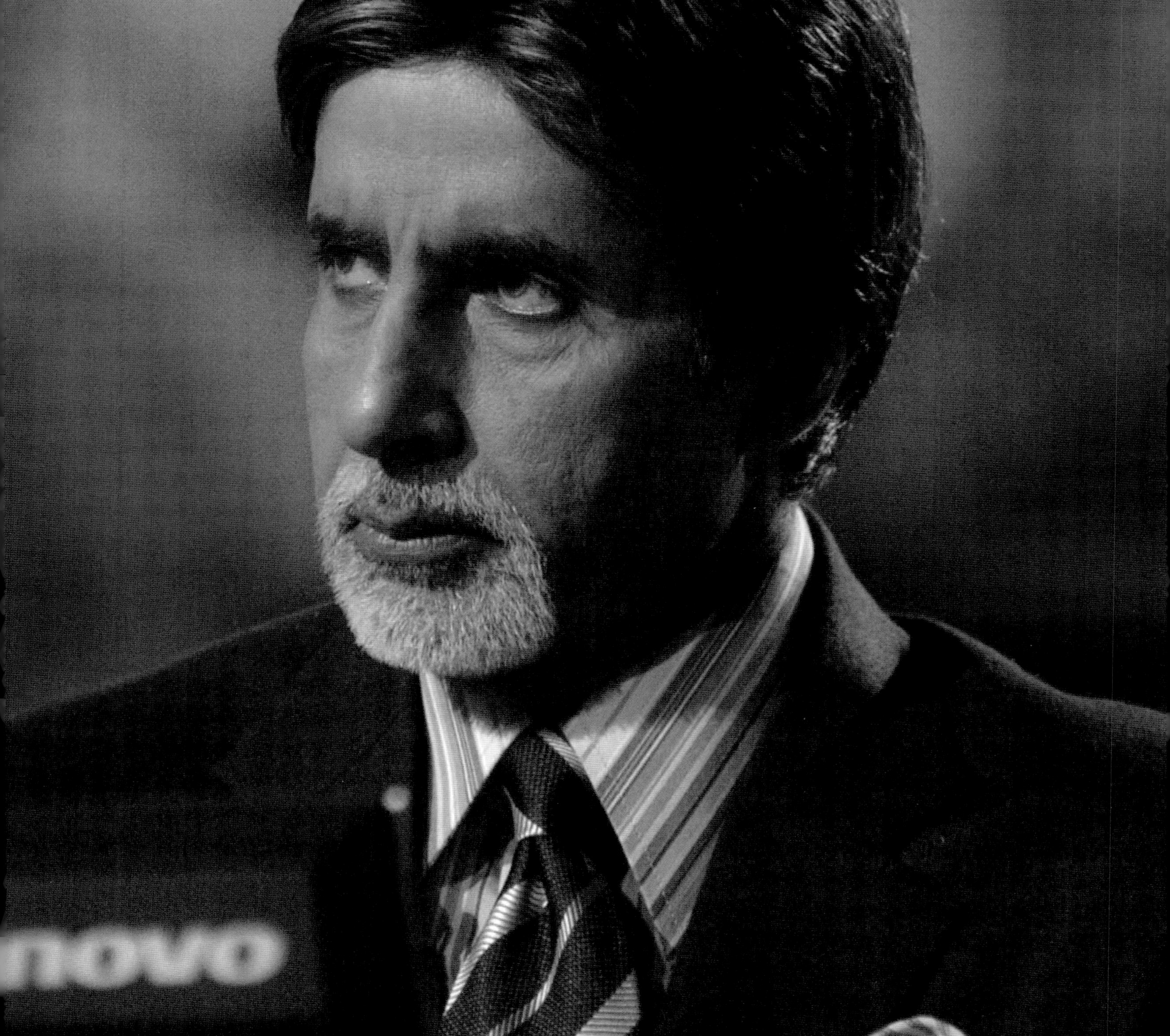

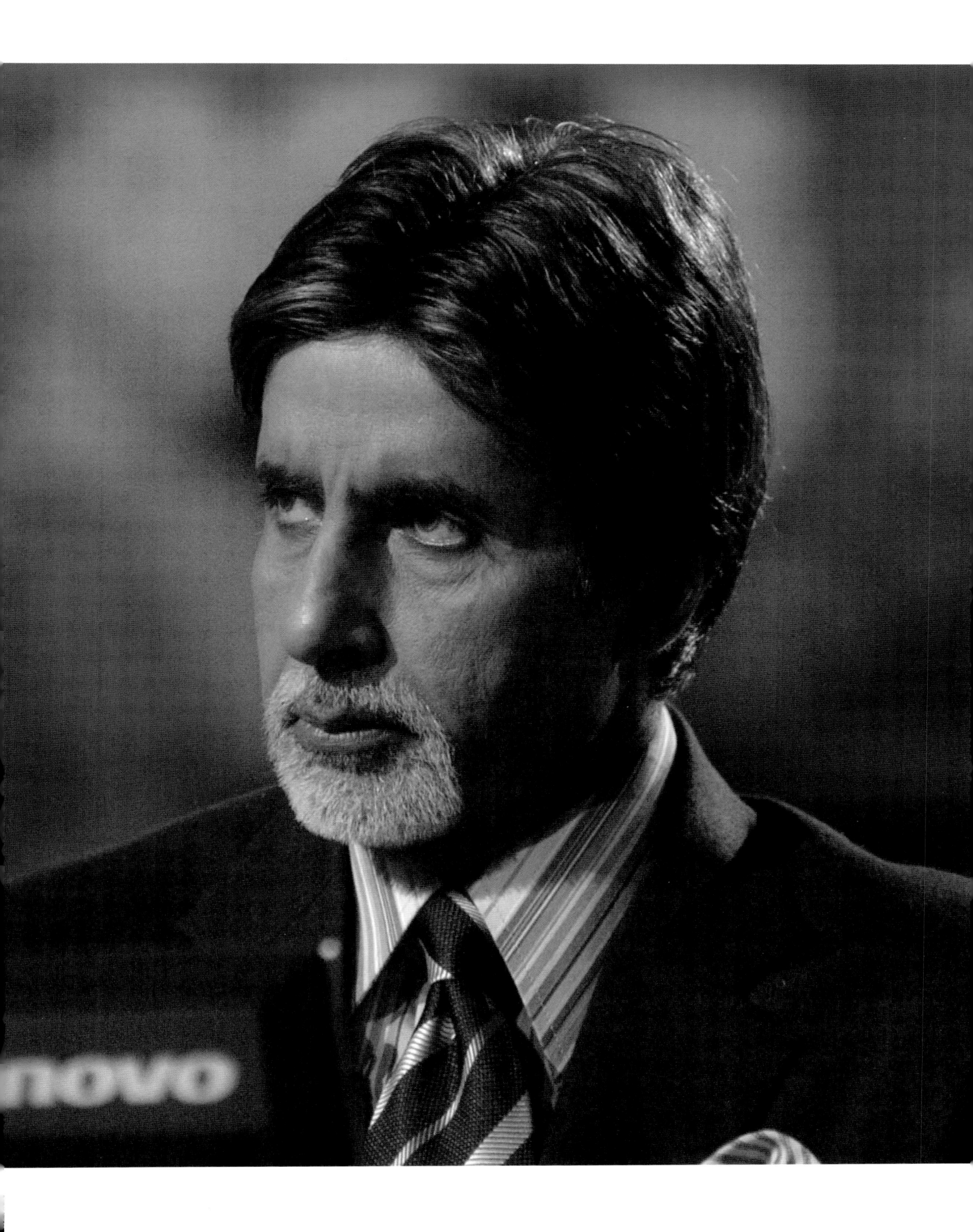

the family still owned a fleet of cars.

It wasn't easy to keep calm and face the struggle without panicking. 'My father's world view taught me the philosophy of life. He used to say *agar tumhare man ka ho to achcha hai, agar na ho to aur bhi achcha hai*. [If you get what you want it's good, if you don't, that's even better.]" This dictum has been my guiding mantra. I had great faith in my father. For a moment, in my despair, I found this ludicrous but soon realised the truth of Babuji's utterance. The goodness lies hidden under the bleakness and so I began the quest for it. I found I had to start afresh in cinema and reorganise myself to the new discipline. This pledge gave me strength and I started my journey from a street where the only other option available was to open a paan shop. I felt my work alone could give me satisfaction and so I approached it confidently.'

Throughout it all, Bachchan never lost his passion for films. To illustrate this, one must go back to Bachchan's 1999 interview with Vir Sanghvi. Sanghvi posed what he told Bachchan was the obvious question. Why didn't he sign seven movies at his then market price of three crore rupees each and make a huge sum of money? Why go into ABCL? Bachchan's reply was, 'The idea wasn't to make money. It was a vision. I wanted India to project its products to the rest of the world. The biggest danger I felt was that if we didn't do it ourselves, foreigners would do it for us because they have more money power. That is the impression I got in some of my meetings with media conglomerates in the US. They had done immense research on India and I could sense that they were ready to move in.'

In the interview, he stood by his decision to start ABCL. 'I believe the profile and vision of the corporation was very sound. In fact we were the pioneers and a lot of others have followed suit[10].'

He was also convinced that the firm made a right decision with regard to the Miss World contest. 'Miss World was one thing which financially caused a big crisis for the company. Despite everything we pulled it off. We were able to do it as a first for India; we were able to project India the way we wanted to despite all the criticism and political victimisation which followed[11].'

Slowly the ad spots featuring Bachchan

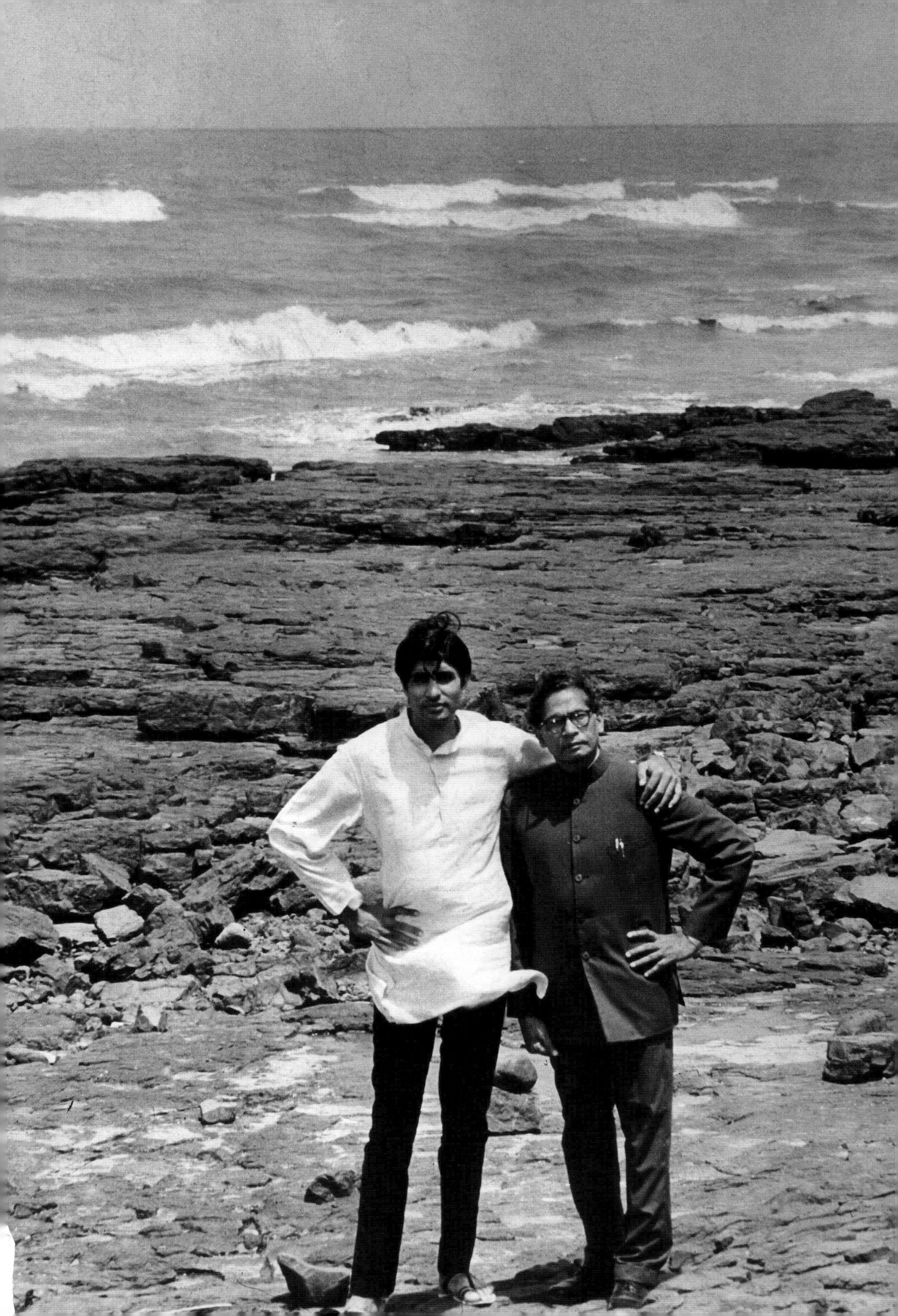

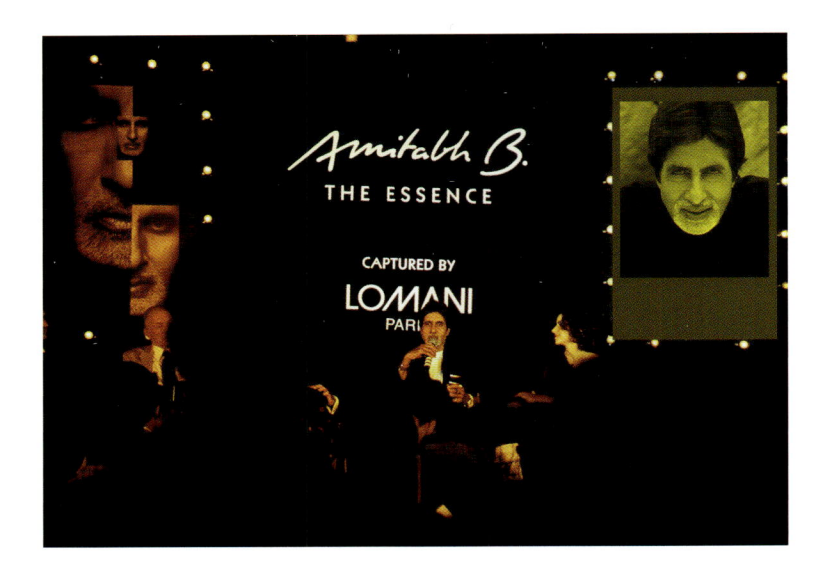

started increasing. He took up all the offers for work that came his way. It was demanding for him in more ways than the obvious. Bachchan, the box office king, had abstained from endorsing products or appearing in advertisements all his life. 'There were opportunities then too [during the Seventies] when ad agencies approached me. I was offered Rs 10,000 for an ad, which was huge money since I was earning Rs 50 a month doing radio spots. But I felt doing an ad would take something away from me and I just resisted the temptation. Eventually, when I had to do ads for the corporation, it was very awkward for me. … [but] people had invested money in the company.' And Bachchan was ready to do anything, cut albums, do ads, to repay the investors.

When the Star network approached him with the offer to host a game show, his family and friends all advised him to turn it down. Never had a movie star of his stature made such a transition to the kindergarten class that television was considered then.

The decision to host *Kaun Banega Crorepati* was a huge risk, but Bachchan didn't shy away from the gamble that the game show offered him. And he won! KBC made him a crorepati too. Never mind that all the money went into paying off his debts. Bachchan was honouring all his dues, and on his own terms, without compromising on his principles.

He took a pragmatic view of the trials he had faced. 'Life is a struggle. There is struggle in every dawn and dusk of day. One of the aims of our civilisation has been an extension of the protective instinct of the parent that teaches the young a certain code of conduct, hoping it shall free them from hardships and dangers. It never happens. We all know the story of Raja Harishchandra. When a mighty emperor like him had to face the challenges of fate, then everyone should be prepared for struggle. It is never completed, never finished. There is no escaping it. It is inevitable. Man must prepare for that.'

Says, good friend, director Tinnu Anand of Bachchan, 'Amitabh has a special quality. He has gone through some of life's worst crises. And he has emerged shining. He has faced death, he has faced bankruptcy. He has faced all this and managed to

The Legend

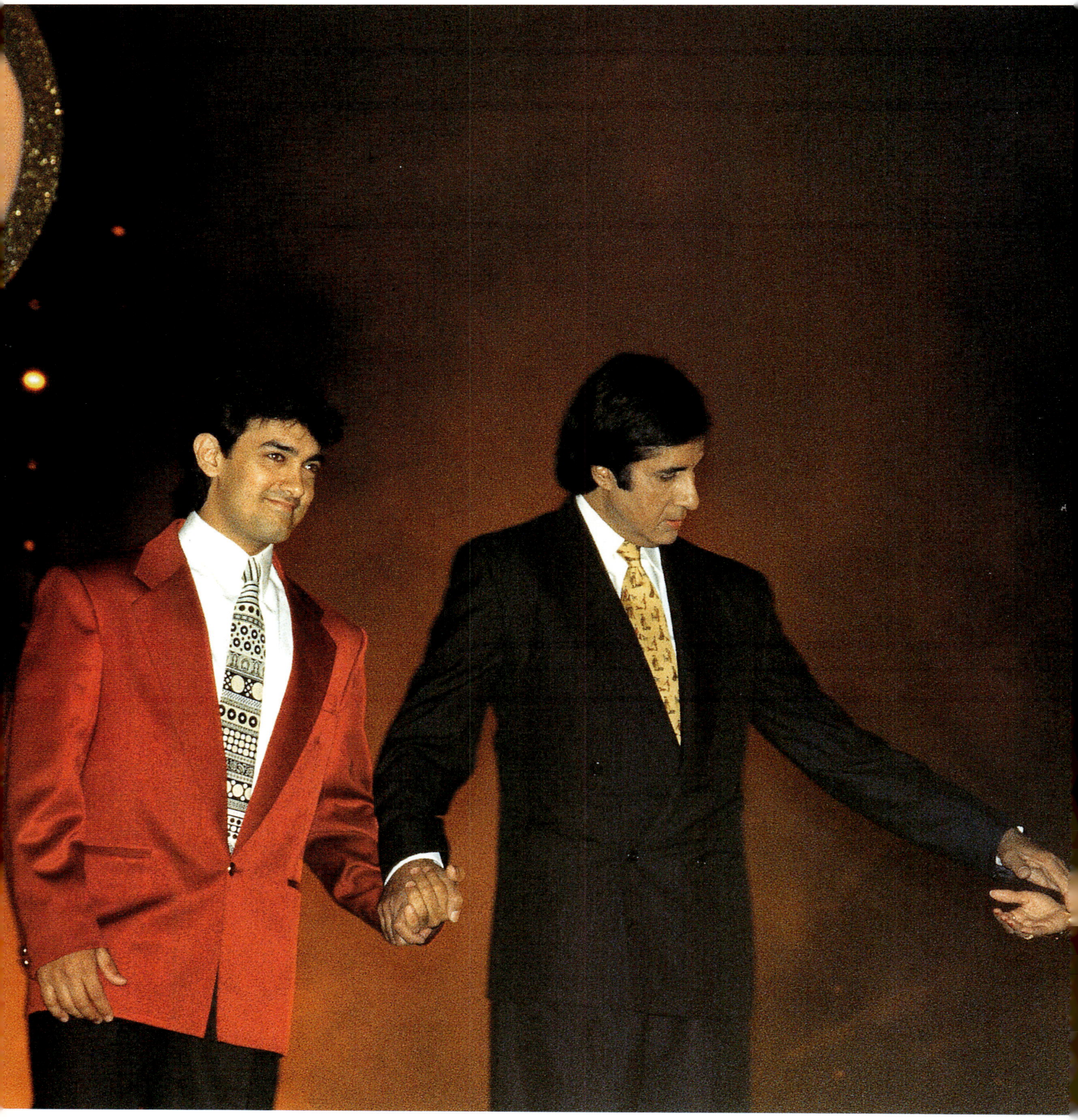

return to his peak. That comes from the prayers of his parents. I am yet to see a human being who is as good a son to his parents as Amitabh. To see him give so much care, emotion and respect to one's parents, it is mind blowing.

'I remember once when I had to meet him for some urgent work. I couldn't do so for eleven days as his father was ill and admitted to the Hinduja Hospital. For all of those days Amitabh had stayed with his father at the hospital and was not taking any calls. I went to meet him there and was talking to his secretary when Amitabh came out to speak to some doctor and saw me. He inquired if I had a problem and I just said that it was okay and he should go back to his father. He replied that since he had stepped out, I might as well tell him what the matter was. Such was his dedication and respect towards his father. And at the same time, he had the decency and courtesy to attend to a friend in need.'

Anand has been around Bachchan during the worst periods of the actor's life. 'He has a tremendous ability to fight back,' he says. 'He had signed my film *Shahenshah* when he met with the accident on *Coolie*. I had spent a lot of money on the promotion of the movie, but because of his accident I had to stop shooting for the film.'

After he recuperated Bachchan heard that Anand was in trouble because of the upset schedules. 'He called me over one day and found out the root of the problem. He decided that he would do a guest appearance in the movie. But when everyone else came to know that Bachchan was doing only a guest appearance in my film, they refused to do the movie.' So Anand went back to him. Bachchan agreed to work as per the old script but said that he would not be able to handle a strenuous schedule. By this time, Bachchan was in the throes of myasthenia gravis and had to take frequent breaks between shoots.

'When I saw the first mahurat shot of *Shahenshah*,' says Anand, 'I was convinced no other person could have pulled that role off.'

Anchoring KBC on television gave Bachchan a new confidence. 'This indeed has made me ready for the greatest of calamities,' he says. He befriended the challenge, looked into the eyes of misfortune, and eking courage out from the core of his being, he faced it all. 'Today I have regained more than the lost ground and am back in films and on TV. Earlier I used to shy away from problems, but now this confidence has given me perfect control over circumstances.'

Hard years do change a man, and on one who is seeking himself, the effects could have been catastrophic, but Bachchan is equanimity personified when asked about the difference between the Amitabh of 1970 and of 2004.

'If I think back I find I still have the same limbs, the same emotions and the same beliefs. In certain aspects, one does mature with time. But when I think back on college days, I still warm up to antics I enjoyed with friends then. I look forward to meeting several of them. They would be the best judge to measure the change that has crept in. Yet, their own personalities might have changed. Their concept of a film-star and his duties might not match with actualities that are mine. As long as we share the same memories, we shall enjoy the same relationship. However as a modern thinker points out — trouble might arise even there for our

The Legend

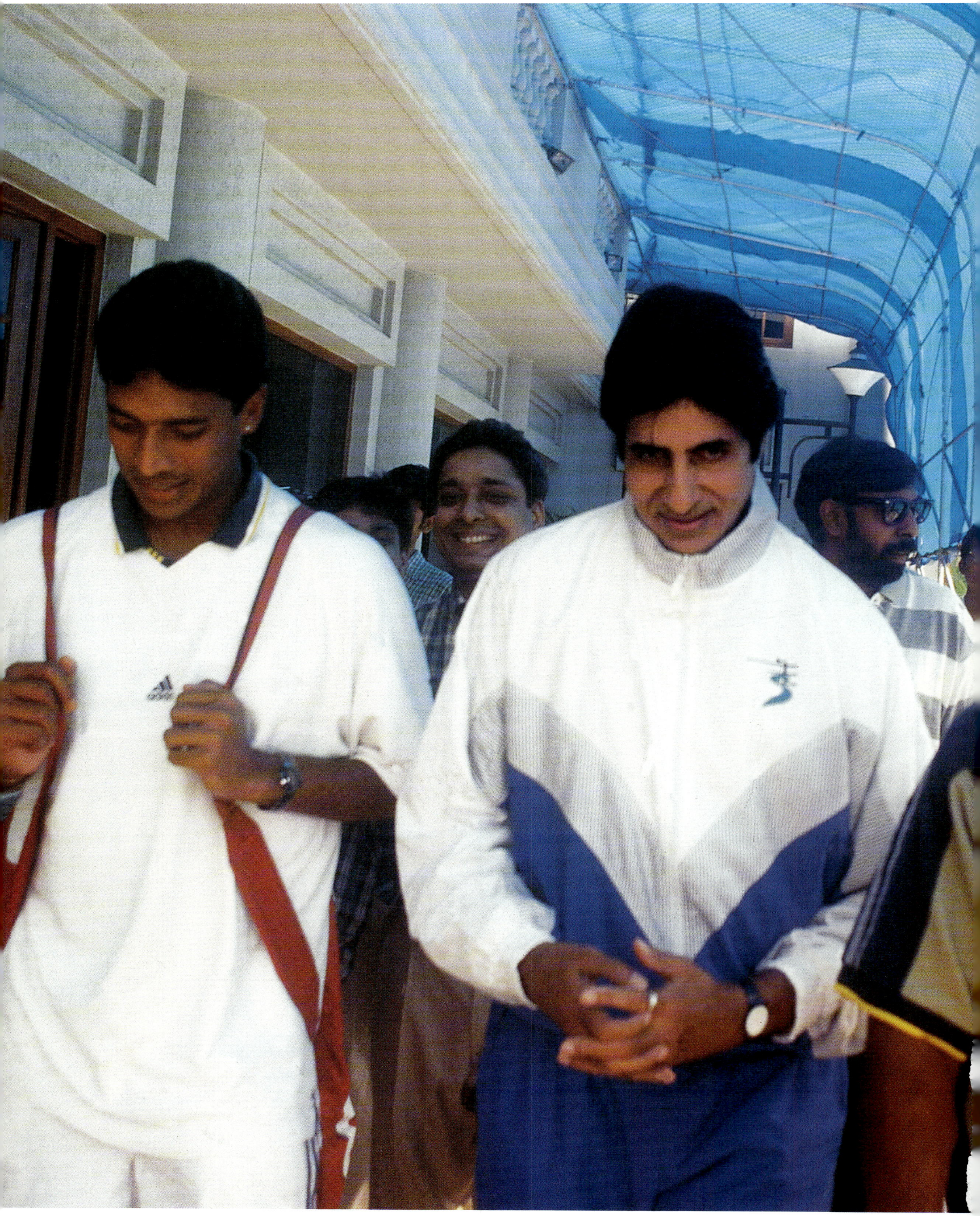

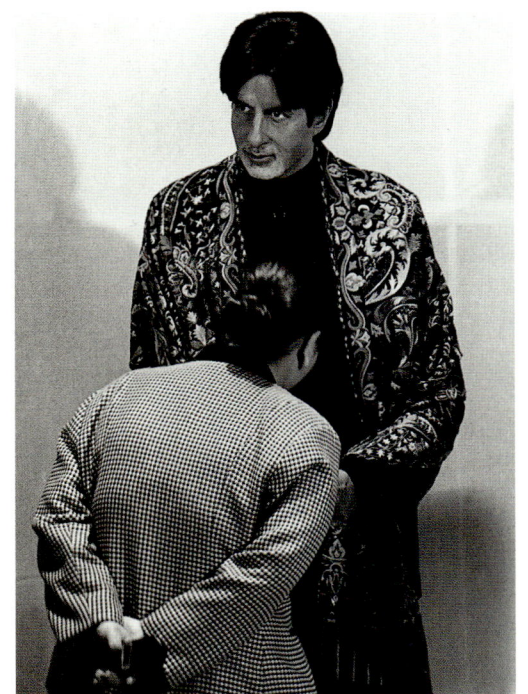

memories are always from a single subjective point of view. Two people are affected by an event uniquely and therefore their remembrance of it may not always be same. Yet, I meet people with the same warmth.

'I just flipped through Kundera's *Ignorance* in which two lovers meet after twenty years. Their expectations are high but they find that their memories do not match with each other. We refuse to recognise that we live in a world where our memories are constantly sinking. If we set great store by them, the result is disappointment — not only with others and the world — but with ourselves too.'

And, when queried about a search for a viable identity, Bachchan says, 'A poet confessed that poets do not have an identity because they are continually striving to fill others. Not being a poet, I do have one; I believe that I am still the person I ever was.'

Guest Writer

Inexhaustible Amitabh

Govind Nihalani

At this stage in Amit *ji's* career, I would describe him as an actor in a state of liberation. He's a liberated actor: liberated from the pressure of maintaining the number one position, from the pressure of always succeeding in a big way at the box office, from the pressure of maintaining any kind of image — whether it's the Angry Young Man, or anyone else. He's been through all these phases, and now he is at the stage where these things don't matter anymore.

Today Amit *ji* is in a position where he can choose his roles. He is perhaps one of the few actors for whom roles are especially written. The way he chooses his roles and the way he enacts them, adapting himself and creating something new for each character he plays, is something that few actors can even dream of doing.

Many people say he is being overexposed because of the number of products he is endorsing and films he's acting in. Yet, every filmmaker, whether the project is a small one or a big one, thinks of him first. That is a rare position for any actor to occupy, and it speaks of Amit *ji's* range and his capacity to hold the audience even today. I say even today because, in his younger days, you had different kinds of glamour. He could play a romantic hero, an action hero and an intense rebel. But now, coupled with his maturity, he adds so much gravitas to any subject.

Amit *ji* is seen in so many films today because he is being offered an incredible number of good roles. I believe he'll have a long second innings. And so much the better for Indian cinema!

Dev came about after we had discussed several projects together: ultimately *Dev* was the subject we both agreed upon. In fact, if he had not agreed to do the film, *Dev* would never have been made. Only Amit *ji* could bring nuances to the role in the way he did.

I particularly remember the scene where he goes to prevent an untoward incident from happening. He discovers that the whole building with people locked inside a room is being put on fire, and the police are allowing it. And he can't do a thing about it. He tries his best to save some people. When he returns home later, he describes his experience to his wife. I think this is one of Amit *ji's* best scenes in the film. And he did it in a single take! It was amazing to watch him perform that scene. For those four-and-a-half minutes, there was pin-drop silence on the sets. Everybody's hair was standing on end. That is the sort of intensity that he can bring to any role.

After the shot was okayed, I suggested that we shoot one more take for safety. Amit *ji* just threw up his hands and said, 'I cannot get that kind of note once again; it was very, very exhausting.'

Today, Amit *ji* seems to have started new genres in films. After the success of *Baghban, Waqt* and *Dil Jo Bhi Kahe,* you cannot think of a family drama without him. In fact, most filmmakers don't think of making a family drama unless Amitabh Bachchan is there. So the whole genre of emotional family drama is in existence only because he is there to play the patriarch. It's like creating or bringing back a genre which was popular at one stage in Indian cinema. It had been pushed into the background, and is now re-emerging only because Amit *ji* is there to act in such films.

The other surprising new trend is, for the first time in Indian cinema, the father-son pair is commercially a viable one. There have been popular hero-heroine pairs, but a father and son acting together and actually being a selling point for a film is an occurrence that is happening for the first time. So a film which has both Abhishek Bachchan and Amitabh Bachchan together is an extremely viable commercial proposition. We are watching a phenomenon form in front of us.

One always wonders how Amit *ji* can manage so much. He is able to put thiry-six hours' worth of work into a twenty-four hour day. Probably because as I discovered while working on *Dev* there is hardly anyone he says no to. Once he finished shooting on my sets at about ten or ten-thirty in the night and he then left for Thane at about one o'clock in morning because that was the mahurat to inaugurate a friend's factory. He was supposed to shoot again on my sets the next morning, and sure enough he was there, on time.

Once I asked him how he manages to do so much. He said, 'It's everything to do with how you manage time.' I think he's not only one of the best time managers, in his own way he creates extra time in the given twenty-four hours. The amount of work he packs into those hours is amazing. He has got social obligations, family obligations, film work, advertising work and more. And yet he obviously manages to do it all because nobody complains.

I come back to the liberated idea. Being free is being liberated from any kind of pressure. And having a different artistic agenda or ambition this time, which is to create very different kinds of roles. And he doesn't have to worry about his image anymore. It's been accepted that he's a legendary actor. All he has to do is go from strength to strength. So he can immerse himself completely in the role and create great characters without worrying about anything else.

In fact he is one person who has become part of the collective subconscious of the nation.

— *Govind Nihalani is a renowned filmmaker*

Chapter Five

The Return Of The King

If you can dream — and not make dreams your master,
If you can think — and not make thoughts your aim;
If you can meet with triumph and disaster
And treat those two impostors just the same ...
... If you can make one heap of all your winnings
And risk it on one turn of pitch-and-toss
And lose, and start again at your beginnings
And not breathe a word about your loss; ...
                                    –Rudyard Kipling

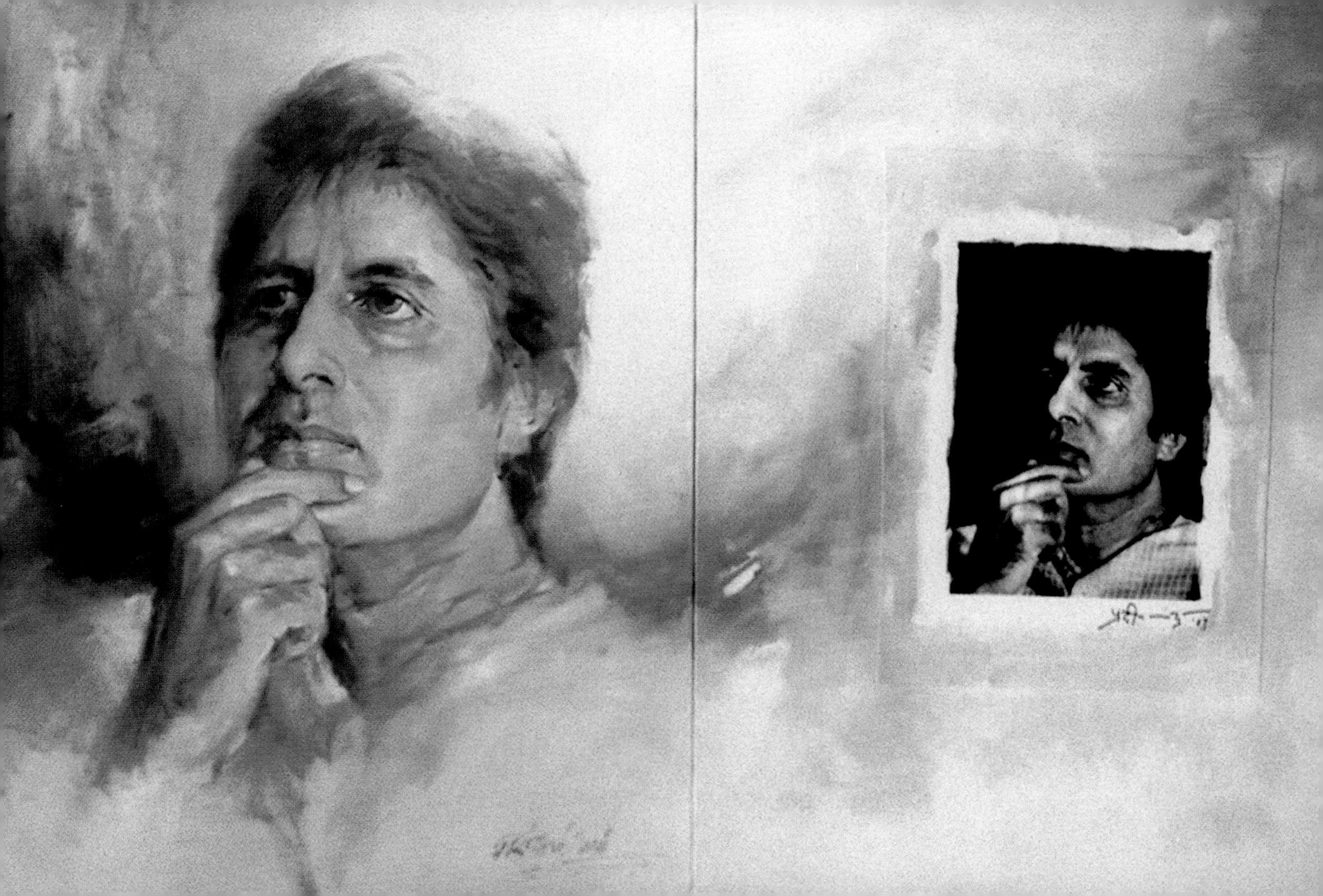

At the start of 2000, Bachchan's company was facing a debt of nearly ninety-nine crore rupees. The situation was made worse because Bachchan did not have too many films on hand. While he was not a bad market proposition — films like *Major Saab* and *Bade Miyan Chhote Miyan* had done well in the interiors — he obviously needed to rethink his roles. Work was a little hard to find though.

In Bachchan's words, 'I was out of work. I went over to my good friend, Yash Chopra's house round the corner. I went over and told him the facts. I was out of work. I needed money and would he give me a job.' Chopra was stunned. However, he said that his son Aditya was going to make a film just then and he was welcome to join the cast. The result was *Mohabbatein*.

In his comeback film, Bachchan shared the

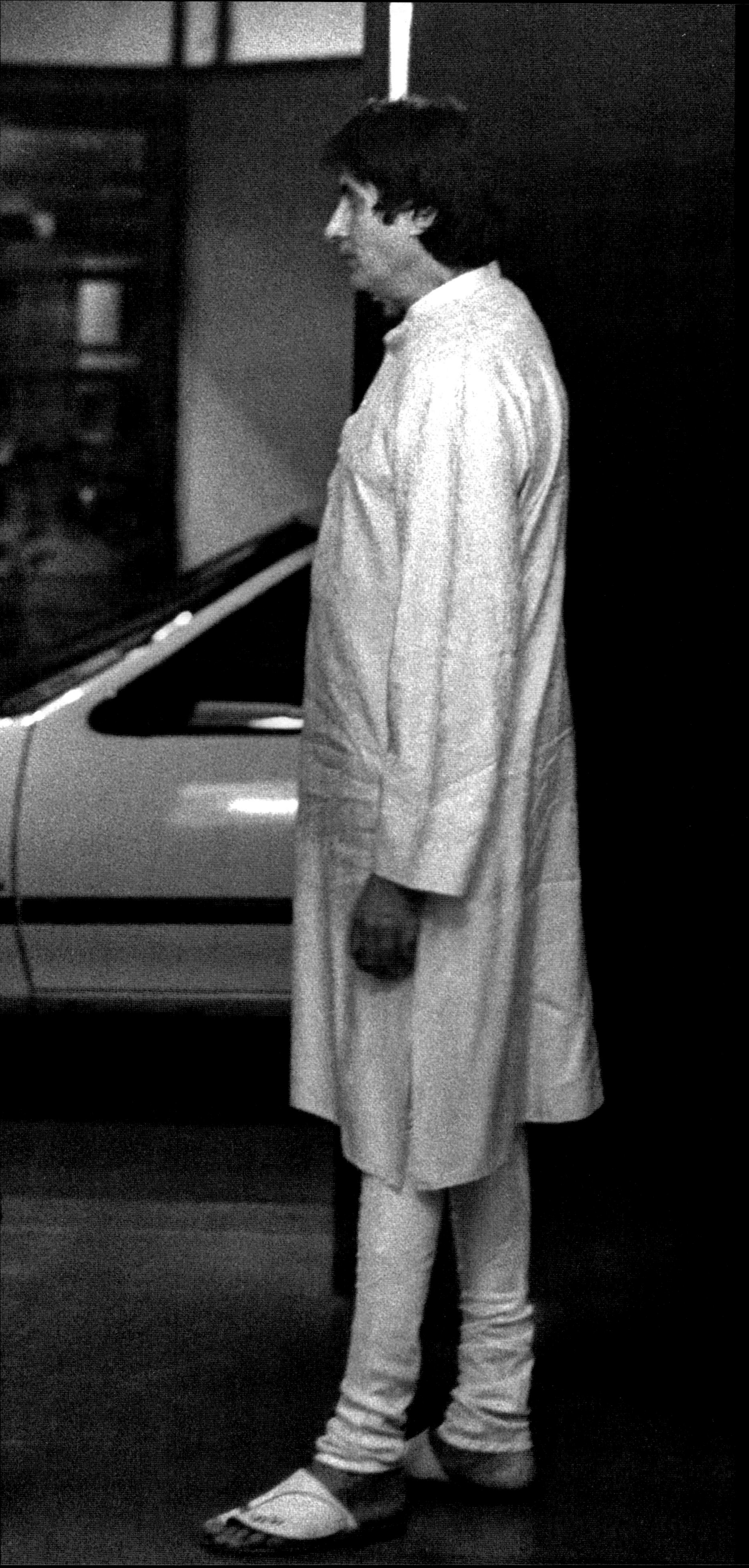

screen with superstars Shah Rukh Khan and Aishwarya Rai. If this wasn't enough, there was not one, not two, but three teenage romances written in the script. Only a hero in the true sense could have stood out in such a scenario. And Bachchan did. He played his age with aplomb.

Says director Govind Nihalani, 'In any actor, the basic talent remains. What enriches it is his experience of life. That also adds richness and depth to your understanding of the human predicament. That certainly helps a sensitive actor, which Amit *ji* is. To be able to interpret roles with a much greater depth of understanding. That's what is happening now.'

Filmmaker Mahesh Bhatt attributes the public's acceptance of this new persona to the game show *Kaun Banega Crorepati*. 'Every movement dies. Civilisations come to an end. Heroes get eclipsed. Even the sun gets eclipsed. Mr Bachchan also faced an eclipse, till he was miraculously resurrected by the Indian version of *Who Wants to be a Millionaire*. It reinvented his persona and got him the new image of a middle-aged man who was affectionate, charming. He signifies a symbol of grace and epitome of dignity. I think KBC really transformed his Angry Young Man image.'

It was in 1999, that Bachchan met up with a man, who was a big fan, and who had an unusual, but admittedly exciting, offer. He wanted Bachchan to host a game show on his TV channel. Bachchan was confused. 'You mean, like Siddharth Basu or Derek O'Brien,' he asked the man. 'Why are you asking me?'

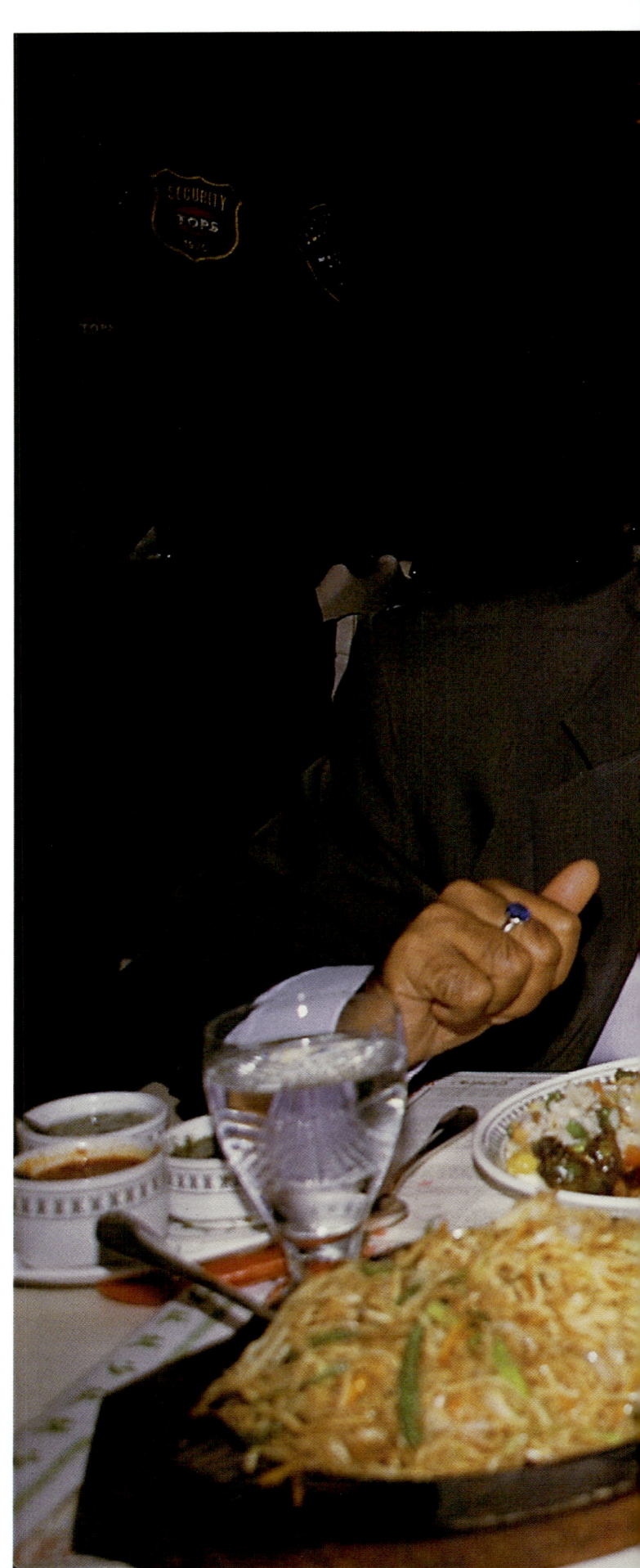

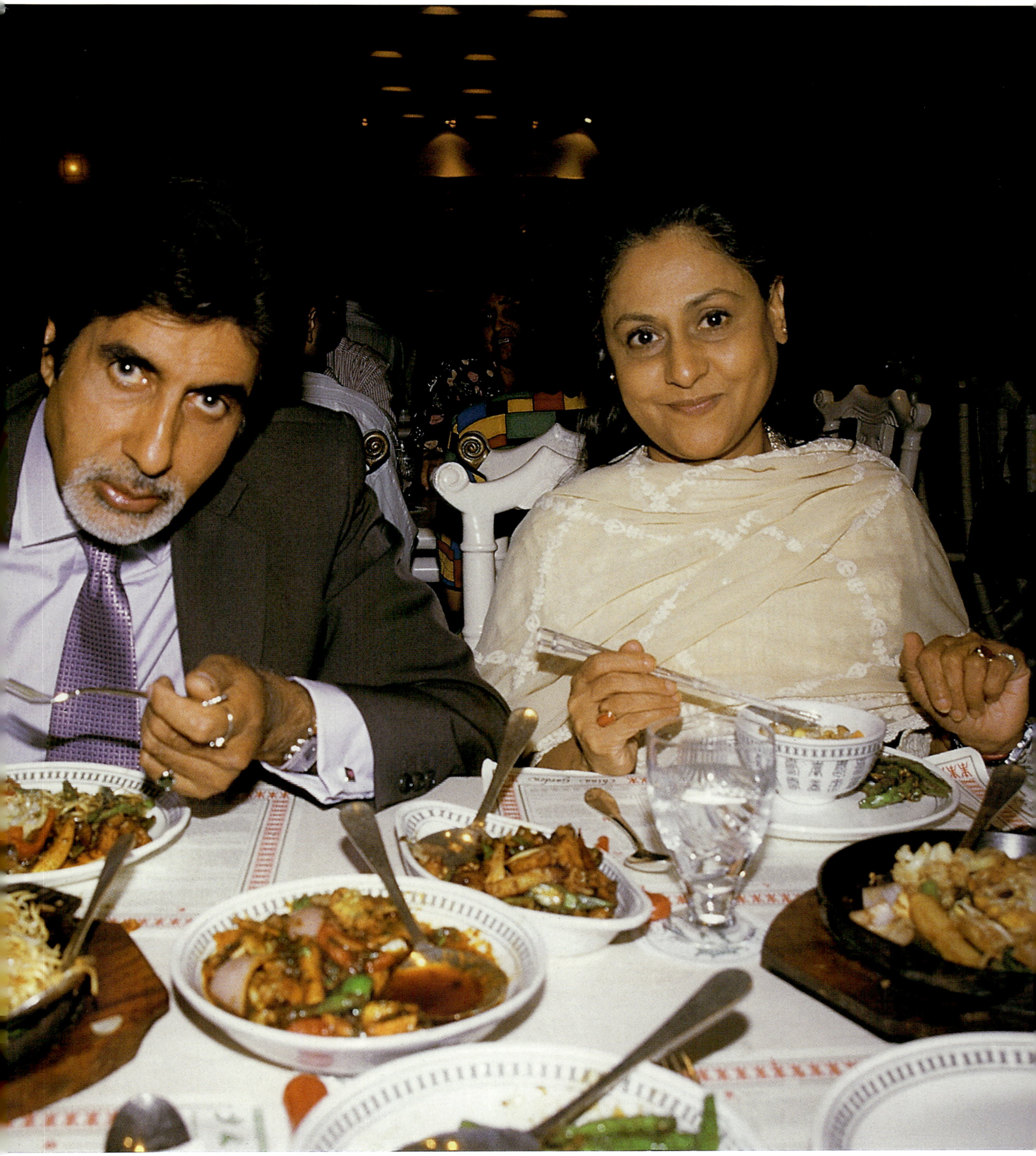

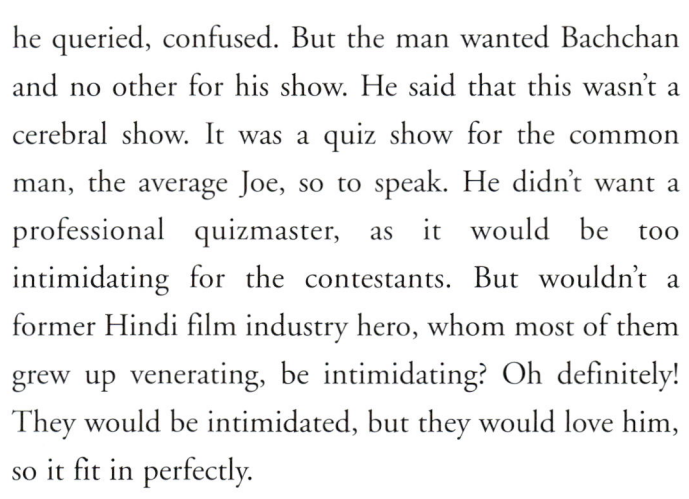

he queried, confused. But the man wanted Bachchan and no other for his show. He said that this wasn't a cerebral show. It was a quiz show for the common man, the average Joe, so to speak. He didn't want a professional quizmaster, as it would be too intimidating for the contestants. But wouldn't a former Hindi film industry hero, whom most of them grew up venerating, be intimidating? Oh definitely! They would be intimidated, but they would love him, so it fit in perfectly.

And Bachchan somehow, in his then image and screen capacity, was the bridge between the concept and the audience. The *sutradhar*, so to speak. A role he has assayed before on screen, several times, in movies like *Shatranj ke Khiladi*.

But it would be a while before Bachchan was convinced. The money was good. The show promised a steady pay cheque for six months but it was a risky proposition for him. He was already on the wrong side of fifty. His film career was a fifty-fifty proposition, but the start still looked auspicious. He was a mainstream Hindi cinema actor. And television was considered the elephant graveyard for film folk. When big screen actors made the transition to telly, no one knew them anymore and everyone knew they were never coming back. It would be a difficult cultural choice to make and an unsound path for him to take given the urban legend listed above. However, what he was about to achieve, went on to make film and television history in India.

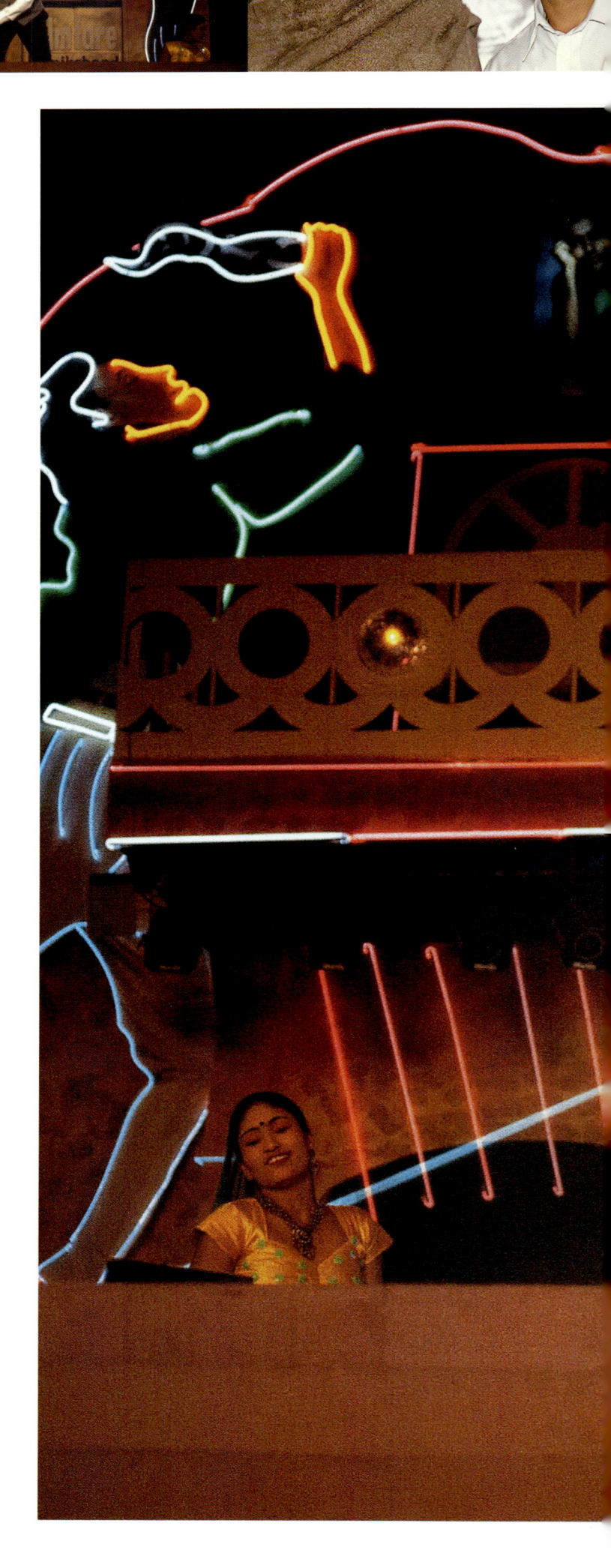

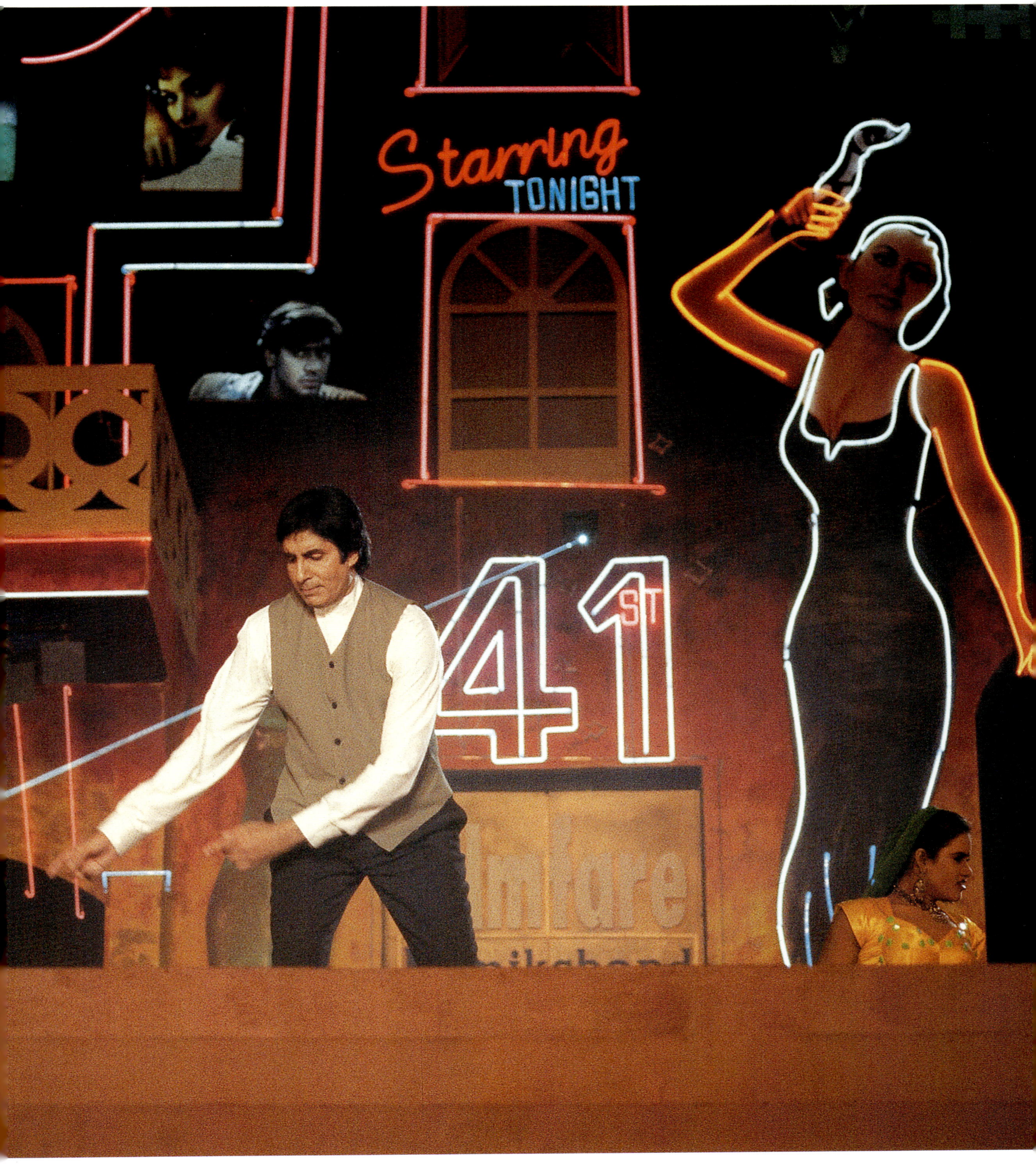
Starring
TONIGHT
41 ST

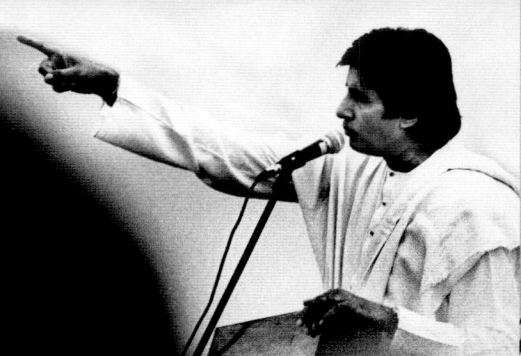

Sameer Nair, the Bachchan fan, and the man who was chief operations officer at Star TV, was convinced that Bachchan could pull it off. Says Chief Executive, Star India, Peter Mukherjea, 'The idea to take Mr Bachchan as the host of our show was conceived by me and my colleague Sameer Nair. He was the one who thought of Mr Bachchan. We went together for the closing meeting as Sameer had gone alone for the initial discussions with Mr Bachchan. I was told that his initial reaction was very sceptical. He was not sure. He was a famous film star and was being asked to leave it. This was something that he needed to come to terms with.

'And then Sameer said I better come along for the meeting with the big man to see if we can get close the deal. It all started at about ten o'clock at night. And we didn't finish till about one-thirty or two o'clock. We talked and we talked. He wanted to know what was on our mind and what we expected to do and how we were likely to resonate with the audience. Basically we discussed all the possible pros and cons. And finally when everything was settled, we knew that it was going to be a big thing.'

In order to convince Bachchan, Star arranged for him to visit the sets of the original Setador show *Who Wants to be a Millionaire*, in London. Recalls Nair, 'While we were returning from London after seeing the *Millionaire* set and watching the shoot of one episode, he told me seriously, "You know, if we do the show right, we'll blow the market apart." Later he

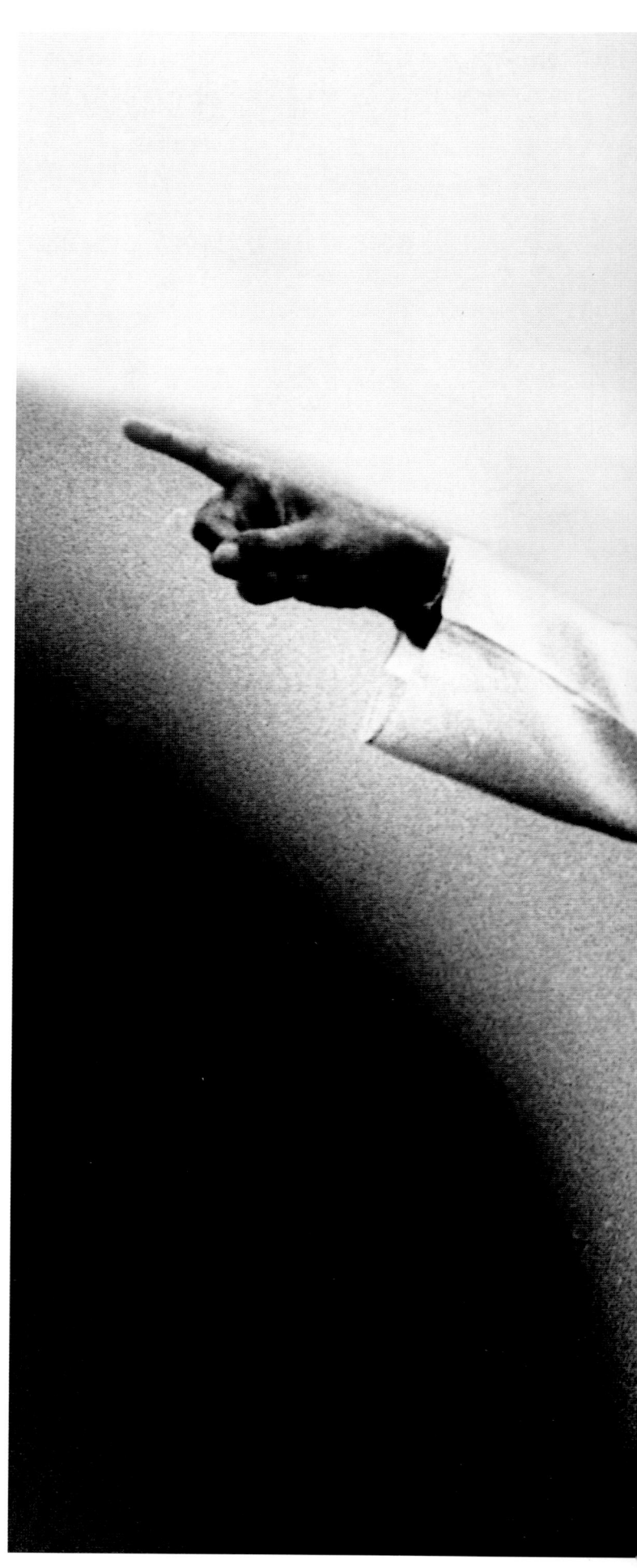

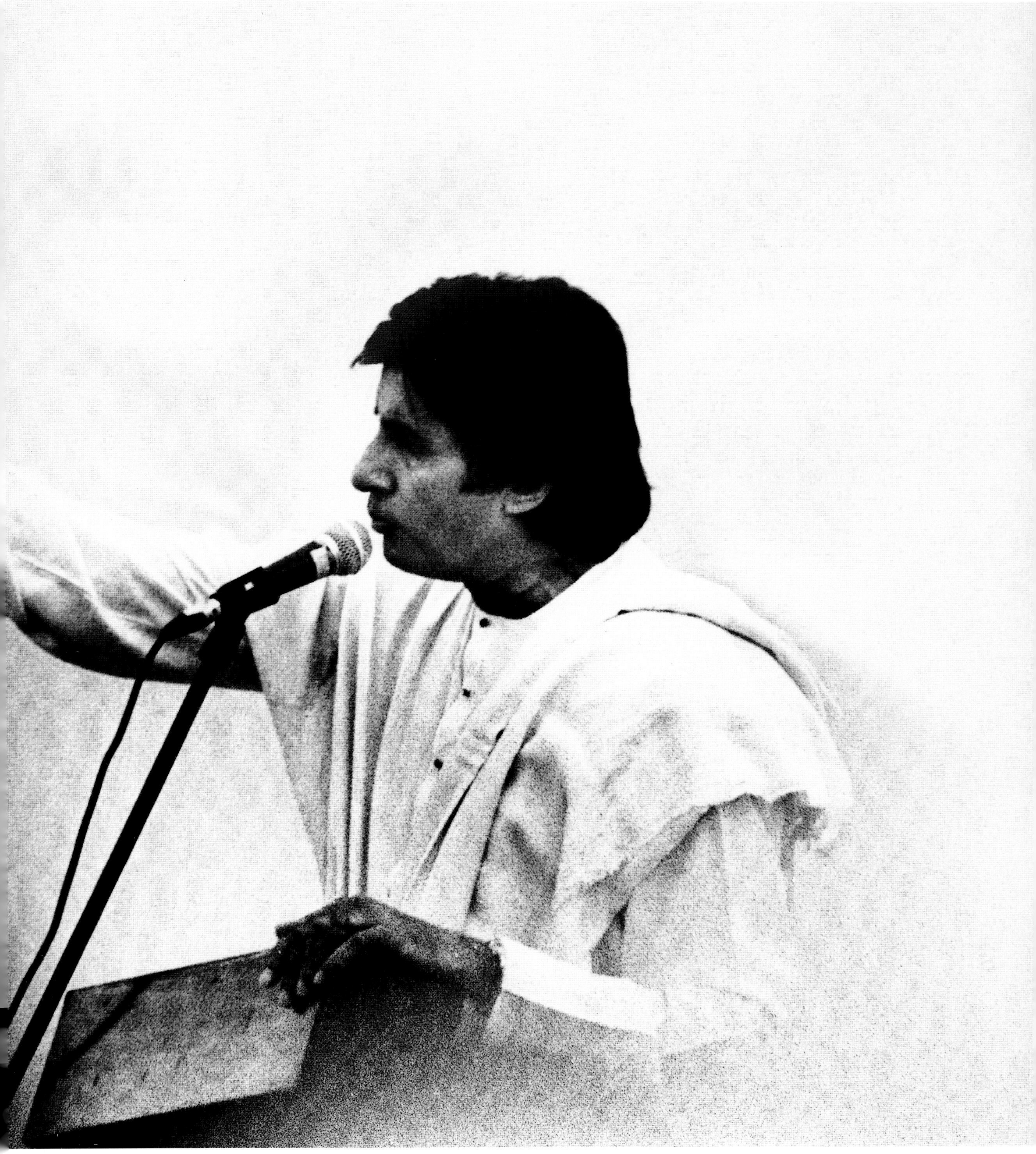

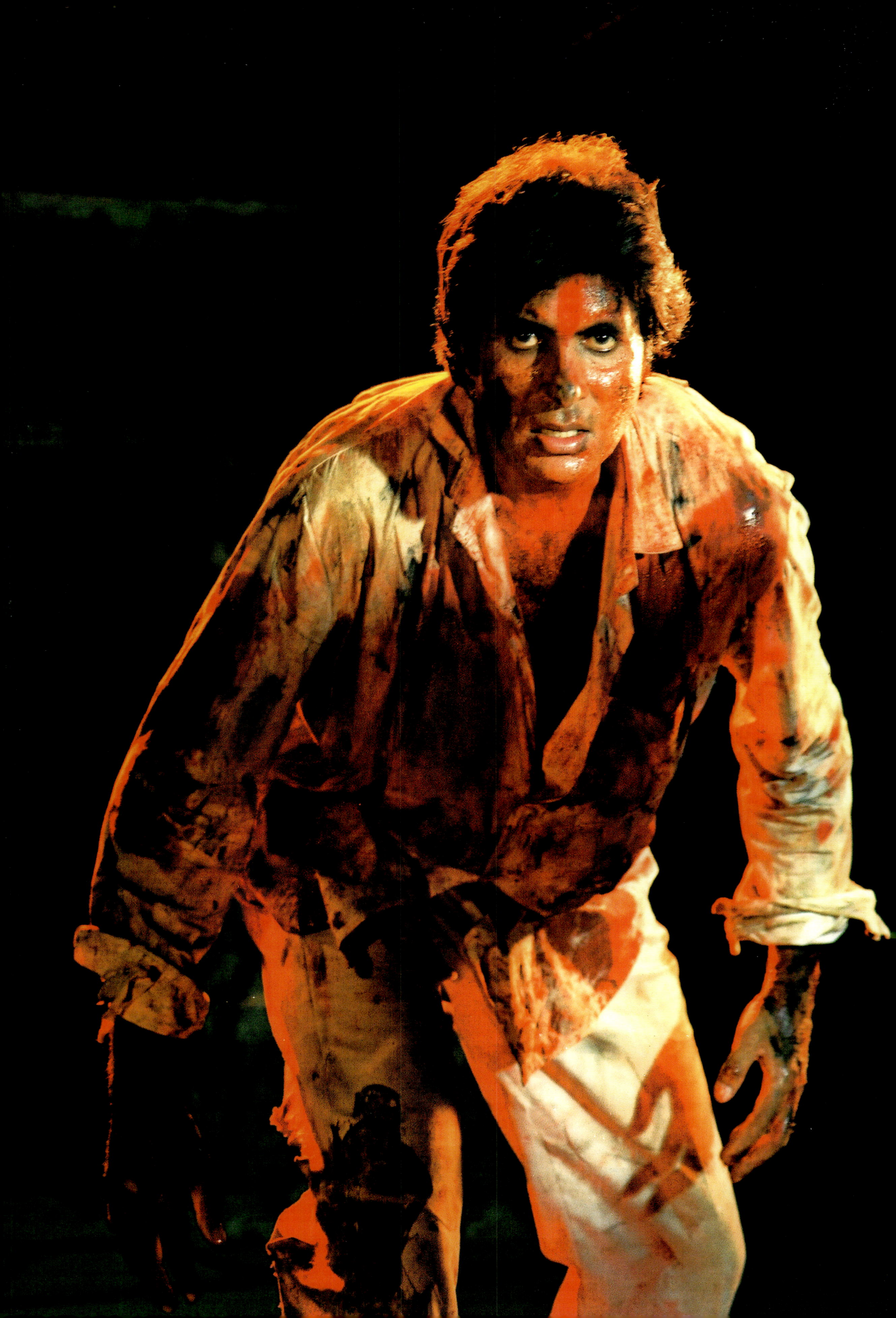

woke me up on the flight and was most insistent about the fact that this had to be the perfect show[1]!'

Bachchan finally agreed, much to the dismay of his close friends and family, all of whom felt that he was signing a death warrant on his film career.

The shooting for KBC eventually commenced in July 2000 with the first episode scheduled to go on air in the first week of August 2000. The audience verdicts started pouring in immediately and they were as Nair expected them to be. The audience was awed by his presence, then they were delighted that he was finally there with them, and when they mentally compared the physical man to the onscreen hero they venerated, they didn't find him wanting anywhere.

When Star India launched KBC, the network was a distant number three, lagging behind Zee Telefilms Ltd and Sony Entertainment Television. But this pioneer game show soon became the most highly-watched programme on cable television, pushing Star TV to the number one slot among Indian television channels.

Bachchan fit the part like a glove. He brought to the basically cerebral role of a quiz show host, the glamour, warmth and eminence of a showman. 'As a performer, he's more open to experimentation. He enjoys the television medium,' says Siddharth Basu, the show's producer. According to him, Bachchan was formal and more of a traditionalist in the first season of the series. He was the image of sobriety, which an Indian audience unused to the free-for-all entertainment that existed then on television abroad were comfortable with. Bachchan walked the show's participants through every baby step that they took across this pioneering layman-oriented game show. The concern was evident in Bachchan's voice every time he queried, *'Lock kiya jaaye?'* to a dubious answer.

So popular was the show, that in a few weeks' time, Bachchan's *'Lock kiya jaaye?'* and 'Is that your final answer?' became a part of the popular lexicon.

However, there were a few rough edges. Filmmaker B.R. Ishara, who made *Ek Nazar* with Jaya and Bachchan in the Seventies, and who has kept up a regular correspondence with Bachchan all these years, remembers sending feedback to him when the show was first aired. 'I noticed that he was a bit stiff in his first few episodes and I wrote to him saying so. Since then there has been a significant improvement and I think he's very good now.'

Bachchan turned out to be an excellent host, very warm and gracious to everyone, and he never lost patience with even the most nostalgic contestant. 'Like most people, even Amitabh Bachchan enjoys praise, but unlike others, he cannot deal with it for more than twenty seconds. While shooting for KBC, contestants would gush about how it was a dream to be seated opposite him and they would just go on and on…and then Amit *ji* would just give his customary deep throated, "ha ha ha…ab aage badhte hue".' He is extremely gracious too. He'd spend forty five minutes to an hour twice a day signing autographs for everyone. Once an eighty-year-old lady, who was wheelchair-bound, came on the sets to meet him. She couldn't sit through the show due to her health. So, when Bachchan heard about it, he went out where she was sitting, spoke to her for quite some time and got photographs clicked with her. She, of course, was thrilled to bits.'

Three months into the shoot and Bachchan was still a stickler for details. Nair recalls a phone call from Bachchan on the sets of KBC, asking for a meeting. 'I went there and asked him what the matter was. He pointed to a spot boy and said, "Look at him. He is wearing chappals. I thought everyone around here was supposed to be wearing shoes. This is what I meant when I said that this had to be the perfect show in all respects." This just goes to show the man's penchant for stringent attention to details.'

153

The Legend

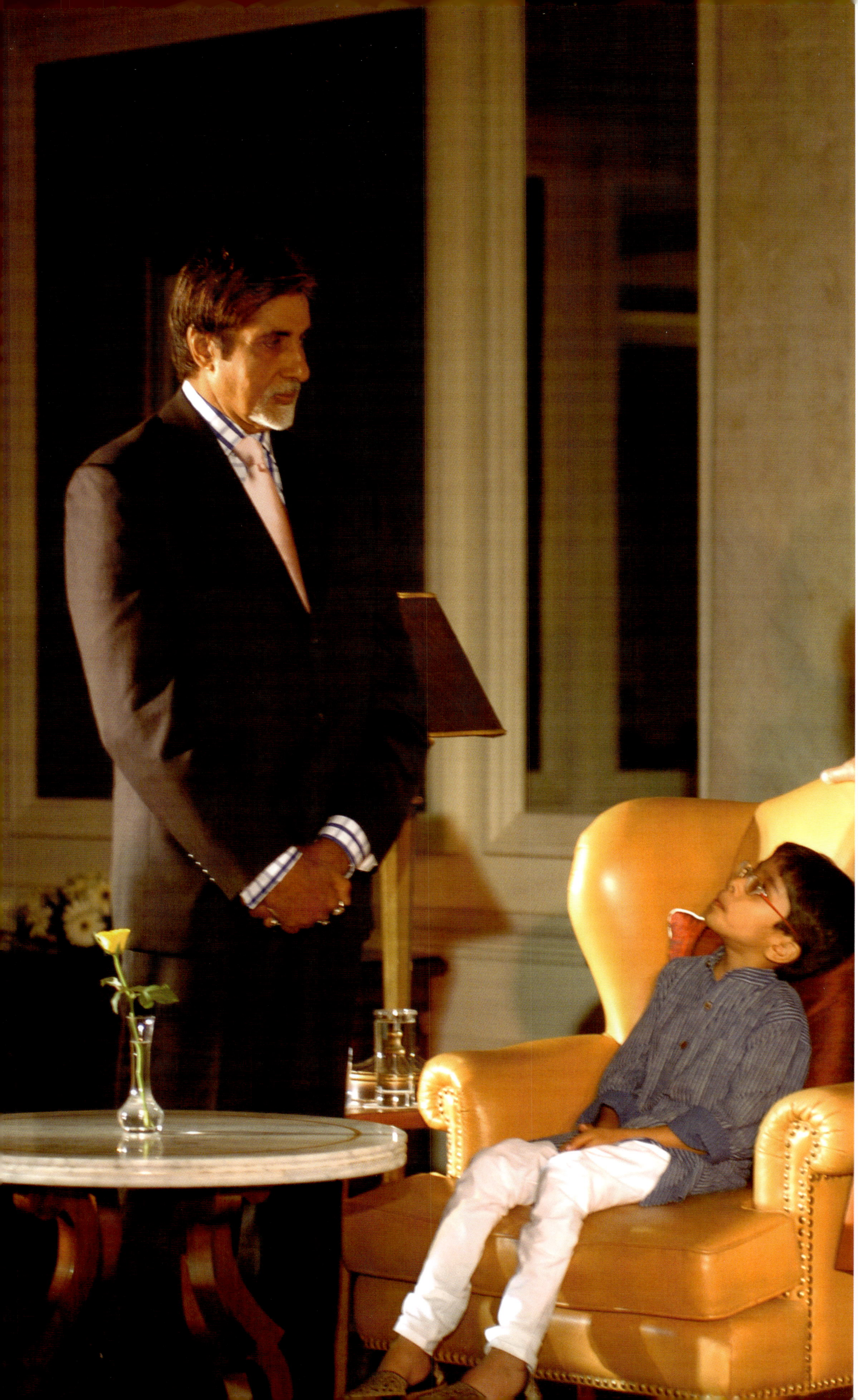

'His presence in the show had such a lot to do with how successful it was,' says Mukherjea. 'The KBC game show was a very unique process. The concept and the thought were one of a kind. But, I can't imagine the show today without Mr Bachchan. His role was absolutely vital, very critical, very significant. He was already a well respected, recognised person that people could look up to, for one reason or another. Whether they liked his films or his acting or his persona, it's part of the package.'

The fact that Bachchan was a down-and-out professional then didn't matter to either Nair or himself, Mukherjea maintains. 'Actors have their ups and downs. It happens with terrific actors all over the world in cinema. At some point Mr Bachchan will go down in history as probably the most towering film personality of all.'

The show was instrumental to some extent in reversing Bachchan's fortunes (he for one maintains that it helped him pay off most of his debts). Mukherjea, however, believes that, rather than the show helping Bachchan, the actor helped the show. 'I would say that KBC succeeded because of Mr Bachchan and not the other way round. We were very fortunate. The show was enriched by his presence and the fact that he had a series of successful films after that was merely coincidental. I think his films were successful because they were really powerful movies. And I don't believe that he was offered the films because of his presence on KBC. In the case of KBC, people tune in to see the show at 9 o'clock. And Mr Bachchan is there with them. They see the contestants make fools out of themselves or win a lot of money. But as far as movies are concerned, people go to see them because they hear the story, they like the songs, they like the actors, they like the actresses, the whole bunch of people. So I think the fact that he had a string of successful movies after the show is fortunate for him. It is not really driven by the success of KBC.

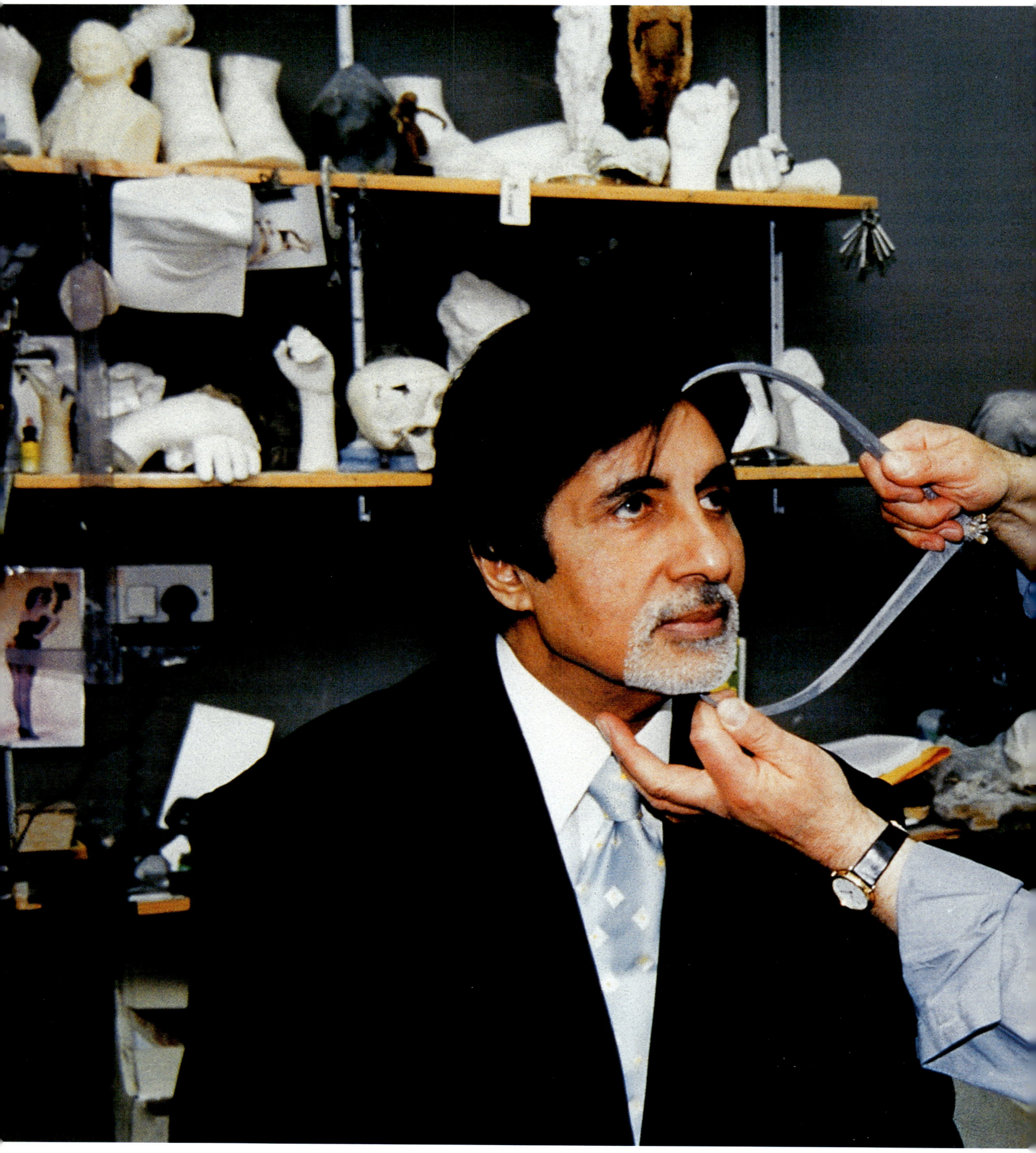

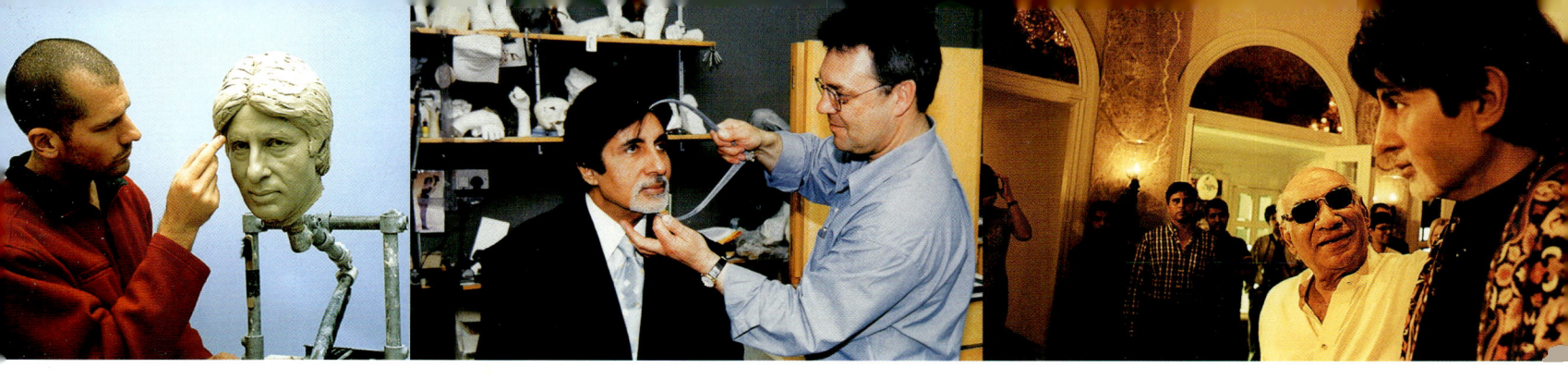

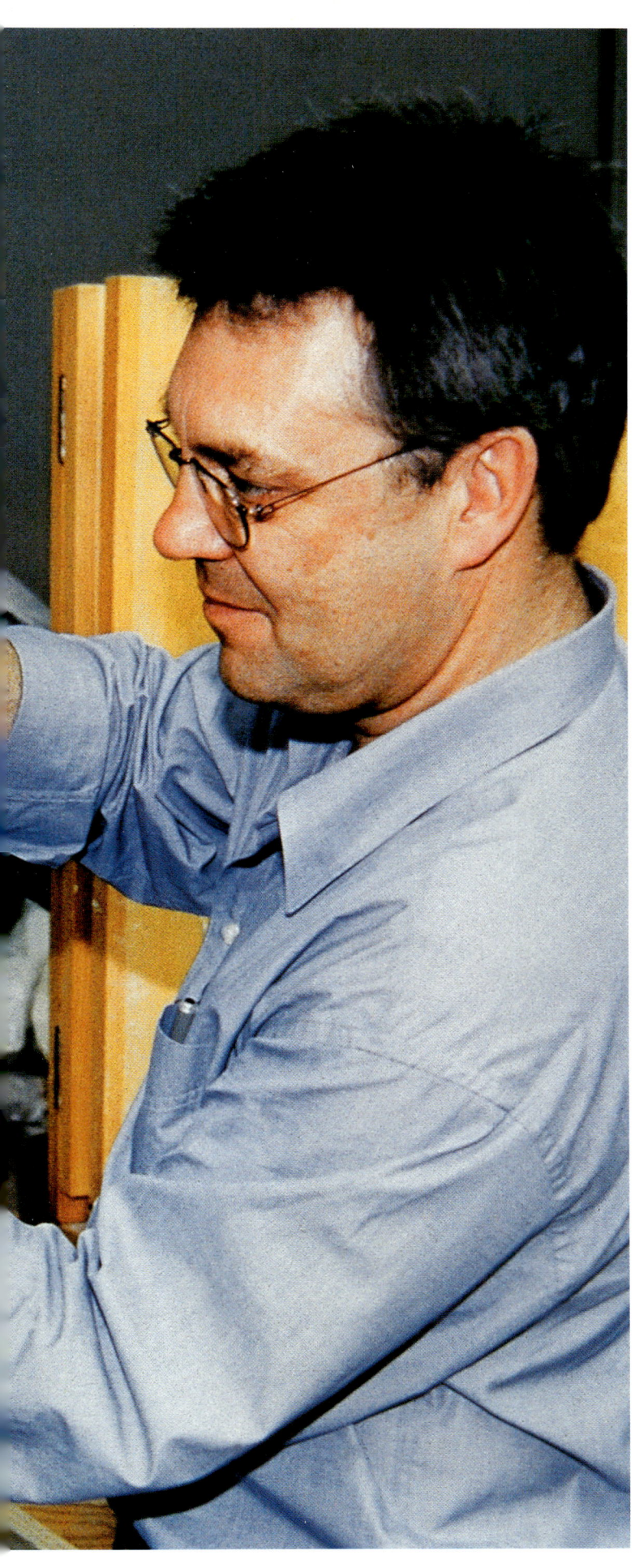

I would be presumptuous if I said it was driven by the success of KBC. We were lucky and the good luck spread to him as well.'

Bachchan was besieged by filmmakers and advertisers after the show's success. The ten-twelve films that Bachchan had done before KBC were unsuccessful. In all these, he played a younger man. After KBC, the public were more comfortable with his new persona and he was able to play his age on screen.

KBC's success inspired a few other games shows such as Zee Network's ill-fated *Sawaal Dus Crore Ka* with Manisha Koirala and Anupam Kher. This show failed despite offering ten times the reward money on KBC. Which seems to prove that it is not the money, but Bachchan, that attracts the viewers.

'It's wrong to compare any show or format with KBC. It became a success because all the planets and the stars were in its favour,' jokes Nair.

'When KBC was aired I did not miss any episode of it,' says Nelson Wang of China Garden. 'Since I worked till 9.30 p.m., I put up a TV in the restaurant. And everyone would stop everything they did and just watch. That was the charisma and magnetic personality of the man and the style with which he conducted the show.'

'In KBC, he plays himself to the hilt,' says ad filmmaker Prahlad Kakkar. 'He couldn't have got luckier. It brought him lots of opportunities.'

The show's second season, *Kaun Banega*

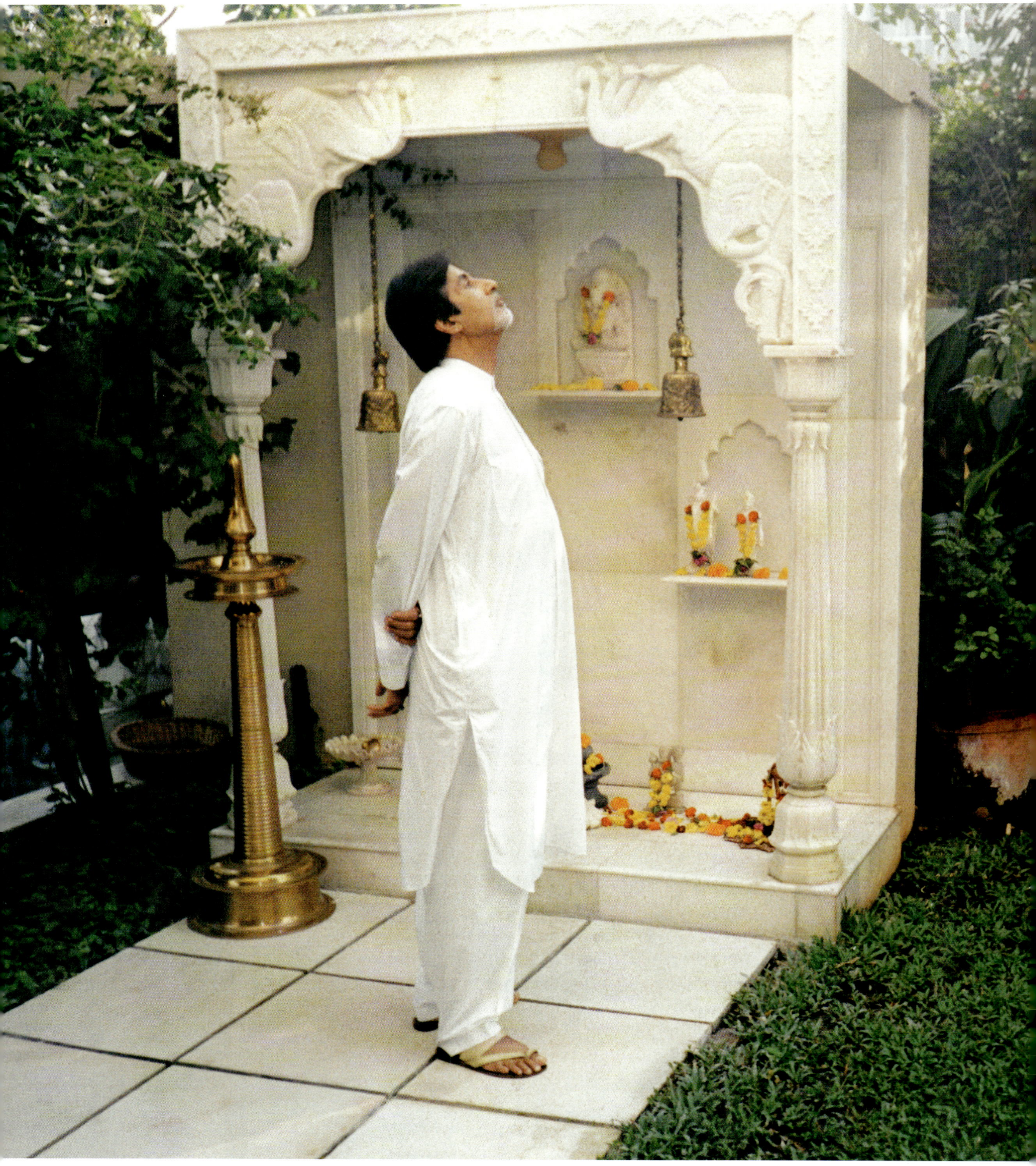

Crorepati 2, which refers to both its second innings as well as the new prize amount of two crore rupees, took wing in August 2005. Bachcan has a fresh, new look, in the show. His trendy eveningwear has been designed by duo Shantanu and Nikhil. His three silver rings have become as much a style symbol as any tattoo worth its ink. What many people don't realise is that these rings are set with precious stones bearing gemmological significance to his body.

Although a healthy sceptic, Bachchan has often used unusual methods of therapy not just for himself but for the benefit of his family members too. A couple of years ago, when his father was seriously ill, he approached renowned spiritual painter Uday Raj Gadnis.

'I had done an exhibition on spiritual paintings at the Nehru Centre. Amitabh Bachchan had read about it and his secretary called me and said that he would like to visit my exhibition. I was more than happy. Mr Bachchan came in the evening and looked at every painting for some time. He then came up to

me and said, "I believe your paintings have the healing touch. My father is not too well and I was wondering if you could advise me on choosing a painting that would help him recover." I suggested a painting and had it sent to his place along with instructions on how to place it.'

KBC 2 airs from Friday to Sunday, instead of the earlier season's schedule of Monday to Thursday, a reflection of the channel's strategy to have more people watch it, especially working people.

'As you know, the show's demographic has changed dramatically since it was last on air. Quite simply, far more people will watch it now than the first time. The number of younger viewers has also increased. Though there are cosmetic changes, the soul of KBC remains unchanged,' says Basu.

And the number of people trying to get on the show has increased manifold. 'More than before, much more,' says Basu, crediting this increase to the success of Bachchan's recent films. 'Between the last time and now, he has experimented and succeeded with so many roles in cinema.'

Bachchan himself is a little nervous about the second coming. 'As usual I am scared, frightened and nervous,' he says, 'and not necessarily in that order!'

He adds, 'I am fulfilling my contractual obligations.' Bachchan had always reiterated that, despite his several film and other commitments, he would be back on the show along with Computer *ji*.

And Bachchan does have numerous commitments. His comeback on the big screen has been a resounding success. After Aditya Chopra's *Mohabbatein,* he worked with directors and projects as varied as chalk and cheese. From Kaizad Gustad's *Boom,* where he played a cranky gangster, to Farhan Akhtar's *Lakshya,* where he is cast as an unbending military officer, he did them all. And he seems to have moved from strength to strength: all his films released in 2005 have gone on to become box office successes.

One of these, especially, was most unlike anything he has done so far in his career: the Alzheimer-affected teacher of a deaf and blind girl in Sanjay Bhansali's *Black*. Mukherjea, who keeps track of his host's parallel career comments, 'I liked *Black*. Of all the roles that Mr Bachchan has acted in through the years, I found this to be a truly astonishing performance. Here he had to drill deep down into himself to be able to perform like that. He was fabulous.'

Bachchan broke every box office norm with this role. For too long now, filmmakers have depended on Bachchan's innate charm. Says director Sanjay Leela Bhansali, '…what he has agreed to do and what he has achieved in this film is truly remarkable. …when they [the audience] come to see them, they at least get a chance to see something different. It is a chance for the actor to show something different.' He was placed in an ambience that was creative, and see how he soars, remarks Bhansali.

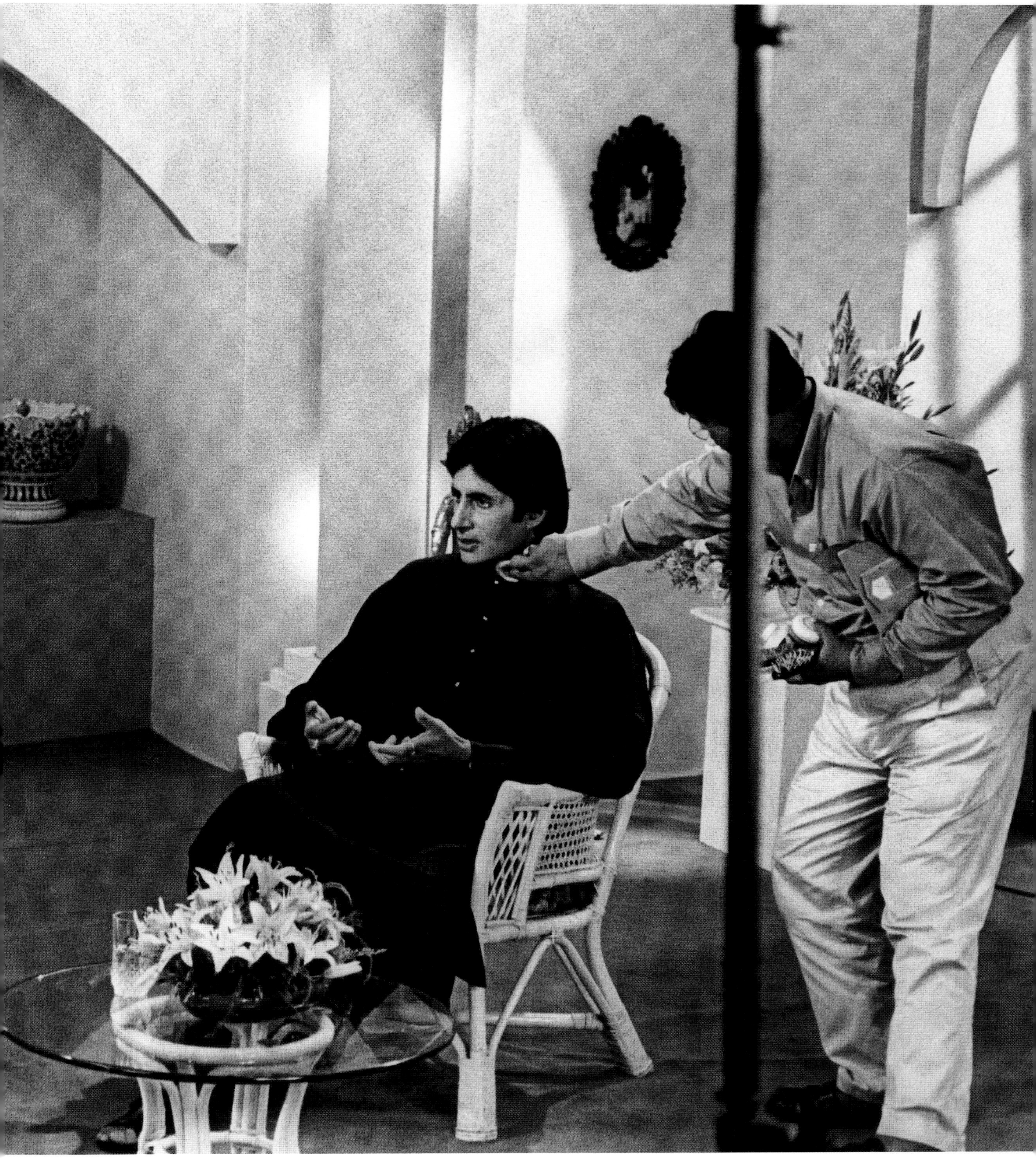

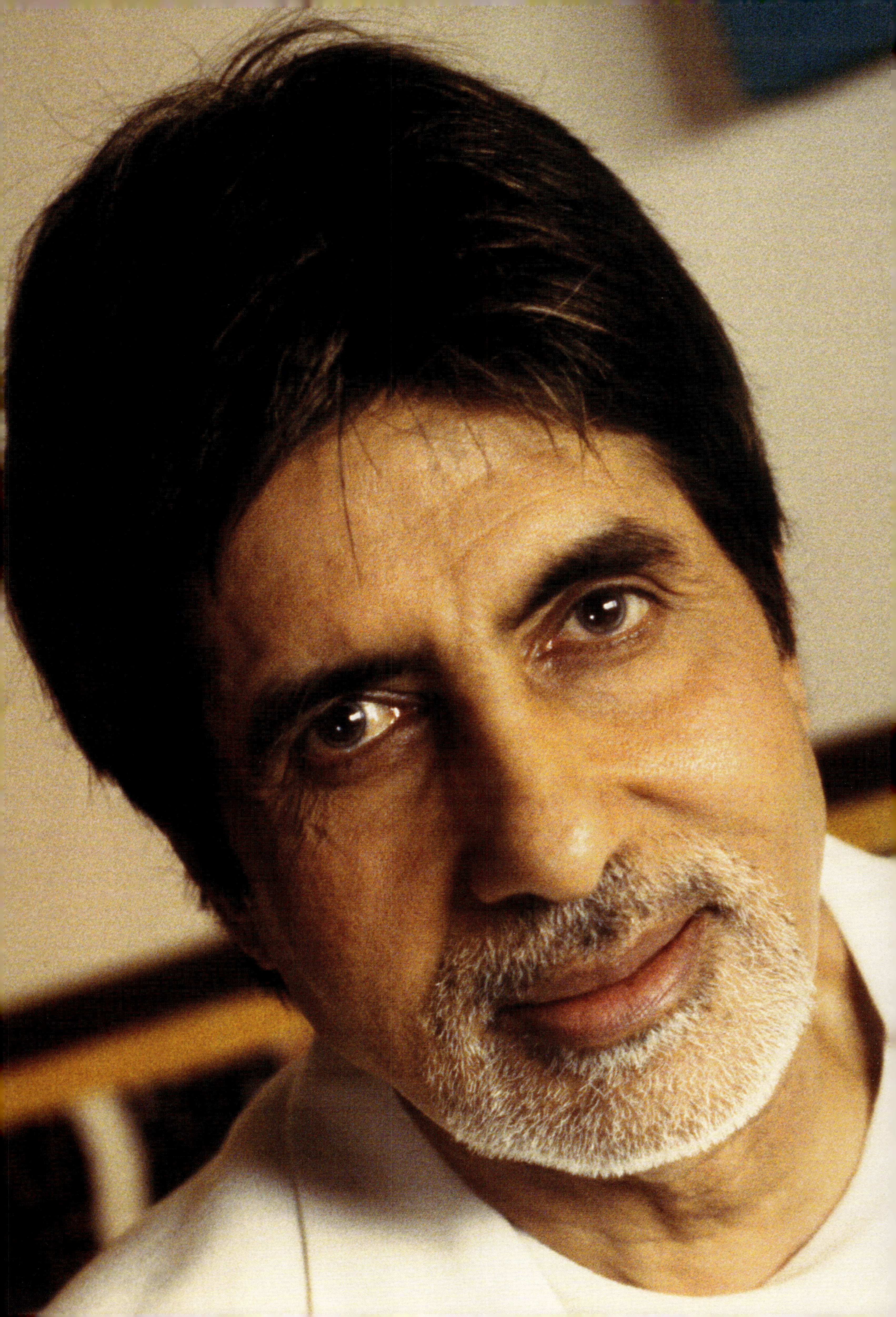

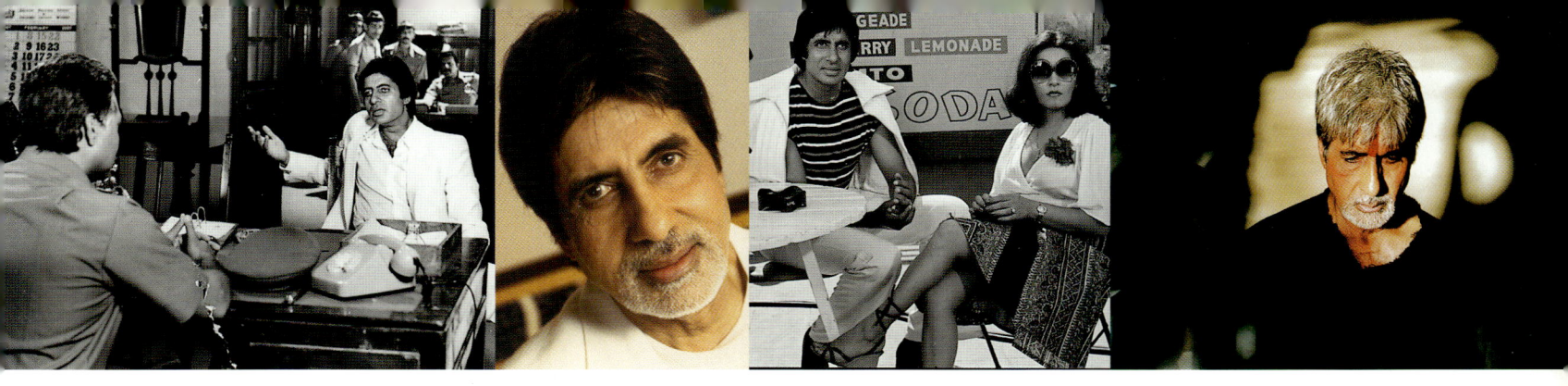

But of all the roles that he essayed in 2005, the one that took him back to the iconic status of *Deewar*, was that of Subhash Nagare in *Sarkar*.

In *Sarkar*, director Ram Gopal Varma wanted to recreate the intensity that Bachchan oozed in *Zanjeer* and *Deewar*, keeping his age in mind. Varma thinks Bachchan is the only actor in Indian cinema who can hold the camera without saying a word. 'To me, [Amitabh] Bachchan drinking tea from a saucer is more incredibly performance-oriented than some other actor doing a complex emotional sequence. Like I said, he can hold the camera with his personality,' says Varma.

Then there was the laugh riot *Bunty aur Babli* with Rani Mukherjee and his son Abhishek. Through the film he seemed to be saying, 'Don't mind me now, I'm just having some fun!' And the entire country rolled in laughter along with him.

Waqt, the first hit of 2005, had him playing a terminally ill father. The movie, an adaptation of a Gujarati play, was a choice that director Vipul Shah had run by Bachchan after the latter had asked him to pick a script that would get them to work together again after *Aankhein*, their last film together.

Then there is Bachchan's 'coming of second age' role in his home-produced movie, *Viruddh,* directed by Mahesh Manjrekar. 'I didn't want Amitabh Bachchan to play a parallel role or an angry middle-aged man,' says Manjrekar, who made the movie as a joint venture between Bachchan's AB Corp and Satyajeet Movies.

'The first thing that Amit *ji* asks after stepping on the sets is, "Mahesh, what do you want me to do?" If I called for a retake, never once did he ask "Why? What's wrong with this shot?"' Besides, says Manjrekar, he never leaves the sets after a shot. He waits till the entire shoot is over. John Abraham, who plays Bachchan's son in the movie, feels the senior actor is fitter and more agile and energetic than most of the younger actors around.

Production and direction responsibilities were clearly demarcated, says Manjrekar. 'Amit *ji* gave me total freedom as a director and not once did he question anything.'

'The very fact that he does not interfere with the vision of the director is also a part of his success,' says Nihalani, who worked with Bachchan in *Dev*. 'He understands, perhaps, that he has to submit or be part of a bigger vision that the director has. There is a certain relationship of faith that gets established between the director and the actor which works best for the film.

'One hears of many actors who participate in designing the scene and dialogue, but we see that the results of their films are inconsistent. I don't say the actor should not discuss these things with the director, because unless they have sorted out their doubts how will the intensity of the performances emerge? But the point is, there is a difference between discussion and interference. And Bachchan never interferes, that's for sure.'

Today, Amitabh Bachchan is a megastar, a legend, and everyone wants a piece of his glory to touch their films or their products. Endorsers are willing to pay crores of rupees for a few seconds of his time. Filmmakers feel that a scene with him, or even a voiceover, will change the destiny of their films. Directors say that it is their ultimate dream to direct

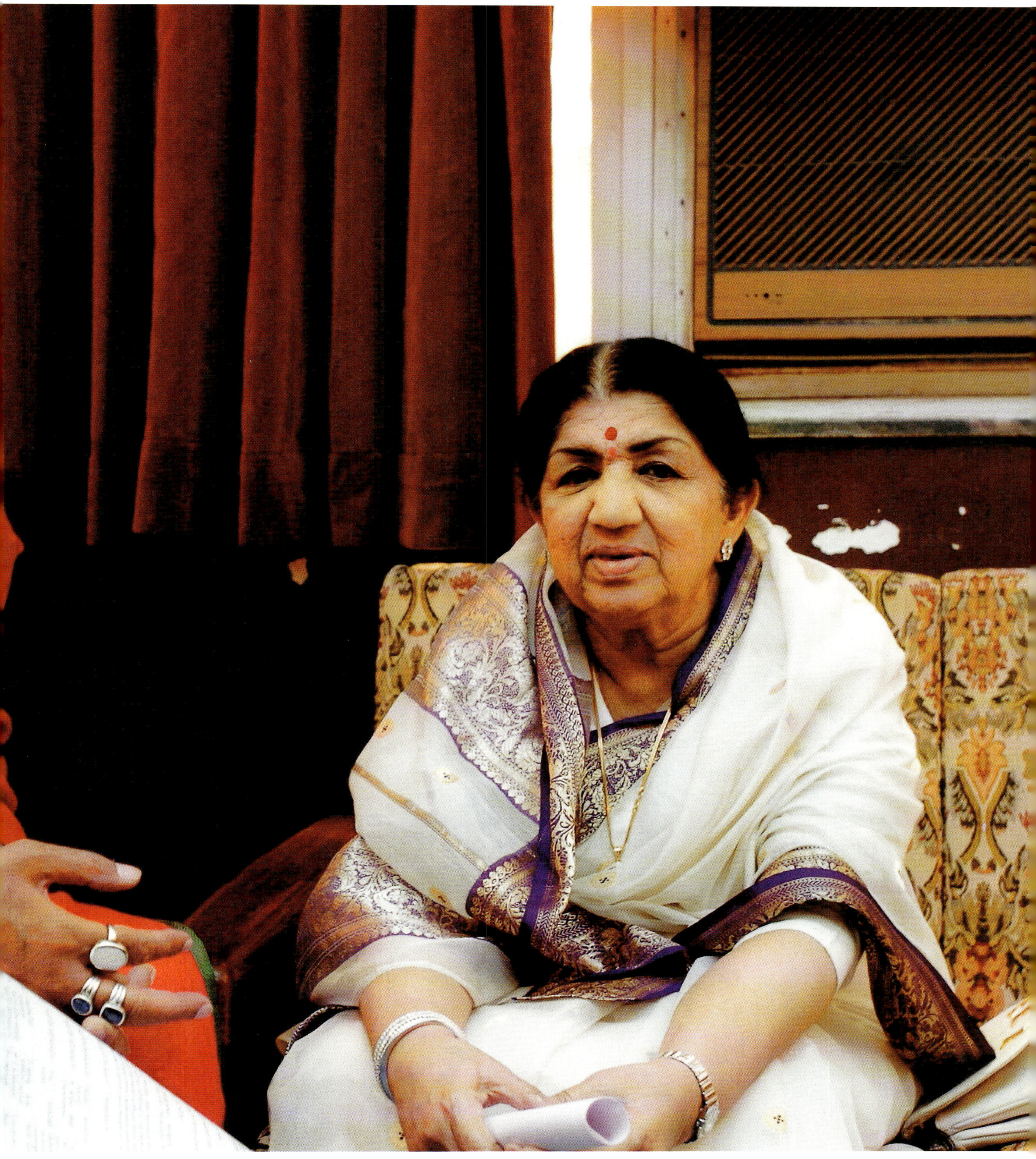

him and even design projects with him in mind. And being the benign soul that he is, Bachchan rarely says no.

So he is found on almost every hoarding, every television channel, and every other movie. And yet the desire to watch and listen to that masterful persona is still insatiable.

But yes, he's mortal: for every movie like *Black,* there are still the no-brainers like *Ab Tumhare Hawale Watan Saathiyon, Kyun! Ho Gaya Na,* and *Boom.* Are we seeing much too much of Amitabh Bachchan? Is he getting overexposed? Or is it just that we love him too much to feel that we could ever get enough of him?

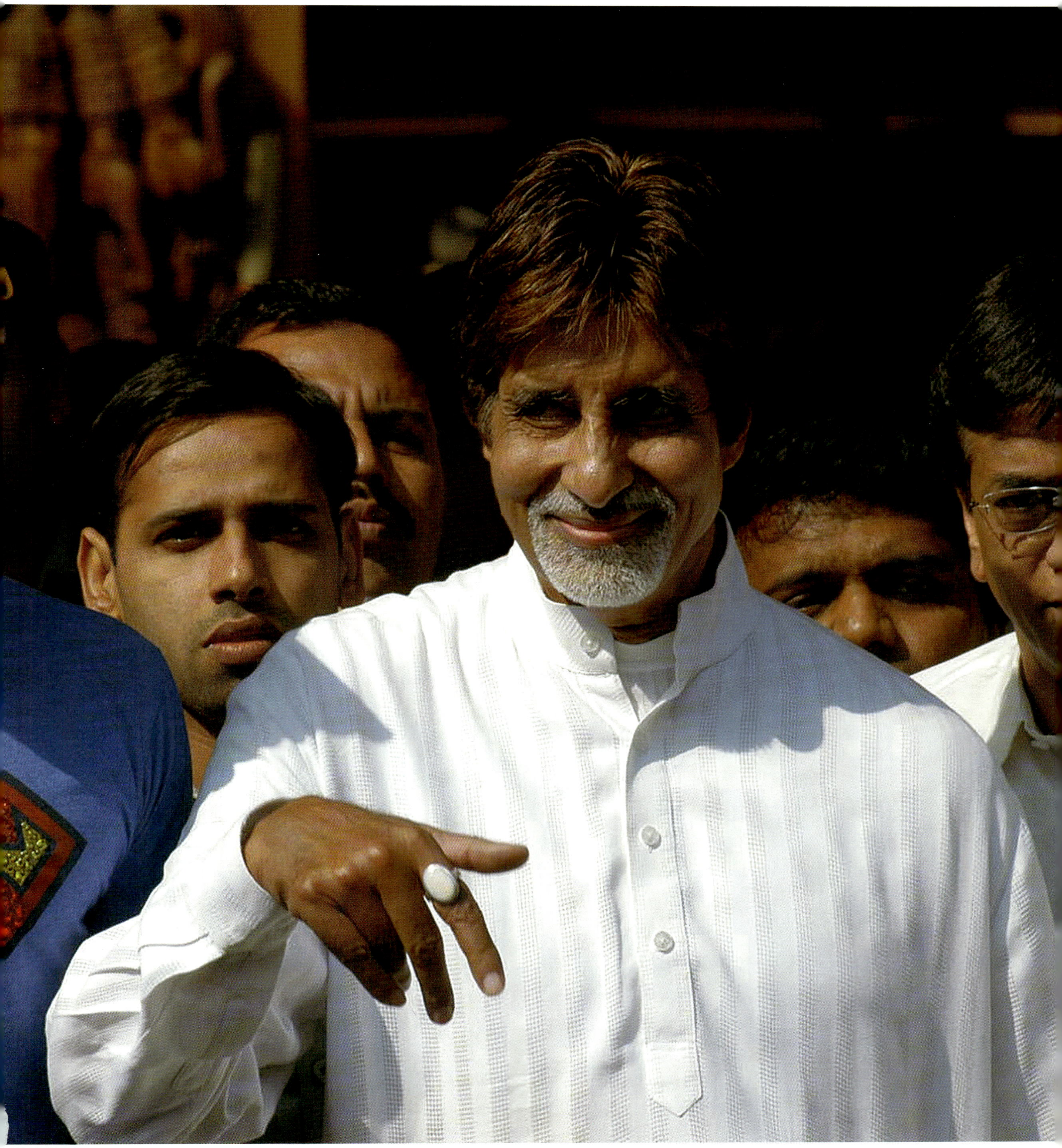

Guest Writer

Brilliant, but hugely lucky too

Srinivas Hebbar

On many counts, Amitabh Bachchan is in a class by himself. Of course, there is his extraordinary staying power. He was way ahead of the pack thirty years ago, and remains on equal terms with a new generation. After a hundred films, he is still in the reckoning, in an industry notorious for typecasting, straitjacketing of actors and the inevitable fadeout. From being the Angry Young Man, he has morphed seamlessly into the funny, but man-of-the-world *Bade Miya,* to romp with a Govinda half his age. That calls for skills rarely seen in the industry.

But durability is not the only reason for Amitabh's cachet. He has shown remarkable resilience in a career that has taken more than a few knocks, some bad enough to lay low even the hardy perennials of Bollywood. Like his brush with politics and his stint as an MP. His proximity to the Gandhi family was such that it could have taken him to the top rungs of politics. Alternatively, it could have singed him. Neither of that happened. Amitabh made a messy foray into politics, decided he was not made for it and withdrew. He has emerged practically unscathed from the searing experience, save some bad memories perhaps and a lifelong lesson. That again is Amitabh Bachchan for you. I wouldn't call him the Teflon man on whom nothing sticks. He is more like an escape artist: handcuff him, tie him up, put him in a box and drop him into the sea and soon you see him emerging, his old hearty self.

The ABCL interlude is another illustration of the remarkable ability of the man to remain untouched by the muck into which he is now and then prone to fall. To even those who have a peripheral interest in the film industry and the lives of its superstars, Amitabh's fall had the makings of a tragic story that the tearjerkers of Bollywood could never match. This was real life stuff, a great actor who had everything going for him bites the dust because of his own vaulting ambitions. Being a legendary actor was not enough. He had to become a producer. He wanted to participate in the great corporate sweepstakes and set up a film company. This was hubris on a grand scale, enough to tempt the Gods.

Even a stranger to business could say it looked like a terrible career move, to throw away what he did well, which was acting, where he did not risk a *paisa* of his own money, and go into film production, a different ballgame altogether. To top it, Amitabh borrowed from banks and mortgaged all that he had. Including the house he lived in.

To an outsider to the industry like me, one who had only seen the Big B on screen, it seemed like a stunning debacle. Banks were moving in to recover their money, which is as bad as it can get, since banks do so only when they are convinced that the client is in a free fall and they had better collect whatever they can as fast as they can. The Big B without even a house was an idea that boggled the mind.

Yet, not very much later, Mr Bachchan had bounced back, more buoyant than the best of Bollywood, firing on all cylinders and the toast of society again. *Kaun Banega Crorepati* was the dream chartbuster that was the envy of every channel. All Amitabh had to do to pay his dues to Doordarshan was endorse a few products. Could repayment be sweeter: appear on the small screen, push a noble cause such as the anti-polio campaign and pay back your debts?

Another famous film figure, writer, actor composer of yesteryear, Chuck Barris, had once said, 'I'm amazed how life takes everything away from you so fast and then gives it right back.' This was more than true in Amitabh Bachchan's case: life gave back, and gave in abundance.

Which brings us to the next aspect of the importance of being Amitabh Bachchan. Is he extraordinarily lucky? It would seem so. This is not to detract from his talent. Very talented, extraordinarily lucky is not an unfair description of the Bachchan phenomenon. Before Napoleon took on anyone in a high position, he would ask his advisors whether that person was lucky. It is an important qualification and it is not unfair to say that Amitabh oozes luck.

It is the L word of extraordinarily successful people. We don't like to associate great success with luck. It is like trivialising talent, diminishing it somehow. His diehard fans might argue that it is sheer talent that has brought Amitabh to where he stands today, assuredly the most successful of all film figures, past and present, monarch of all he surveys, a patriarchal figure with a fan following that borders on the worshipful.

There is son Abhishek, who started off shakily and seemed likely to go down the path so often taken by sons of famous fathers. It's an old story, of sons permanently doomed to live in the shadow of their fathers and finally breaking down. But Abhishek, perhaps with many helpful nudges from a doting father, did finally make the grade. So, many attempts later, he has finally emerged into the light. That perhaps is as much a tribute to the father as it is to Abhishek. Let's grant it: Abhishek had the daunting challenge of not being overwhelmed by his father's huge reputation and the resulting expectations from him that it created. Abhishek as an actor may not be a patch on his father, or even match up to current Bollywood biggies, but he had the grit that made him cling to his dream of following in his father's footsteps. He is no superstar, but that he still commands a price in a market that is notoriously hard-nosed, is no small achievement.

So, getting back to Amitabh: lucky again with his children.

It is hard to get away from it, this amazingly lucky streak that runs through the Amitabh persona. Talented he is, unquestionably. An ability to avoid the sordid temptations that life in Bollywood is replete with, he surely has. The savvy to handle the Press and successfully establish an image of being aloof from it all, avoiding the tawdry gimmicks to remain in the public eye, the tantrums that go with superstardom, the last desperate efforts to keep alive a sputtering career — Amitabh has done it brilliantly.

Yet, after having attributed all those admirable qualities to the great man, it is hard to get away from the fact that Amitabh has had his scrapes, but has always managed to land on his feet. The generous thing would be to say that, along with all his great qualities, such as his screen presence, the famous voice, a fine sense of balance in his acting, a feel for comedy, the ability to convey the feeling that he is not acting at all, our own Marlon Brando (the sadness that he retains throughout in his *Sholay* role, nothing overt but always there, is one of the high points of his acting career), he also has savvy.

People say this of Amitabh Bachchan, that scratch the aloof, very private actor and you find a calculating, savvy person. Perhaps. That might explain his proximity to politicians even after he had sworn off politics. But those connections could have carried him only so far and no further. They may have delayed his creditors who were closing in on him, but they couldn't have bailed him out. That unfinished task would still have required a *Kaun Banega Crorepati*. That's the fortuitous element in his life that stands out, the lucky streak. It re-launched Amitabh, an all-new Amitabh, with many new features, exuding warmth and charm, getting along famously with his adoring contestants in the programme, irrespective of age, displaying an off-screen confidence that would do a politician proud.

Would Amitabh have accepted the *Kaun Banega Crorepati* offer had he not hit rock bottom after the ABCL fiasco and been desperately hard up? Odds are that he wouldn't. Why would he risk a reputation built over half a lifetime for something dubious on the small screen? An actor's success, at least in India, depends to an extent on his off-screen image. If Amitabh on screen was larger than life, in people's minds he was larger than even his screen image. Why risk all that for the trivial temptations of TV? Well, the decision was forced upon him. Call it destiny, call it luck. A reluctant Amitabh, whom the Press had already written off, bankruptcy snapping at his heels, suddenly rose out of the ashes and walked away to hurrahs from the public and stunned silence from critics. Even the dream purveyors of Bollywood couldn't have scripted a better success story. And you surely can't do it in real life. You've got to be lucky. It's what Chuck Barris said about life taking everything away and giving it all back again. Certainly, it happens to so many people, but in Big B's case, it is like his film persona — larger than life.

This turnaround in fortunes also makes Amitabh a maverick of sorts in the film world, which abounds with tragic tales, of talent that did not live up to promise, of careers cut short in their prime. In the crowded, breathless, make-believe world of Bollywood, tragedy too has a certain sad sweetness about it. The only thing worse than being tragic is being mediocre. Tragedy in film folks' life has its compensations, which can be counted in column inches in the glossy film rags. Broken marriages, alcoholism, sudden deaths have a certain acceptance in this parallel universe.

But tragedy is the price of fame. Amitabh perhaps stands out as an example of success that came without the price tag. A father famous in his own right (and famous for all the right reasons, being a respected poet, a friend of the Nehru family), a wife, famous in her own right, a marriage that did not break up, a son who had the courage to become an actor without being intimidated by his father's fame and doggedly held on—that's success undistilled. That perhaps adds to the Bachchan persona in the public mind, in an India that is predominantly young, that is on the make and hungry for success. Unlike in the US where the public sometimes takes pleasure in demolishing a legend, the Indian people hate their heroes and heroines to be brought down from their pedestals. Not all the negative stories about Jayalalithaa or MGR or NTR can change public opinion. We are able to perform a mental sleight of hand that makes all that is unpalatable about our legends disappear. We use a Botox on our idols that irons out their wrinkles. But in Amitabh, the public sees someone who does not demand that of them. They believe they have what they see: a man who has everything going for him, not tainted by politics, sleaze or scandal, a regular family man like any of them, religious, like any of them, and hugely successful, like any of them would dream of being. That, to my mind, is the Bachchan saga.

— *Srinivas Hebbar is a Mumbai based journalist*

Chapter Six

Still Here

I been scarred and battered.
My hopes the wind done scattered.
Snow has friz me,
Sun has baked me,
Looks like between 'em they done
Tried to make me
Stop laughin', stop lovin', stop livin'—
But I don't care!
I'm still here!

–Langston Hughes

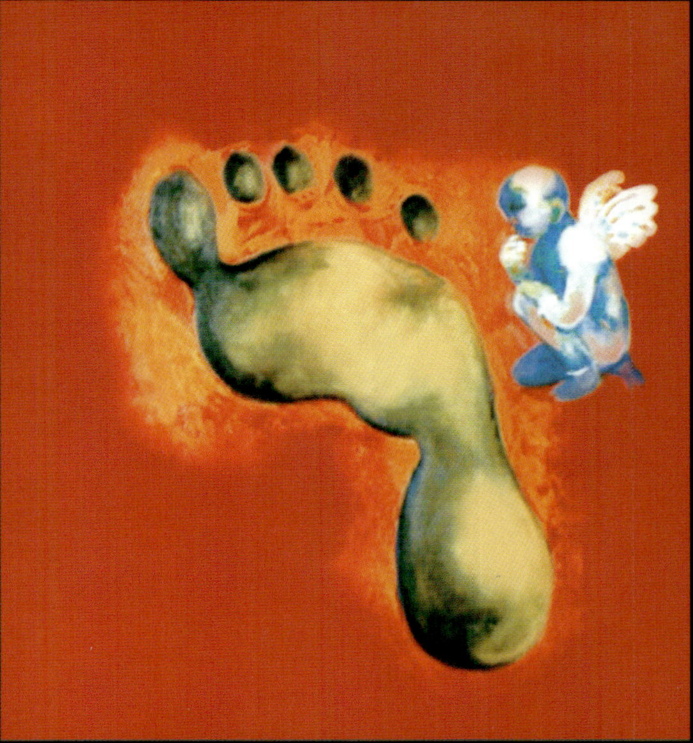
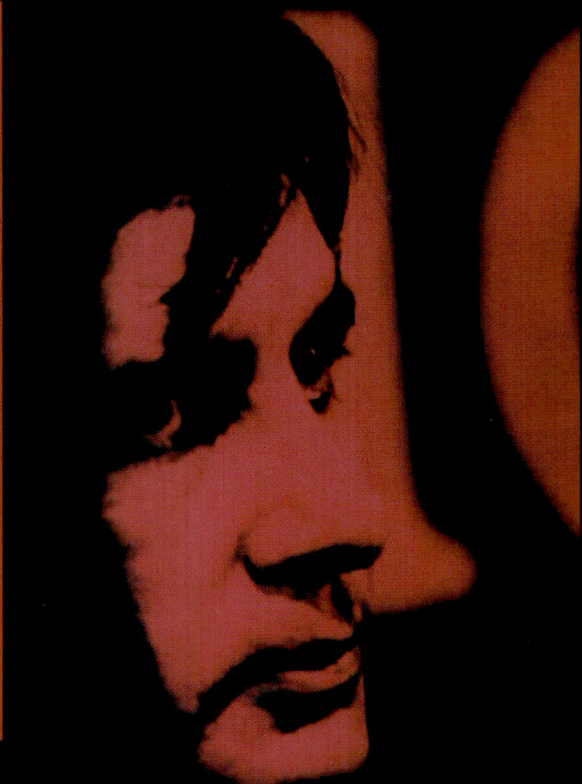

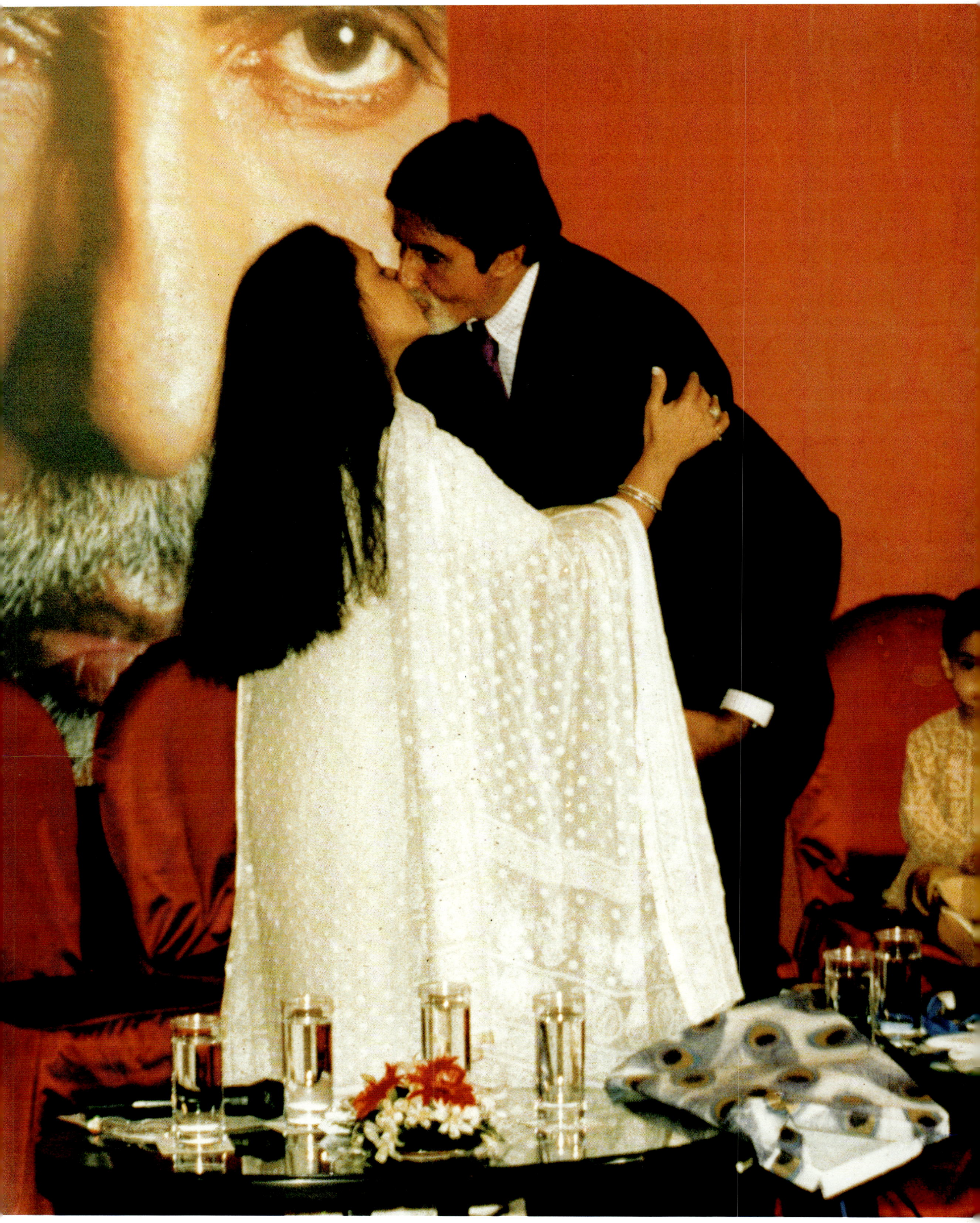

When people around him tried to convince Bachchan to let go of ABCL and declare bankruptcy, the superstar refused because he believed that precious little was possible without trust, and it went against his principles to let down someone who had placed trust in him. According to Stephen Covey, in his book *Principle Centered Leadership*, 'If there is little or no trust, there is no foundation for permanent success[1].'

In an earlier book, *Seven Habits of Highly Effective People*, Covey talks about two approaches that a person uses in his/her interactions with other people: a 'Personality Ethic' and a 'Character Ethic'. The Personality Ethic is essentially transaction based. '…where success is more of a function of personality, of public image, of attitudes and behaviours, skills and techniques, that lubricate the processes of human interaction…'

But, according to Covey, the Character Ethic is 'the foundation of success — things like integrity, humility, fidelity, temperance, courage, justice, patience, industry, simplicity, modesty… The Character Ethic taught that there are basic principles of effective living, and that people can only experience true success and enduring happiness as they learn and integrate these principles[2].'

The way Bachchan has lived his life as an actor and a human being seems to exemplify a person whose interactions with people have been governed by the Character Ethic. Bachchan has also managed to set himself apart from other people in the Hindi film industry through his principles and personal integrity. 'He's a complete contradiction to the industry he's in,' ad filmmaker Prahlad Kakkar says. 'His values remain unchanged in an industry that's increasingly ephemeral in its principles. He's always stood for them, he's always worked for them.'

Once Tinnu Anand had signed Bachchan on for a film. After shooting for the film for about a week, Bachchan's *Ganga Jamuna Saraswati* was released. Anand realised that the character Bachchan had played in the film was very close to the one he was doing in his film. He asked Bachchan why he hadn't told him about it. Bachchan's reply was, 'I've played Anthony many times over so I didn't think there was any need to tell you.'

However, Anand felt that the characters were too similar and he discontinued the film. Bachchan said in case Anand thought it was his fault, he was prepared to bear the losses arising from the film's production. 'And he gave me the money though he had shot only for five days. He and Rajnikanth are the

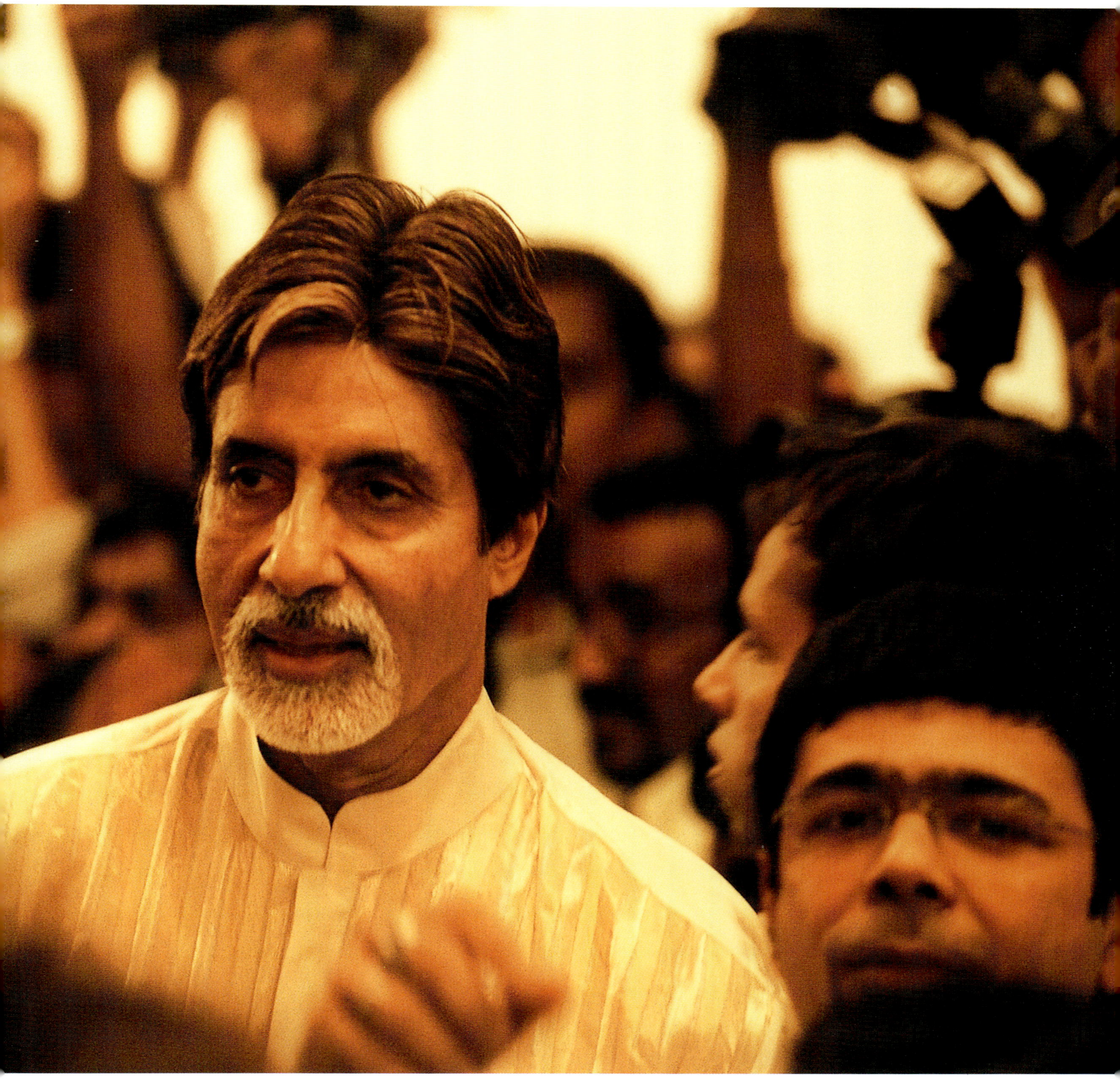

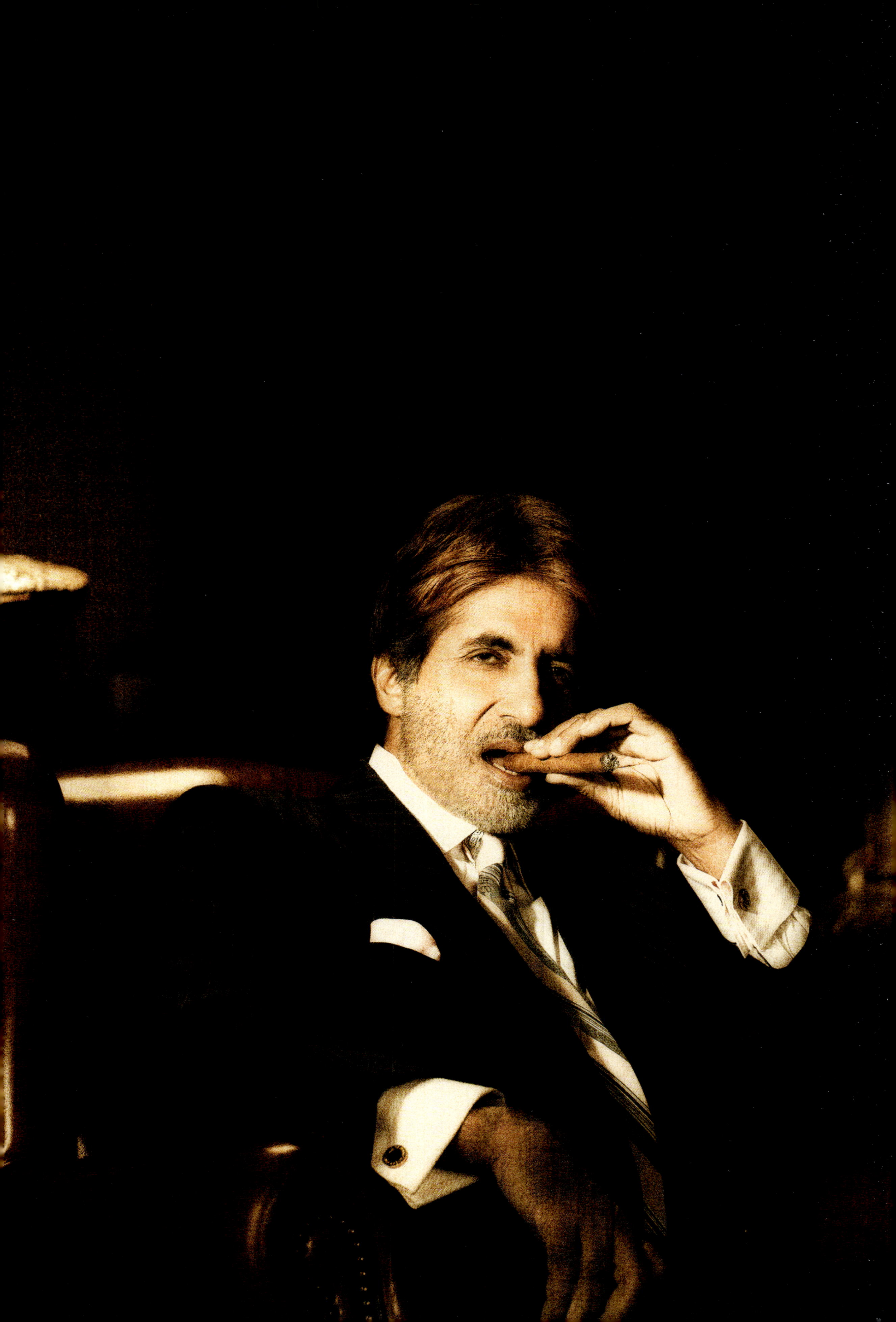

only two men who don't think of their food, their money,' Anand said.

Facing the darkness, and living through trying times has endowed Bachchan with a newfound confidence. The kind that blossomed from within. 'I have not differentiated between life and struggle; I've felt more vibrant, more alive when the challenge got tougher, meaner. It has created a deep faith within me. Now I like struggle and can appreciate life better,' he says.

'An artist looks forward to something new everyday. I feel the moment one is satisfied, one likes the imagination in the self. This attitude of self-satisfaction is wrong. I want to face new challenges each day, and be daunted by new ideas and roles which force me to use my innovative capabilities to do something I have never done before.'

'The new Amitabh Bachchan has emerged. He's proved to the world that he is a durable part of the industry. Not many people have had the kind of long innings he has. To have survived many a death. There was a physical death to be survived. There have been so many deaths where he has been written off as a has-been, but he has survived that,' says filmmaker Mahesh Bhatt.

'He goes beyond the moment, he goes beyond

the sentence. He goes beyond the question. That is how he analyses the role and the film. These are the great gifts of Amitabh Bachchan,' says Gerson DaCunha, director, Bombay First.

Bachchan is, in fact, very humble about his talent. 'As an artiste, I believe that I should never feel satisfied. Perfection is a state only for God. If he considers himself perfect then the artiste begins to impersonate God. But when a man finds contentment, he really attains godhood. An artiste always has to search for ways to improve. A divine discontent is always necessary for creative achievement. It leads to that moment of creativity — the moment of daring surrender by which all things new in this world have taken form.'

Says restaurateur Nelson Wang, 'I recognise expressions and body language because people are unguarded when they are eating. If I were to estimate this man, I think he doesn't care much about money. It is not the driving force of his life. It is what he has achieved and is going to achieve that propels him. He knows that if he does what he does best right, then money will come to him automatically. He has an urge to satisfy himself more than anybody else with his work.'

It is this kind of integrity that has enabled

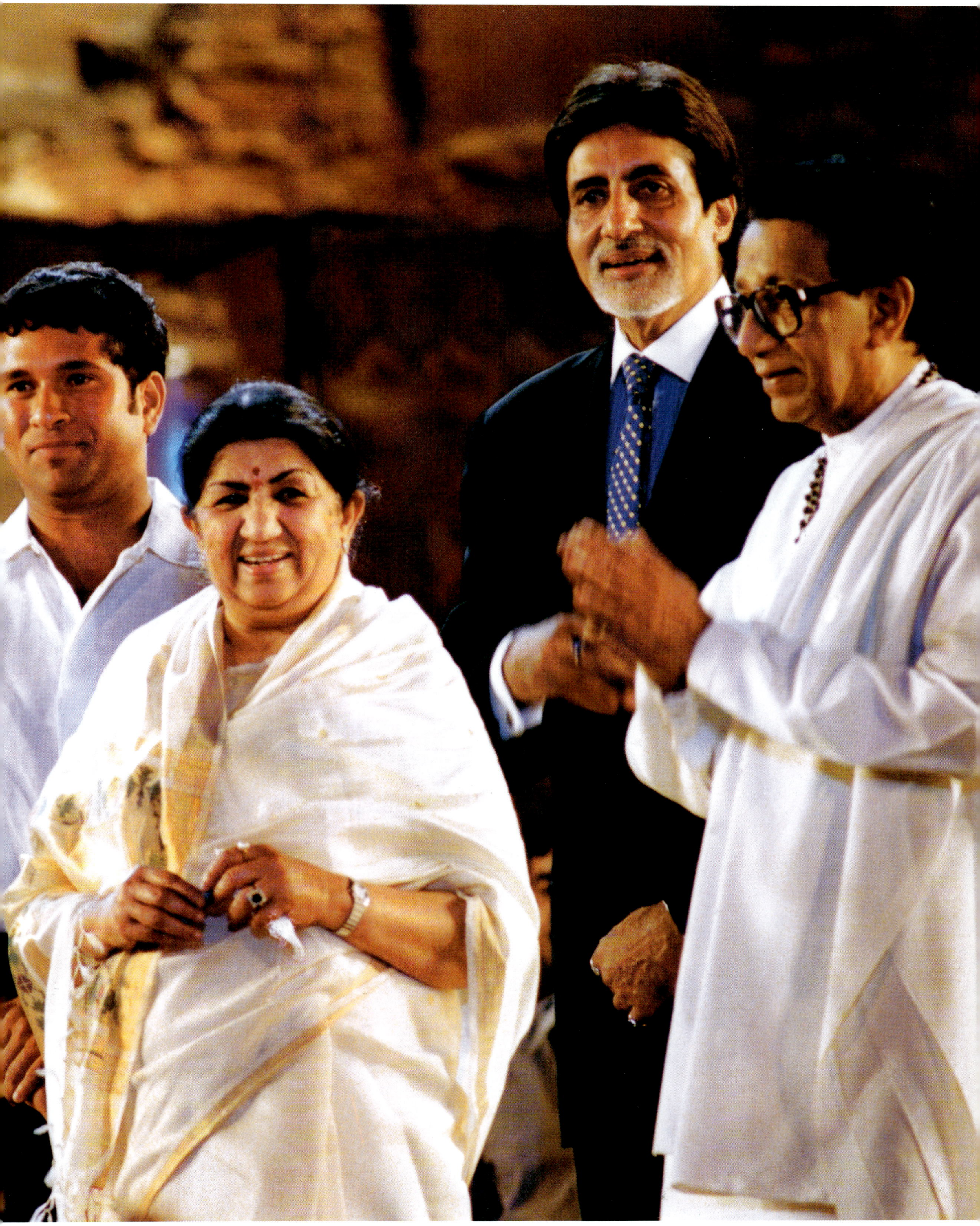

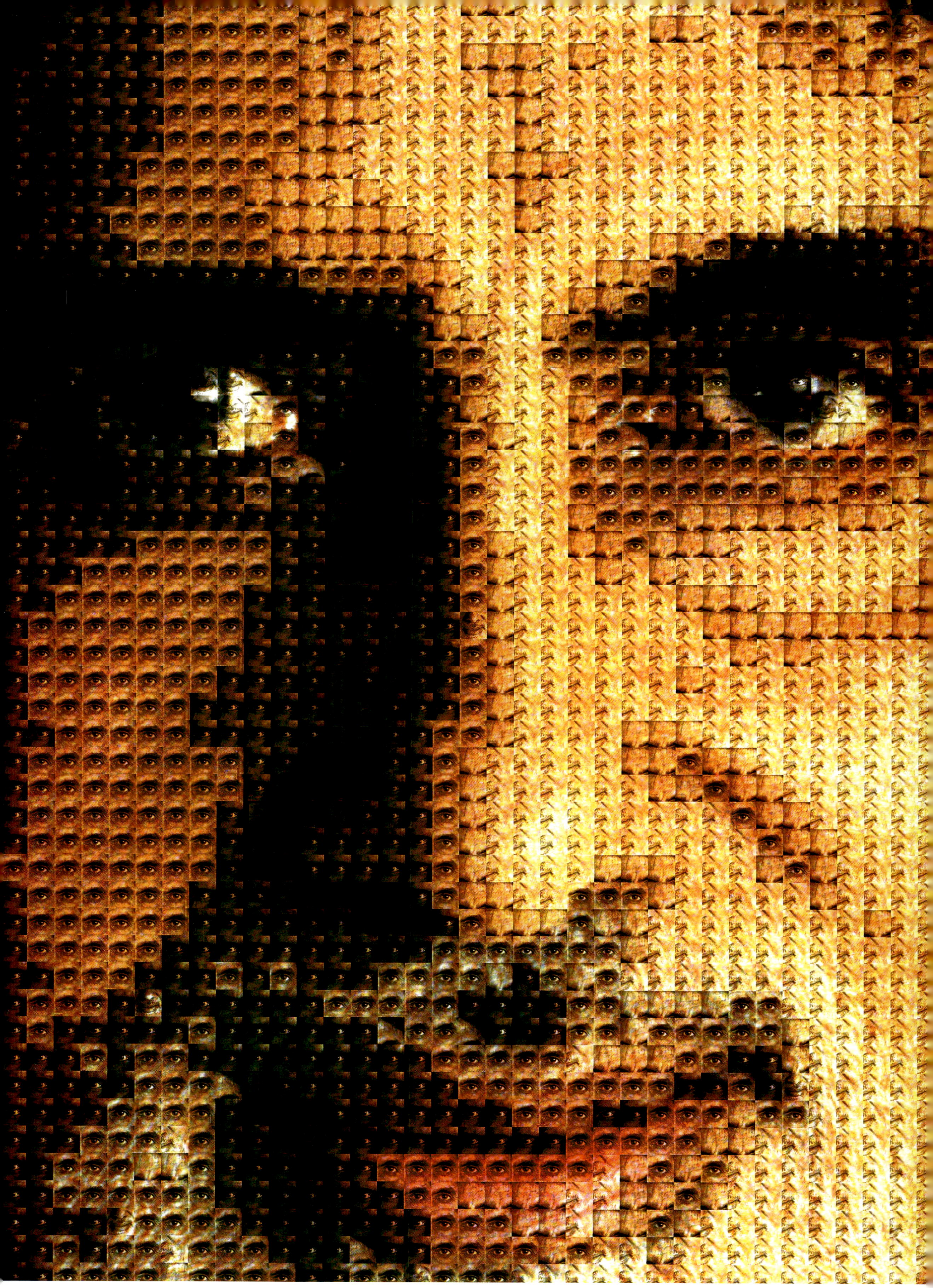

Bachchan to be the icon that he is today. A status that companies have been quick to cash in on. The actor must hold a record of sorts for being the brand ambassador for around thirty to forty brands at the same time. This is a first even worldwide. 'The reason he is probably the best actor on the Indian screen is, other than Dilip Kumar, I can't remember anyone with such tremendous talent and ability, that he can convince an audience in whatever role he plays. That's the beauty of Amitabh Bachchan and that's why Amitabh has also become an advertising icon,' says ad guru Alyque Padamsee.

'And all the people ask me "do the products sell?" And I have to answer with a resounding yes. They do sell. All brands that Amitabh Bachchan has endorsed, as far as I know, have increased their market share, increased their sales.'

Bachchan today is an icon for everyone right from the little child looking trustingly up to him on matters as serious as chocolate, to the elderly septuagenarian plagued by joint pain. And ad gurus like Padamsee heave a sigh of relief that they have a trustworthy ad motif. 'I say thank God we have had an Amitabh Bachchan in our lives,' he says.

'He's a one man industry!' says Kakkar.

Prasoon Joshi, poet and creative director,

McCann Erikson, also believes in the influence Bachchan has over the masses. 'There is nobody else I can think of who can do so much justice to an advertisement. He is a superman and super people can do things which ordinary people can't.'

Incidentally, a testimony to his stature in advertising is the fact that he is never referred to as a model or an endorser, but always as a 'brand ambassador'. And Bachchan has always reiterated that he does use the products he endorses.

'Anything he recommends, you know you can put your bottom dollar on. I think he did a fantastic job for Cadbury when they were in a spot of trouble. When Amitabh said, "I went to the factory, I know that the best packaging has been used for Cadbury chocolates" it was absolutely credible,' Padamsee says.

The ad man spoke to many people after the advertisement started airing. These people had initially stopped their children from eating Cadbury chocolates after worms had been found in a couple of chocolate bars. After the advertisement, though, these people unanimously believed that, if Amitabh Bachchan said the chocolate was safe, it truly was. 'This is an incredible kind of trust and confidence in Amitabh's integrity,' Padamsee states.

In real life, Bachchan is unlike the usual

The Legend

187

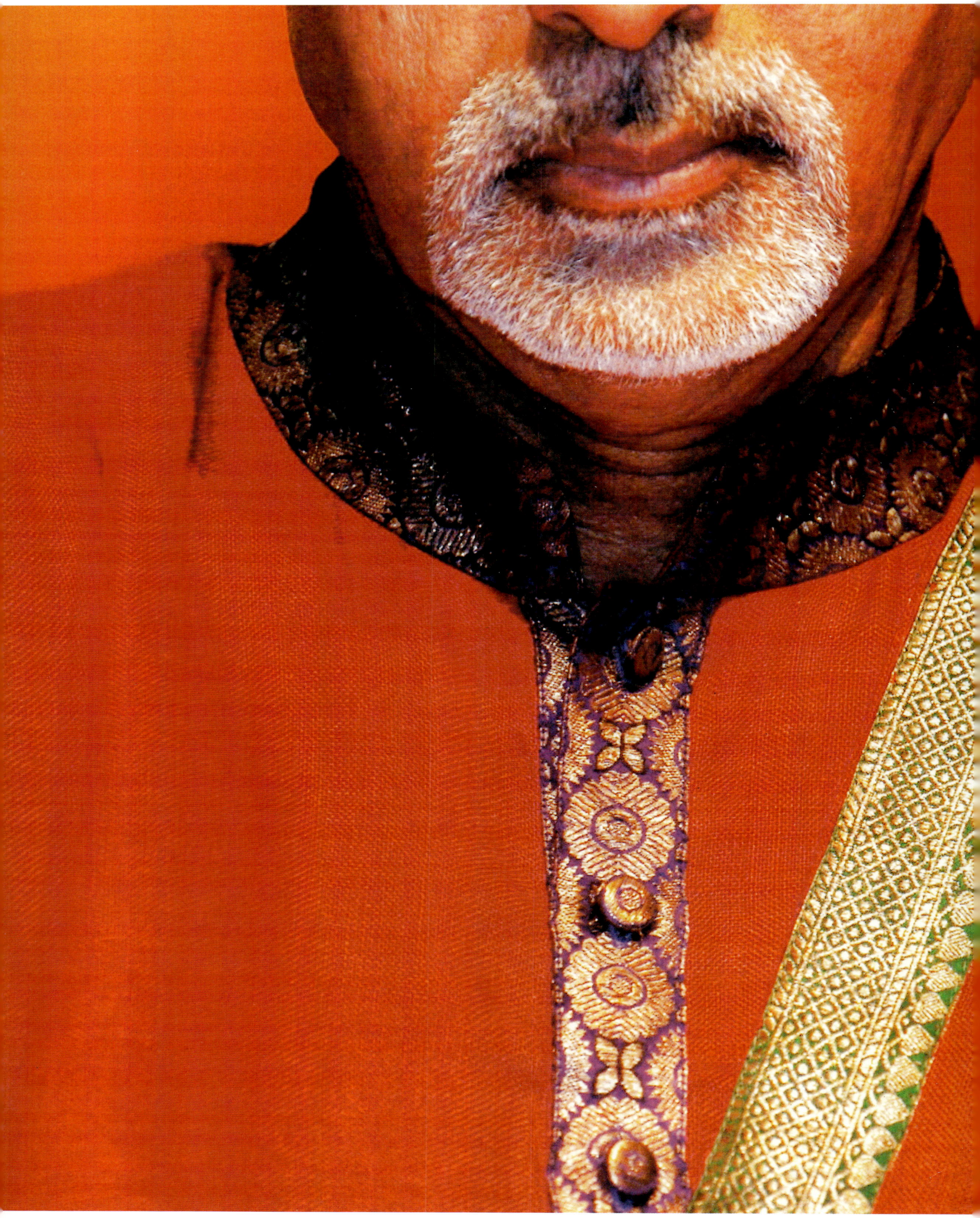

flamboyant Hindi film star prevalent today. So his quiet, almost introverted, personality tends to take on mythic status. 'As far as public persona is concerned, when he was a big star as the angry young man, he tended to shun publicity, because he said he was always being misquoted. Today, Amitabh is in the spotlight more than the prime minister of India,' muses Padamsee. 'It's wonderful to see Amitabh as a less reclusive and more extroverted public persona.'

Bachchan is exacting when it comes to his job, always approaching each day with a dedication and discipline that is admirable. 'I wish there were more disciplined actors like him. Instead we find many of them who are more interested in fooling around. His is an amazing success story,' says Om Puri. 'He always comes to the sets fully prepared, never makes anybody wait, never interferes on the set. Maybe the key to his success is that he hasn't taken his success for granted. He is still very passionate about his acting. Consistency is most important, which you will find in Bachchan's performance. A part of it also goes to his upbringing and literary background but his own contribution to the success cannot be denied.'

Says theatre personality Dolly Thakore with whom he had acted during his college days, 'If you call or SMS him on his mobile phone, he will always reply.

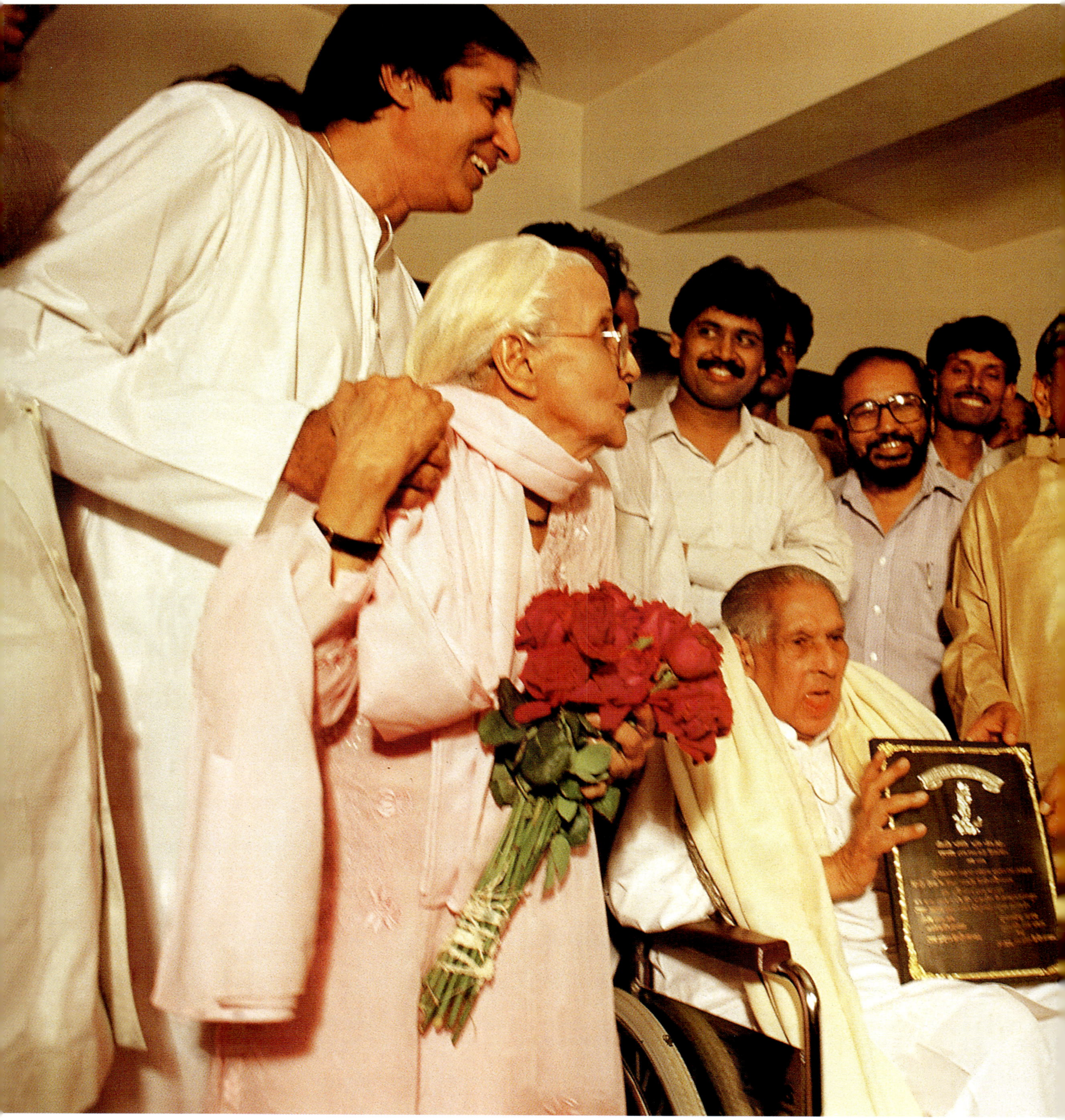

He may not do it within ten minutes, but he will always call you back irrespective of whether he is abroad or in India. And his secretaries are on call twenty-four hours. Once I sent him a message at three in the morning thinking that he will get the message the first thing in the morning. But I was shocked to get a reply within ten minutes. I asked the secretary why she was awake and she said that they have to be on call throughout the day.'

Bachchan is as gracious with the media. Once when Dolly Thakore met him at a function in a Mumbai hotel, there were hordes of photographers taking pictures of him. Two days later, she met him in his home and told him that in case she ever had a programme with him in future, she would allot fifteen minutes for the photographers to take the mandatory pictures. Post that they would have to give way to the other people who could then see him and hear him. Bachchan turned around and told her, 'They also have to earn a living.'

'I thought that was a very gentle and sensible thing to say,' says Thakore. 'This man has been with the media for so long that there's maturity in that sentence. I was quite touched.'

But Bachchan has also learnt to hold his own in the various press interviews that he has to face without giving away any more information than he wants. He has learnt to protect himself during interviews. He has gotten nifty at getting around a query, flooring many a green journalist who doesn't realise till much later that a question has not really been answered. Another trick is the famous interrogator's ploy of keeping quiet so that the other person gets flustered and asks another question to cover the uncomfortable silence. To overcome this, a journalist has to keep his or her cool and wait it out, which only a seasoned journalist is likely to be able to do.

Vir Sanghvi, also a good friend of Bachchan, has managed to get fairly detailed interviews from him, but he says that it isn't easy to get a good interview from him because of this. Sanghvi feels that Bachchan will answer difficult questions only if he respects the interviewer.

With most people being interviewed, the journalist is usually conferring a favour by giving them access to publicity, but with Bachchan the roles are reversed. It is he who is being gracious to the journalist by agreeing to do an interview, so the odds are stacked against the interviewer right from the start.

Perhaps it is a sense of gratitude for their love and adoration that makes Bachchan so gracious and so receptive to his fans. Indeed, people feel they are a part of his family. And Bachchan does take his fans very seriously. He signs autographs for about an hour twice a day. He hires secretaries to go through the mounds of fan mail that he receives every day.

Says Thakore, 'He hasn't surrounded himself with fashionable people. He has very simple people around him. You would think that Amitabh Bachchan's secretaries would be like film stars themselves, but they are not. They are simple people and obviously loyal because they have been there with him for so many years.'

'He is a terrific professional,' says Kakkar. 'He's embarrassingly punctual. Whether it's a small ad film or Oscar-nominee material, he gives it the same attention and effort. It is not the money that makes him pay attention, it is the attitude and his personal exacting standards. He's always five minutes ahead of everybody. If you are incompetent, then he makes you feel incompetent just by being the way he is.'

In the same twenty-four hours available to everyone, Bachchan manages to include in his schedule his TV show, his film career as well as the numerous shoots for his various advertising

UGYEN CHOPEL
BINOD PRADHAN, GOPAL
JAVED AKHTAR
SHANKAR EHSAAN LOY
BHI

endorsements. Then there are his commitments to AB Corp, and his family. He also manages to sign autographs, take phone calls and meet people. And we haven't even covered the half of it. Why this frighteningly exact sense of efficiency? The key may lie in something he said to Vir Sanghvi in an interview that took place some years ago.

In reply to a question about his age, Bachchan replied that he had always been anxious about it. 'Oddly enough, as your physical capacity decreases with age, the expectations go up. That's the most frightening part. People's expectations are so high that it scares me. And it's almost impossible to live up to it[3].'

Bachchan isn't afraid of overexposure, 'I want as much exposure as is possible. I am absolutely desperate to work. I consider myself fortunate that I still get work at the age of sixty-three. And, honestly, I feel thrilled to be able to portray diverse characters.'

He has ruled out the possibility of re-entering politics. 'I knew nothing of politics, I still don't know. I've been a misfit there. I don't know the game.... Temperamentally I am not suited for it and that is why I find myself where I am.... There is absolutely no chance of returning to politics[4].

'I get up at five, five-thirty. Go for a walk. Then

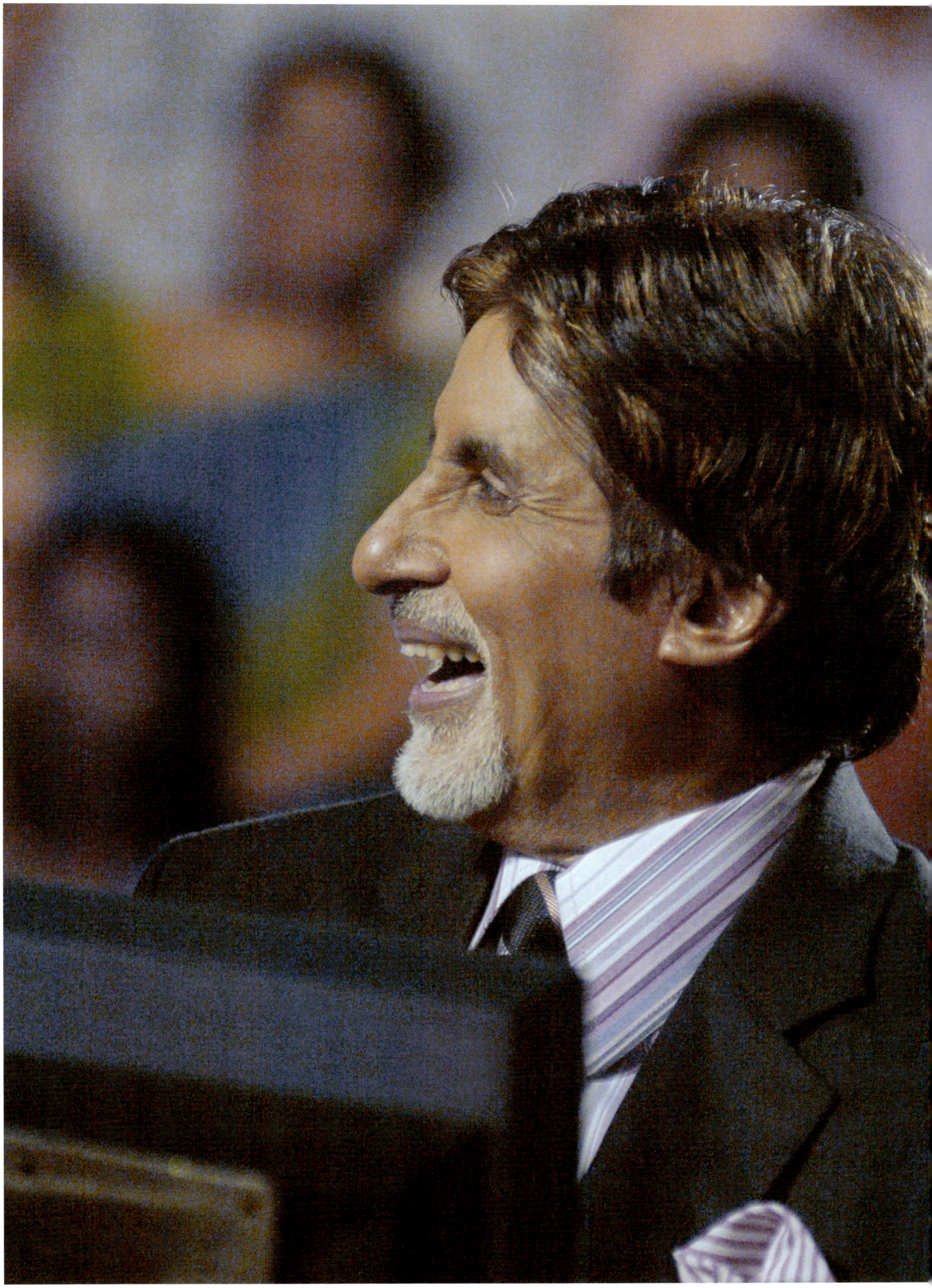

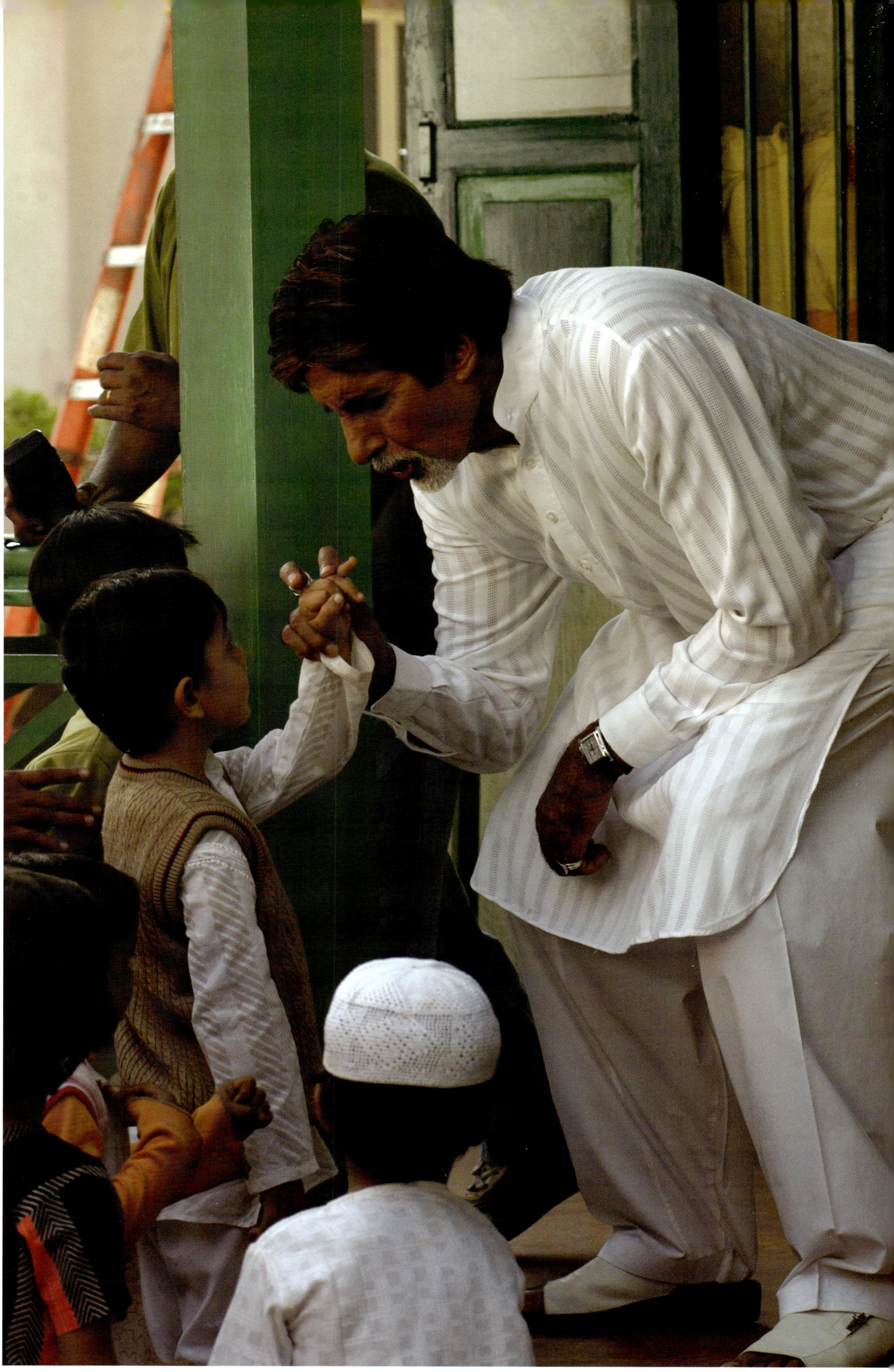

visit the gym at the J.W. Marriott hotel across the road. Do a workout for almost two hours. I then go back home and relax with the newspapers — national, local, Hindi, I read them all. After my bath, morning prayers, yoga etc, I get ready for work — the day's shoot. Now that it is so easy, I also surf the Internet while on location. Read messages, send a few mails. I go for make-up, do the take, attend calls, meet people all along the way. I have a working lunch of simple vegetarian home-cooked food. Then I get back home to dinner with the family.'

How does he do it?

'Busy-ness is just an attitude. A man can perform all if so he wills. Otherwise even thirty hours in a day would not suffice. The twenty-four hours available in a day are ample to do one's job. One should take care to plan his day well.'

Almost four years past the age of mandatory retirement in a corporate life, Bachchan is content with what he has achieved so far.

'As an artiste I may always nurture a small discontent with my performance, but I shall always be content with what I have got. I shall never wish for my life to have taken any other course. What I have received is beyond my expectations.'

'Amit *ji* has been a very principled and sincere person all his life. He has no qualms about being a film actor… He has given respectability and status to a Hindi film hero right from the start,' says Jaya Bachchan[5].

'Today he has become a character actor. But vis-à-vis the box office, he remains the boss among the numerous lead stars today.… One thing that is commendable is that he has made character actors' roles significant and equally important today. His role in a film like *Mohabbatein* is as important as Shah Rukh's,' she adds.

'I just chose a profession and tried to be as sincere to the profession as is possible. I have no regrets, and am happy the way I am[6],' Bachchan says. The same is the case with his family life. 'I am happy being by myself, or with my family. When I leave the studios I have my own life[7].

'There is always room for improvement in every role. I have never been totally satisfied with any of my roles…When you give a performance you cannot measure it. You just do it. Later on you assess it and find a lot of shortcomings.

'I am content. I have faced difficulties of all sorts and now I can face anything with equanimity. I am moved by people's love. I can never thank my

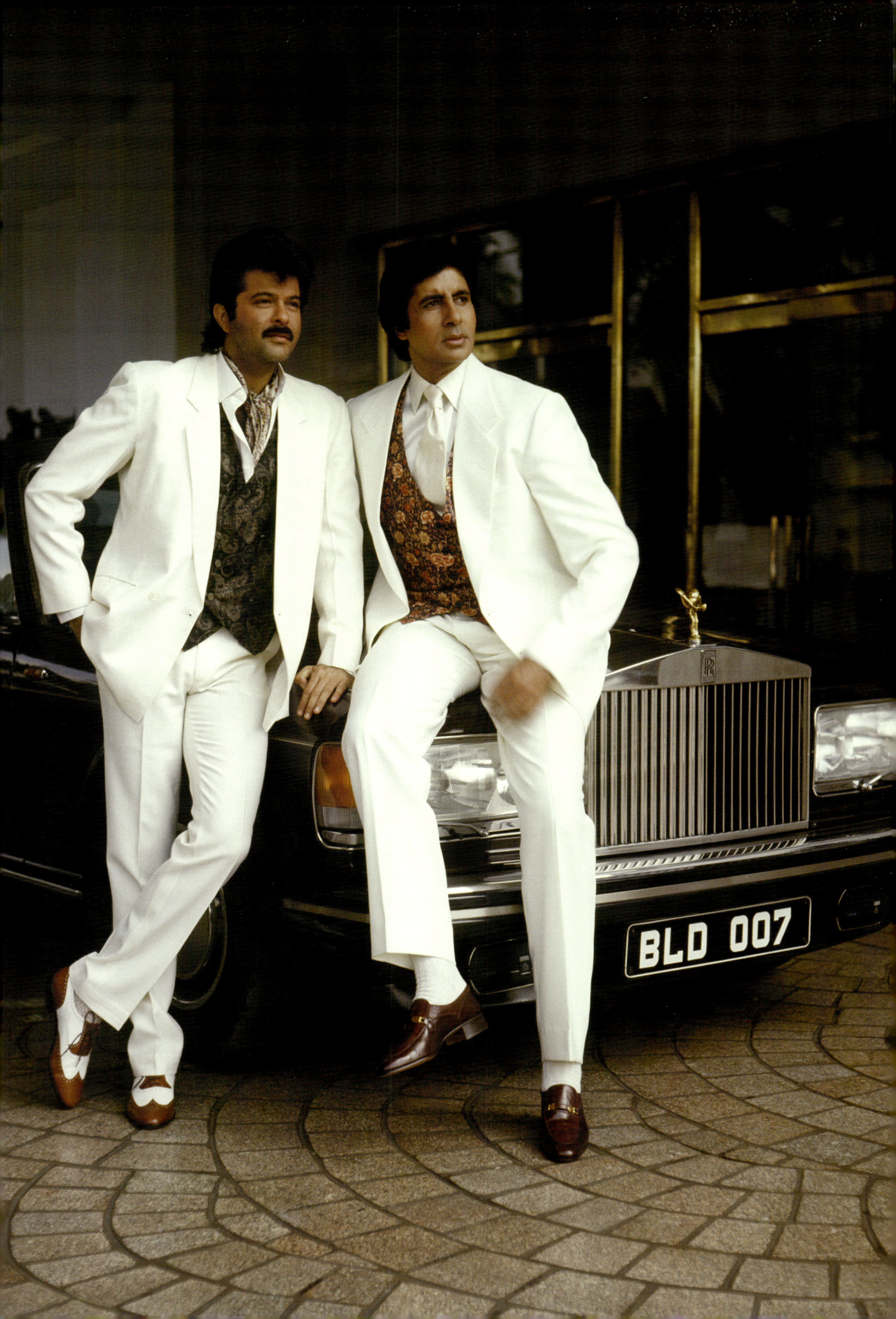
BLD 007

admirers enough. I am lucky to be born to such parents. My father belonged to a lower middle-class background while my mother was from a rich Sikh family. So the East and West did meet in my family. I learnt a lot from my parents and they are the ideals of my life.

'Their faith and self-discipline influenced me the most,' he says, speaking about his parents, the most enduring idols to him. 'The values my parents inculcated in me egged me on to become a good human being.'

Bachchan doesn't take his star status seriously at all. 'With open eyes, I do not find anything special as you fancy. I consider myself to be part of a powerful medium that can rivet the attention of people. The credit lies with the medium and not the individual… People still love me but that shouldn't turn my head.'

He doesn't believe that he is gilt edged. Even being awarded BBC's Actor of the Millennium doesn't cut too much ice with him. 'There was disbelief. I was surprised, but I am grateful that there are people who voted for me and I graciously accept their verdict. But yes, it was very surprising…. Awards and rewards are the opinions of some people. I don't entirely want to criticise the system, but if somebody is happy to reward me I will happily accept it.

'I don't subscribe to the hype. It's the business I am in the industry that everything is presented with great glamour and glitter. I am an ordinary man, like everybody else.'

But this does not mean that he is blasé about the public veneration and selfless love that he has received from the Indian people for over thirty years. His biggest gain he says over his entire career is 'their unfettered love. It is their selfless adoration which has provided me with the will to live in the face of dire calamity.'

He is definitely a man who has earned the right to speak with authority about personal calamity. 'Pilots and sailors face many storms in their extensive voyages across the skies and seas. When thunder roars and the clouds gather, one instinctively tries to rush through it. But this is a dangerous and inept attempt at escape. The seasoned navigators are trained to decrease their speed, yet, keep on going. Don't rush it, but don't stop either. Keep moving and a time will come when you would have left the darkness of the storm clouds and the thunder will clap harmlessly behind you.'

Guest Writer

Will the Real Amitabh Bachchan Please Stand Up?

Shobhaa Dé

Does anybody at all know a man called Amitabh Bachchan? The man. The human being, not the manufactured icon worshipped by millions across the world? I would seriously doubt it. In fact, I wonder whether even he can tell the difference between the public persona and his true self. Who is he in the privacy of his own room? What does he see in the mirror when he brushes his teeth in the morning? More importantly, does he like the image staring back at him, does he even recognise himself? Assuming he does, is there a smile on his face? Or a grimace? And when he hears his own voice – THAT voice – the one his admirers go weak in the knees listening to, what is his response? 'Hey…I know that guy. Hmmm – what's he saying now?'

To call Amitabh Bachchan an enigma, is to fall back on a cliché. But he, more than any other actor of our times, truly fits that description. I have watched him with interest (most of the time) and some indifference, over a period of 30 years. That's a whole lot of watching. But even after three decades, I cannot claim any special insights. As an actor, his career graph is fascinating. But as Mr Stone Wall, his emotional graph is as challenging as it is fascinating. He started off as a big-time flop, a loser. Then ruled as the Angry Young Man for twenty years, (ironically enough he was well past his prime when he found himself stuck with that sobriquet). It is only in the past two years, that the Angry Young Man has gracefully morphed into the Grand Old Man. If I were asked to pick just one cinematic moment that perfectly encapsulates his transition to the present state, I'd say it was that brief but compelling scene in *Viruddh* where he mocks the tragic comedy of life, with a hollow laugh. It was almost as if he was laughing at his own complex journey in the movies – and at all of us. Brilliant. Just as he seemed to be chortling over his indifferent performances in all those idiotic films he has 'acted' in. We don't know his compulsions or constraints for accepting those lousy movies. But those duds certainly didn't make his report card look good.

Today, this actor who reportedly makes a crore of rupees a day, has no real rivals left. His own contemporaries are tired, out-of-work grandpas nobody as much as recognises, except to say in wonder, 'God! I thought he was dead!' The younger Khans have their own following, but hey – even those guys are getting on. But even with a yawning twenty year age-gap between Bachchan and say, the latest Khan (Saif, not 'The Rising' Aamir), Amitabh's career graph runs a parallel course. Nobody has thought in terms of creating a Senior Citizen slot for him, and regardless of the roles he plays (Daddy Cool or 'Grandpa Cool'), he continues to be viewed as a regular hero, not an actor on an extended life line. Bachchan does not need an artificial respirator to breathe life into his roles, and that's saying something for a screen professional who has always claimed he is a mere puppet in the hands of his director and will do as instructed, no questions asked. This is a strange attitude coming from an intelligent, sensitive person, who more than all other mighty individuals from the film industry, is respected enough to push for change and raise the bar with his own inputs. Why would he want to settle for anything less? Why would he be happy with mediocrity? Should a man in such an elevated, exalted position go along passively with a poor script and lousy director? Is it enough to say, 'I do what I'm asked to. That's it.' Perhaps, Bachchan has finally woken up to his own response and responsibilities as an actor. This is evident from his recent superlative performances where he is going well beyond his director's brief. What is it that has finally freed him from the earlier binding/limiting forces? I'd like to hazard a guess – maybe he is now financially secure enough not to care. With the kind of money he is making, he doesn't have to worry about his *daal-chaaval*. Or old, accumulated debts. At a crore of rupees a day, the next couple of generations can keep those sort of anxieties on hold. Liberated from past ghosts and high debts, Bachchan is in a position to experiment, innovate and explore – which is good news for his fans, who, in any case, never seem to get enough of the man, or tire of his repetitive routine.

His is truly a remarkable story and a very unique one. No other actor in India has undertaken even half the journey he has, nor had the same impact on our collective consciousness. People talk about Dilip Kumar. But he is history, already. Shah Rukh Khan…?? Give him another twenty years, we'll talk then. Aamir Khan – hugely talented, but also equally hugely over-rated. That leaves just one guy – and he is everywhere. On the small screen and big. On billboards and stickers. On radio and websites. In wax and on canvas. Books, films, news clips…gosh – I'm breathless. Poems, songs, essays…there is hardly any space left that has not in some way been impacted by him, directly or indirectly. All this, and a temple in Kolkata too. What does this make Amitabh – a living deity?

For all that, he remains an enigma. He speaks only when spoken to. And even then, the conversation is restricted to a few, short sentences. Nobody has seen him drunk or anything less than in Supreme Control. He is punctual and polite, gentlemanly and well-mannered. If he does have emotions, they remain strictly under wraps. What one sees is a disciplined robot, a worker ant, someone who goes about life without too much of a fuss. Silent, brooding and melancholic. One wonders what brings the man some honest-to-goodness joy? What makes him smile? Laugh? Relax? Enjoy himself, like other mortals? I think I know. Amitabh Bachchan has an inheritor in mind. Like any other savvy business tycoon, his succession plan is very much in place. His nominee? Come on, the name is obvious enough. Keep the surname and switch the first one. The day Abhishek Bachchan ascends the throne vacated by his father, will be the day Amitabh Bachchan will roar like the Lion King. And finally relax. Over to you, Simba…

— *Shobhaa Dé* is a media personality

Notes

Chapter One

1. Martin Zerlang in the essay titled "A close-up on Salman Rushdie's Midnight's Children", Published in City Flicks: Indian Cinema and the Urban Experience, Edited by Preben Kaarsholm, Seagull Books 2004.
2. Pushpa Bharati, interview published in Dharmayug magazine, 1979, excerpted in Super Film Weekly, December 1981.
3. Super Film Monthly December 1981.
4. Super Film Monthly December 1981.
5. The Hero with a Thousand Faces, Joseph Campbell, Copyright 1949 Bollingen Foundation Inc. Princeton University Press, 1973, pg 30.
6. The Hero with a Thousand Faces, Joseph Campbell, Copyright 1949 Bollingen Foundation Inc. Princeton University Press, 1973, pg 30.
7. K. A. Abbas, Blossoms caught in cobwebs, Super Film Weekly, February 1982.

Chapter Two

1. Jalalludin Rumi quoted from "Essential Rumi" translated by Coleman Barks with John Moyne, Copyright 1997 Castle Books.
2. Super Film Monthly December 1981.
3. Super Film Monthly December 1981.

Chapter Three

1. The Hero with a Thousand Faces, Joseph Campbell, Copyright 1949 Bollingen Foundation Inc. Princeton University Press, 1973, pg 110-111.
2. Mahabharata by Kamala Subramaniam, Bhavan's Book University, Bharatiya Vidya Bhavan, 2001 edition, p 453.
3. James Lane Allen, King Solomon of Kentucky, Great Short Stories Of The World, 1947 edition. The World Publishing Company, Ohio, Copyright 1925, Robert M. Mcbride and Company, pg 1000-1001
4. Jean Anouilh, Becket, or The Honor of God, (translated by Lucienne Hill).
5. The Hero with a Thousand Faces, Joseph Campbell, Copyright 1949 Bollingen Foundation Inc. Princeton University Press, 1973, pg 130. "The ogre aspect of the father is a reflex of the victim's own ego—derived from the sensational nursery scene that has been left behind but projected

before…Atonement consists in no more than the abandonment of that self generated double monster–the dragon thought to be God (superego) and the dragon thought to be Sin (repressed id)".

Chapter Four

1. The Week, Cover Story interview by Maria Abraham and Sejal Shah, November 20, 1994.
2. Interview with K Srinivasan for Onlooker magazine, July 1985.
3. The Week, Interview with T R Gopalakrishnan, May 20, 1990.
4. Interview with Vir Sanghvi, May 17, 1999.
5. Interview with K Srinivasan for Onlooker magazine, July 1985.
6. The Week, Interview with T R Gopalakrishnan, May 20, 1990.
7. Interview with Vir Sanghvi, May 17, 1999.
8. Interview with Vir Sanghvi, May 19, 1999.
9. Interview with Meera Joshi, Filmfare, September 1995.
10. The Week, Interview with Sejal Shah, July 25, 1999.
11. The Week, Interview with Sejal Shah, July 25, 1999.

Chapter Five

1. Sameer Nair, interview with Abha Srivastava, Amitabh Bachchan Sweet Sixty, October 11. 2002, TOI.

Chapter Six

1. Stephen R. Covey, Principle-Centered Leadership, Summit Books, Copyright 1990, 1991, Stephen Covey, pg 17.
2. Stephen Covey, The Seven Habits of Highly Effective People, Simon & Schuster.
3. Interview with Vir Sanghvi in 1994-95.
4. The Week, Interview with T R Gopalakrishnan, May 20, 1990.
5. Interview with Ramesh Nirmal, Aha Zindagi.
6. The Week, Interview with Maria Abraham and Sejal Shah, November 20, 1994.
7. The Week, Interview with Sejal Shah, July 25, 1999.

Captions

The Early Days

Pg 21 –	With Jaya Bhaduri in a still from B.R. Ishaara's *Ek Nazar*
Pg 23 –	Amitabh in Ram Gopal Varma's *Sarkar*
Pg 24 –	Amitabh and Jaya Prada in Prakash Mehra's *Sharabi*
Pg 26 –	Attending a press conference as the corporate boss
Pg 27 –	Top – With Amar Singh and director Raj Kumar Santoshi; Below –With Jaya Bachchan, Abhishek and Leander Paes
Pg 29 –	With Jaya Bhaduri in *Ek Nazar*
Pg 33 –	With Tina Ambani and her children
Pg 34 –	With Hema Malini in *Baghban*
Pg 36 –	With Sachin and Anjali Tendulkar
Pg 38 –	With Dimple Kapadia in *Ajooba*

The Struggle

Pg 41 –	With Jaya Bachchan
Pg 43 –	With Raakhee in Ramesh Behl's *Kasme Vaade*
Pg 50 –	Top L – R – With Manisha Koirala, being interviewed by Javed Akhtar(Akhtar not in picture), with Nana Patekar, with Shah Rukh Khan and Hrithik Roshan
Pg 52 –	Top L – R – No 3, In *Bombay to Goa*; No 4, with Manisha Koirala in K.C. Bokadia's *Lal Badshah*
Pg 54 –	With Utpal Dutt, Jalal Agha, Shahnaz Anand, Anwar Ali and — in *Saat Hindustani*
Pg 56 –	Top No 3 – With Hema Malini and Esha Deol
Pg 59 –	L – R – Mahaveer Adhikari, Manmohan Saral (standing), Kamleshwar, Dr Harivanshrai Bachchan and Amitabh at Dr Dharamveer Bharati's house; No 2 – In a still from *Reshma aur Shera* with Jayant, Sunil Dutt, Vinod Khanna and Sulochana; No 3 – With ShatrughanSinha in Shaan
Pg 61 –	L – R – No 1, With Hrishikesh Mukherjee; No 2 - with Jaya Bhaduri in *Guddi*
Pg 62 –	Top L- R, No 1 – With Jaya Bhaduri in *Bansi Birju*; No 2 - with Kajol, Tanisha and Rani Mukherjee, No 3 – In a still from Mahesh Manjrekar's *Virudh*
Pg 65 –	Top – No2 – With Jaya Bhaduri in a still from *Zanjeer*; No 3 – With Moushmi Chatterjee in *Benaam*
Pg 66 –	Top – No 1 – With Dev Anand, With Jaya Bachchan, Teji Bachchan, Dr.Harivanshrai Bachchan at a function, No 3, With Sharmila Tagore in *Virudh*
Pg 68-69 –	Being measured for his statue in Madame Tussaud's wax museum
Pg 70-71 –	In still from *Black* No 2 – With Sharmila Tagore in Shankar Mukherjee's *Faraar*, No 3 – With Zeenat Aman in Chandra Barot's *Don*; No 5 – With K.K. Menon, Supriya Pathak, Abhishek and Rukhsar in *Sarkar*

The Angry Young Man

Pg 78 –	No 1 – With Prahlad Kakkar, No 3 – With Salim Khan
Pg 79 –	With Jaya Bhaduri in *Zanjeer*
Pg 82 –	With Shatrughan Sinha in *Kala Patthar*
Pg 84 –	L-R - No 1 – With Raveena Tandon; No 2, With Salman Khan
Pg 85 –	With Rekha in *Ganga ki Saugandh*
Pg 86 –	With Akshay Kumar in *Ek Rishtaa*
Pg 86-87 –	Campaigning with children at a drive to eradicate polio
Pg 89 –	With Parveen Babi in *Deewar*
Pg 90 –	With Waheeda Rehman in *Kabhie Kabhie*
Pg 99 –	No 1 – With Dilip Kumar; No 2 – With Dilip Kumar in a still from *Shakti*

A Search for Identity

Pg 106 –	With Puneet Issar in the fateful scene from *Coolie*
Pg 107 –	With Ajitabh and Manmohan Desai while leaving Breach Candy hospital
Pg 109 –	Ketan Desai welcoming Bachchan back to work on the sets of *Coolie*
Pg 110 –	With Sridevi in *Khuda Gawah*
Pg 110-111 –	At an election rally in Allahabad
Pg 112 –	With Amrita Singh in *Mard*
Pg 114 –	With Jaya Bachchan at the launch of ABCL
Pg 116 –	No 1 - With Jaya Bachchan and a guest at the ABCL launch; No 2 – With Amar Singh and daughter Shweta
Pg 118-	L- With Govinda, Above- With Mallika Sherawat
Pg 118-119 –	With son Abhishek at a concert in aid of tsunami victims
Pg 121 –	No 1 - With Parveen Babi in *Kaalia*; No 2 – With Nita Khayani and a co-star in Mukul Dutt's *Raaste ka Patthar*
Pg 122 –	With Sahara Shri Subrata Roy and his wife, Swapna Roy
Pg 122- 123 –	Reciting Dr Harivanshrai Bachchan's poems at the NGMA, Mumbai

Pg 126 –	With Smt Indu Jain
Pg 128 –	With Parmeshwar Godrej at the unveiling of the 1997 Miss World logo
Pg 129 –	With Dr Harivanshrai Bachchan at Bandra Bandstand in the early days
Pg 130 –	At the perfume launch by Lomani, bearing his name
Pg 131 –	On the sets of *Kaun Banega Crorepati Dvitiya*
Pg 132-133 –	With Aamir Khan and Madhuri Dixit on the launch of ABCL's *Rishta* (the film never got made)
Pg 133 –	With daughter Shweta walking the ramp at a fashion show
Pg 134 –	With Shah Rukh Khan, Raveena Tandon and Aishwarya Rai at a Sahara function in Lucknow.
Pg 136-137 –	With Mahesh Bhupati and Leander peas
Pg 138 –	With Govind Nihalani on the sets of *Dev*

The Return of the King

Pg 144 – 145	Top L-R No 1 – With former PM Chandra Shekhar; No 2 – With former PM Rajiv Gandhi; No 3 – With Jaya Bachchan at China Garden, Mumbai; No 4 – Receiving the Observer award from filmmaker Prakash Mehra
Pg 146 – 147	Top L-R, No 1 – With Parvez Damania, No 2 – Performing at the Filmfare awards function No 3 – With Nana Patekar
Pg 151 –	Top L-R No 1, With Mukesh Ambani; No 2, No 3, With Kokilaben Ambani
Pg 152 –	Top L-R, No 1- With painter Laxman Shreshta; No 2 – With Jaya Bachchan; No 3 With Anil Ambani and Amar Singh, No 4 - With Vijay Kalantri and Kumarmangalam Birla
Pg 154 –	With Ishaan Puri (Om Puri's son) at a book launch at the ITC Grand Maratha, Mumbai
Pg 155 –	Top, L-R, No 1 – With a group of Russian children at his residence Prateeksha; No 3, Sushmita Sen with Abhishek, No 4 – With Chhagan Bhujbal, Amar Singh and Subhash Chandra
Pg 156-157 –	Posing for his wax statue; No 4 – Director Yash Chopra with Bachchan's wax face at Le Royal Meridien, Mumbai
Pg 160-161 –	L-R No 1 – With Jaya Bachchan, grandchildren Navya and Agastya and son Abhishek at JW Marriott, No 2 – With Amar Singh, Jaya Bachchan and Abhishek, No 3 - With Jaya Bachchan, No 4 – daughter Shweta and Jaya Bachchan
Pg 162 – 163	No 1 With Kumaramangalam Birla; No 3 – Preparing for a TV interview with Javed Akhtar
Pg 165 –	L-R, No 1 – In a still from *Agneepath;* No 2 –With actress Sheetal; No 3 – In a still from *Sarkar*
Pg 166 –167	No 1- With Jaya Bachchan and grandchildren, No 2 – Pritish Nandy, Jaya Bachchan and Abhishek, No 3 – With Amar Singh, Kokilaben, Anil Ambani and a guest, With Lata Mangeshkar
Pg 168 –	Top, No 1 – With Karan Johar, No 2 – Abhishek with Ajitabh No 3 – With Jaya Bachchan and Salman Khan, Below – Amitabh with a diamond trophy at a function held for honouring him
Pg 169 –	Amitabh Bachchan with Abhishek coming out of Lilawati Hospital Mumbai

Still Here

Pg 176-177 –	Left – Celebrating his sixtieth birthday with Jaya Bachchan, Agastya and Abhishek
Pg 178 – 179	At sculptor Arzaan Khambatta's show at Jehangir Art Gallery
Pg 180 –	Amitabh Bachchan in a still from *family*
Pg 181 –	With Zeenat Aman in *Don*
Pg 182 –	With Jaya Bachchan and Nelson Wang at the restaurant China Garden, Mumbai
Pg 182-183 –	With Sachin Tendulkar, Lata Mangeshkar and Balasaheb Thackeray
Pg 185 –	With poet lyricist Prasoon Joshi
Pg 186 –	With Rekha in Yash Chopra's *Silsila*
Pg 189 –	With Abhishek, mother Teji and Jaya Bachchan at their residence
Pg 190-191 –	L-R (standing), With mother Teji, Govind Swaroop (with beard), Mulayam Singh Yadav, Amar Singh, (sitting) Dr Harivanshrai Bachchan, with the UP award presented to him by Mulayam Singh Yadav.
Pg 191 –	With Nita Ambani, Amar Singh
Pg 192 –	With Rekha, Abhishek and Aishwarya at the premiere of *Sarkar*
Pg 194 –	With Jaya Bachchan at a stage show Hope 86 in Mumbai
Pg 195 –	On a set of KBC 2
Pg 196 –	With children at Film City
Pg 197 –	With Jaya Bachchan in Allahabad
Pg 198 –	With Anil Kapoor
Pg 199 –	Celebrating 63 years with family and close friends at the JW Marriott, Mumbai
Pg 208 –	Signing autographs on his 57th birthday at his residence Prateeksha

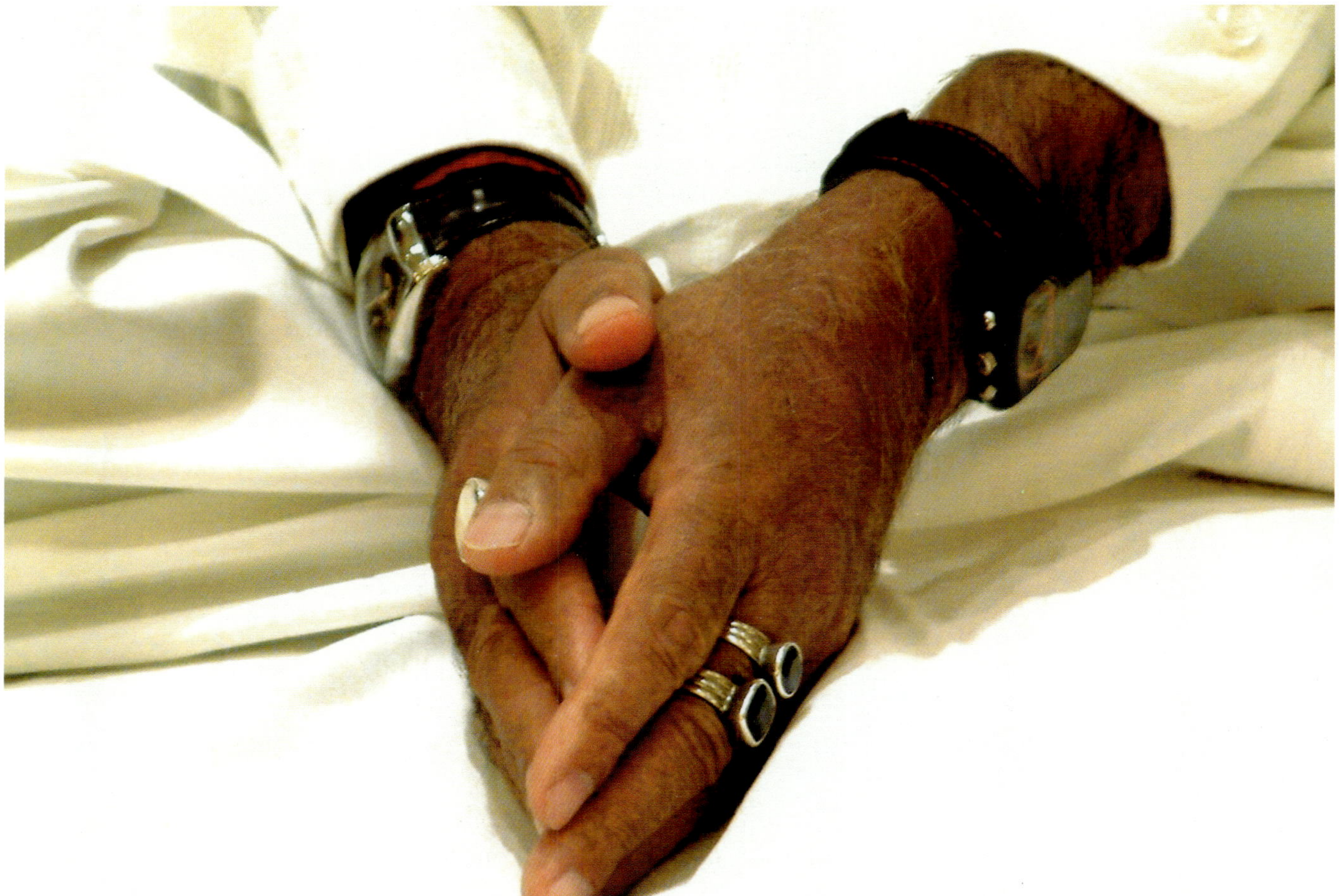

Acknowledgements

The text and photographs used in this book have been based on numerous sources and interviews I have conducted. People from various fields have been of great support to me. I am blessed to have so many old colleagues and friends in the media who have helped me source information on Amitabh Bachchan. These include Om Gupta, T.R. Gopaalakrishnan, J.P. Singhal, K. Srinivasan, and Rauf Ahmed among others.

I wish to thank all the guest writers - Shobhaa Dé, Govind Nihalani, Rauf Ahmed, T.R. Gopaalakrishnan and Srinivas Hebbar - for their valuable contributions and inputs and Pritish Nandy for writing the foreword.

I wish to express my sincere gratitude to Smita Naniwadekar for providing editorial help and assistance in writing the text. I would also like to thank Priyanka Chandra-Sinha for being involved with this project since its conception to editing.

I am especially obliged to the people I have interviewed. Without their co-operation, this book could not have achieved richness in detail. Anupam Kher, Om Puri, Gerson DaCunha, B.R. Ishara, Alyque Padamsee, Prahlad Kakkar, Dolly Thakore, Nelson Wang, Shahnaz and Tinnu Anand, Vashu Bhagnani, Ketan Desai, Subhash Awachat, Udayraj Gadnis, J. P. Singhal, Peter Mukherjea, Shyam Benegal, Poonam Dhillon, Yash Kohli, Dheeraj Kumar, Sangeeta Kathiawada, Govind Swarup and Prasoon Joshi thank you so much.

I appreciate the effort put in by painters, artists and sculptors J. P. Singhal, Subhash Awachat, Charan Sharma, Baiju Parthan, Chintan Upadhyaya, Safdar Shamee, Ravindra Pabrekar, Prithvi Soni, Vrindavan Solanki, Buwa Shete, Arzaan Khambatta and Pratyashaa Bole.

A big thank you to J. P. Singhal, Mukesh Parpiani, Yogen Shah, Gautam Patole, Durga Prasad, Vijayan Raghvan, Pramod Srivastava, Umesh Goswami, S. K. Yadav, Jagdish Mali Pratyashaa Bole, and Farzana Contractor for being very kind in giving their photographs to use in my book.

Also thanks to film producers and still photographers who have been kind enough to part with film stills and Tussauds Museum, London for their pictures from archives.

Special thanks to Arun Sawant for his excellent input in designing.

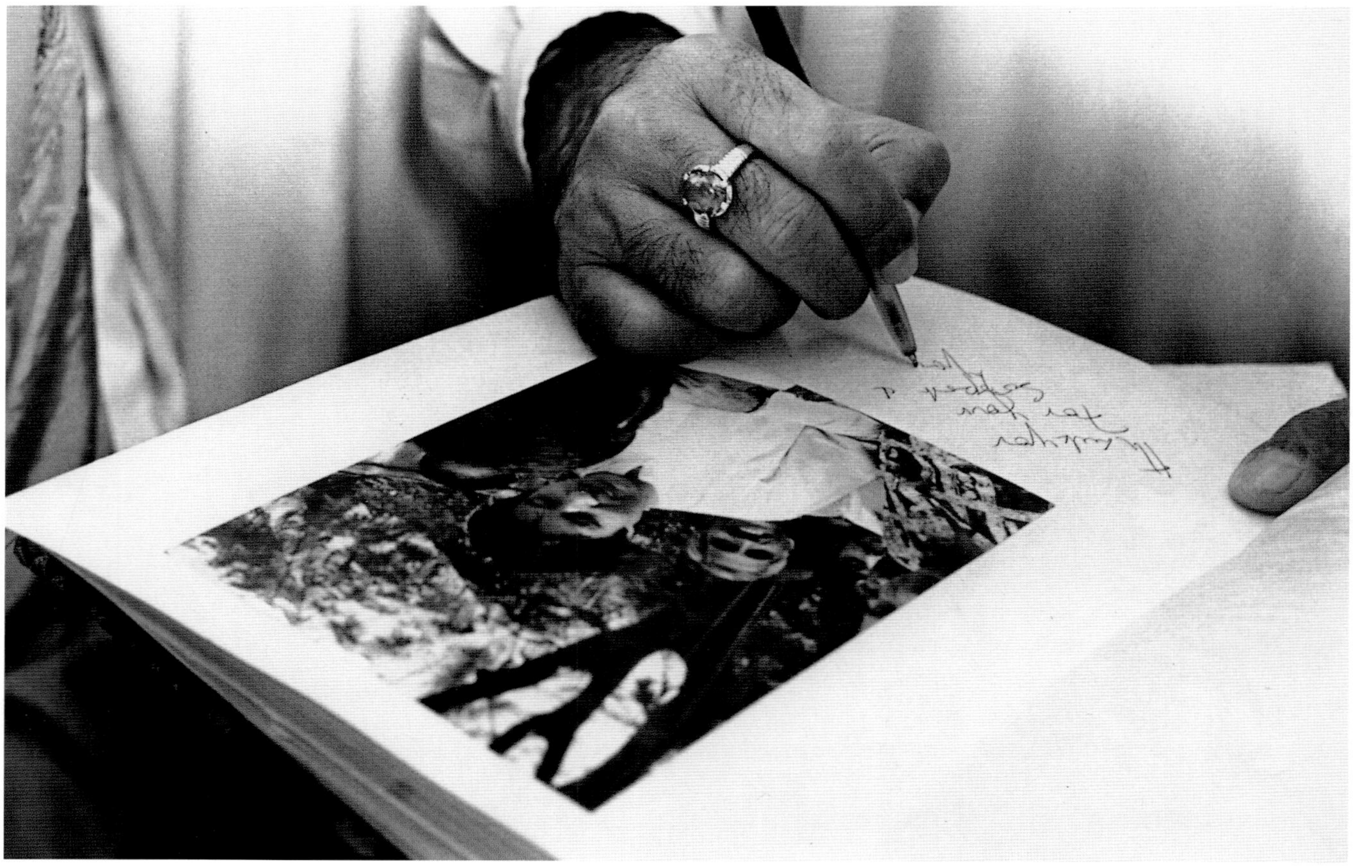

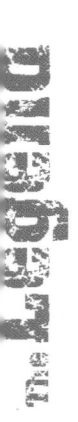

तू गीत है तुझको नमन

बन्दिशों में बँधा निर्झर हो गया
कन्ठ से जब बहा हृदय भिगो गया
गुनगुनाने लगी पंखुरी पंखुरी, शाखों ने सुना
सर हिलाने लगी खामोशी सून कर, रातों ने सुना
मुस्कुराया गगन ईद सब खो गया

कलश भाव का डबडबाता हुआ, थामे रहा
शब्दों की गरिमा छलकने नदी, सँभाले रहा
जाग भी गया स्वप्न से खो गया
आँधियाँ भी चलीं जब यह सारी धरा, डगमगाने लगी
गीत की लौ मगर टिमटिमाती रही, सुर सजाने लगी
लहर सा उठा सारे तट धो गया

Prasoon Joshi wrote this poem as a tribute to Amitabh Bachchan